# PETER LOEWER

### *and*

# ANNE MOYER HALPIN

*SUMMIT BOOKS*

*NEW YORK • LONDON • TORONTO*

*SYDNEY • TOKYO • SINGAPORE*

# SECRETS
# OF
# THE
# GREAT
# GARDENERS

*How to Make Your Garden
as Beautiful as Theirs*

SUMMIT BOOKS
Simon & Schuster Building
Rockefeller Center
1230 Avenue of the Americas
New York, New York 10020

Copyright © 1991 by Anne M. Halpin and Peter Loewer
All rights reserved
including the right of reproduction
in whole or in part in any form.
SUMMIT BOOKS and colophon are trademarks
of Simon & Schuster Inc.
Designed by Edith Fowler
Manufactured in the United States of America

10  9  8  7  6  5  4  3  2  1

Library of Congress Cataloging in Publication Data

Loewer, H. Peter.
  Secrets of the great gardeners: how to make your
garden as beautiful as theirs/Peter Loewer and
Anne Moyer Halpin.
    p.  cm.
  Includes index.
  1. Brooklyn Botanic Garden.  2. Gardening.
I. Halpin, Anne Moyer.  II. Title.
QK73.U62B765  1991
580'.74'474723—dc20                        90-27123
                                                CIP

ISBN 0-671-69590-8

# CONTENTS

# FOREWORD

The people interviewed in this book are professional gardeners, and it is amazing to me how quickly they have become authorities in their areas of specialization. The pride of gardening responsibility is evident, and the open nature in which each person expressed "secrets," observations, and philosophies was no less than I expected.

The Brooklyn Botanic Garden gardeners are always striving for improvements—whether it be of displays, introduction of new plant varieties, refinements of horticultural systems, or more emphasis on biological controls. Their appreciation of and concern for the environment and ecology is evident—and heartwarming to me.

For eighty years the many gardens within the Garden and the high level of maintenance have impressed visitors from across Washington Avenue as well as from around the world. Visitors often call BBG "an oasis" and I have heard used such terms as "a jewel" and "a gem." What this Botanic Garden is today is in great part due to the well-documented principles expressed by the first director, Dr. C. Stuart Gager.

According to Dr. Gager, the Garden was established "to stimulate and to gratify an interest in plant life, to promote public education in all aspects of botany and horticulture. The plantations are intended to serve as an outdoor museum. . . . Besides its scientific and educational activities, a botanic garden serves the public in two ways—aesthetically and environmentally (by affording a locus or background for profitable leisure)."

Every director has since espoused Dr. Gager's views. The second director, Dr. George S. Avery, expressed the idea that if the Botanic Garden is maintained with the pride and attention we would give to our own front yards or living rooms when company is expected, then visitors will respect it. His observation was that no one wants to be the first to litter. Elizabeth Scholtz, our fourth director, used to wear a button with the letters "I B.O.T.P.U.L." (I bend over to pick up litter), which she still does.

With such leadership we are imbued with the spirit of Dr. Gager's dream and akin in concern and goal.

Not only is this Botanic Garden what visitors see but also what they feel. No small part of this impression is due to the people they meet and how they are treated. Our visitors are guests, and they are always welcome when the Botanic Garden is open. Each one of us on the staff is a host. Our well-trained volunteer Garden Guides are the frontline hosts who conduct group tours by appointment. They personalize the Garden experience and are appreciated and admired by all of us.

However, a visit to the Garden can also be a very personal, contemplative respite, a chance to commune with nature. Dr. Gager wrote that BBG should also serve this purpose, and the authors of this book have given a number of examples of how this purpose is still being satisfied.

It has been a pleasant experience working with Anne Halpin and Peter Loewer. They have been accommodating and sensitive to concerns, and they thoroughly researched the history and plant collections of this institution. This book not only relates "secrets" of Botanic Gardeners but also gives some glimpse into the characters and personalities of the individuals interviewed. They pres-

ent BBG as more than a living museum by sharing their insight
into the essence of the Garden we love.

Edmond O. Moulin,
*Director of Horticulture,*
*Brooklyn Botanic Garden*
*October 26, 1990*

# PREFACE

Some years ago the authors met in a small town in Pennsylvania. While enjoying lunch in a popular restaurant there they overheard a conversation at a nearby table. A middle-aged woman was describing the art of making tussie-mussies, or nosegays, small hand-held arrangements of sweet-smelling flowers used in colonial times to brighten air that was often not as pleasant as it should have been.

"You know," said the lady, "I only went to the Brooklyn Botanic Garden once, where I visited their Fragrance and Herb Garden. I'll never forget it, and it was those flowers that started me on my interest in dried herbs and fragrant plants. It's such a beautiful—and unexpected—place."

Then last month Eugene O'Neill, a friend in New York, sent us a clipping from the *Nippon Club News,* a Manhattan-based organization of Japanese and American businessmen. He has been a member since 1979, but his interest in Japan began with the following:

"In 1955, quite by accident, I wandered into the Brooklyn Botanic Garden's Japanese Garden. It seemed as though the wind had stopped howling, the snow was falling gently, and my face no longer felt chapped and cold. Perhaps it was one of those times when what my eyes witnessed was so absorbing that no sound or discomfort could possibly distract me. I remember being profoundly moved by the pristine gentleness of a landscape whose beauty spoke directly to my soul. There was a small foot bridge that crossed a narrow stream that meandered through the garden to a large pond. The snow was at least four inches deep and formed delicate white banks on either side of the stream. I stood on that foot bridge and drank in that scene for a long time, alone with my thoughts and the sweet pain that comes from realizing that beauty is to be beheld but not possessed."

The Brooklyn Botanic Garden has such an effect on people. In the midst of a world-class city, the trees and lawns are there to be enjoyed and marveled at, by generation after generation.

One of us has memories that go back to an art scholarship at the Brooklyn Museum. The Garden joins the grounds of the museum, and many wonderful afternoons were spent walking the landscaped pathways as a short respite from the long hours spent in studio classes. The other of us lived for a time in Manhattan and delights in memories of days spent doing research at the Garden's library and emerging from the black-and-gray subway entrance to confront a blue sky and a forest of trees, dotted here and there with beautiful floral displays.

But the Garden was responsible for something else in our lives as gardeners. Over the years it has published over one hundred handbooks in its *Plants & Gardens* series. As a result, throughout this book there is garden advice not only from the interviews with the talented gardeners of today's BBG, but also from information that we've either learned ourselves from reading the handbooks over the years or other hints picked up while doing research in the Garden's marvelous library.

And as to "secrets," there is a story behind that word in the title of this book.

We don't mean to say that this book is full of secrets in the usual meaning of the word, that of something kept or intended to be kept from the knowledge or view of others. No. These are secrets of a different sort. They mean a method, usually not known to everyone, for attaining something valuable, like the secret of good health. Or in this case, that little bit of advice that turns a good garden into a great garden. We hope that all gardeners who read this book will find at least a few interesting plants or ways of gardening that they didn't know about before.

And here we must thank all the wonderful staff at the Garden without whose cooperation this book would not have been possible. They include Edmond O. Moulin, Director of Horticulture, for his marvelous sense of humor and unflagging help with plants and people; Brenda K. Mulligan, Operations Office Manager, for balancing the many appointments; Barbara Pesch, Director of Publications, for her advice and for all those wonderful publications; Elvin McDonald, Director of Special Projects, for his beautiful photographs; and Stephen K-M. Tim, Vice President, Science and Publications, for his welcome advice and aid in finishing the manuscript. Finally our thanks to our editor at Summit Books, Dominick Anfuso, and to the gardeners interviewed on the following pages.

PETER LOEWER,
Asheville, North Carolina
    *and*
ANNE MOYER HALPIN
Hampton Bays, New York

# CHAPTER ONE

# A SHORT HISTORY OF THE GARDEN

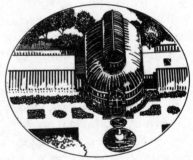

When dealing with great institutions, there is always a difficulty with separating legend from what really took place. In the case of the Brooklyn Botanic Garden it would be pleasant to think that the idea for the garden sprang fully developed like Athena from the forehead of Zeus, and that in a short period of time walkways appeared under the magnificent trees, and well-dressed ladies and gentlemen rambled there and talked of flowers. Unfortunately that's not the way it happened. Between the original proposal for the establishment of a botanic garden in Brooklyn and the day the Garden finally opened its doors, exactly fifteen years elapsed.

The initial idea of having a botanic garden was actively pursued by the members of the Brooklyn Institute of Arts and Sciences, and on February 26, 1897, a committee was appointed to help draft a legislative act reserving the East Side Lands, an area of some thirty-nine acres, known as Institute Park, for a botanic garden and arboretum. The committee worked quickly, and on

May 18 of that year, a bill in support of the proposal was passed by the New York State Legislature.

"A botanic garden and arboretum for the collection and culture of plants, flowers, shrubs, and trees, the advancement of botanical science and knowledge, and the prosecution of original researches therein and in kindred subjects; for affording instruction in the same, and for the prosecution and exhibition of ornamental and decorative horticulture and gardening, and for the entertainment, recreation, and instruction of the people . . ." New York State Law, 1897.

Between 1902 and 1903, the East Side Lands were graded and border mounds along Washington Avenue and Flatbush Avenue were raised and then planted with trees and shrubs. The dedication took place on November 14, 1903.

Then, in June 1905, the Institute received the sum of $25,000 to be used in equipping a scientific botanic garden, chiefly to teach botany to both public and private students in the city, provided that the garden would be established on grounds adjacent to the Brooklyn Museum. Another bill went to the state legislature authorizing the city to establish and maintain a garden and arboretum in Institute Park and was approved and signed by the Governor on May 24, 1906.

In December of that year another $25,000 was added, and by the spring of 1907 a form of agreement was prepared between the city and the Institute. But it was not until the summer of 1909 that the Board of Estimate approved the plan, and the contract between the city and the Institute was signed on December 28. On July 1, 1910, the Brooklyn Botanic Garden was born, with Dr. Charles Stuart Gager as its first director.

Dr. Gager had obtained his initial bachelor's degree in 1895 from Syracuse University, and he spent the following seven years teaching botany and doing research in a number of institutions until he received his doctorate from Cornell in 1902; he remained there until 1904.

The years 1904–1910 were spent in research and teaching botany. Dr. Gager was a laboratory assistant at the New York Botanical Garden, acting Professor of Botany at Rutgers College for a year, taught summer sessions at New York University for two years, and in 1906 became the Director of Laboratories at the New York Botanical Garden, where he remained until his appointment in September 1908, as Professor of Botany at the University of Missouri, where for two years he was in charge of the general courses in botany and also taught advanced courses in physiology and morphology.

So, at the age of thirty-seven, a comparatively young Dr. Gager took charge of the fledgling Brooklyn Botanic Garden and proceeded to chart its course until his death on August 9, 1943.

Today trees are everywhere, the various theme gardens are in place, and the walkways wind with authority between acres of green grass, all with the sparkle of the new conservatories in the distance. It would be intriguing to imagine what Dr. Gager saw when he first looked over the scene of his new responsibilities.

Standing on the southeast corner of the Prospect Hill Reservoir, now Mount Prospect Park Playground, he would see most of the land that later became incorporated into the Garden. A few years before, the Parks Department had made some improvements, raising the border mounds mentioned earlier and planting a few trees and shrubs; but toward the east was an uninviting pond, and in the distance toward Empire Boulevard, the area was used by the same Parks Department as a dumping ground where, usually daily, rubbish bonfires burned.

In his first annual report, Dr. Gager presented a list of possible theme plantations. These included sections on the systematic arrangement of plants; a local flora area consisting of herbaceous and woody plants found growing within a hundred-mile radius of New York City; plantings to illustrate the variations in morphology and the ecological requirements of plants; and areas devoted to economic and horticultural features. He also developed an outline of organization for the Garden by departments, including staff members for administration, research, instruction, and other activities.

As a first step a topographic survey of the thirty-nine acres was prepared, followed by the appointment of the Olmstead Brothers of Brookline, Massachusetts, as landscape architects to lay out the grounds, including roadways, paths, and the esplanade vista.

Most people take the ground they walk on for granted. Level, soft rolling hills and that artful creek that meanders in and about a loose profusion of boulders is assumed to be entirely natural. The reality of that landscape is entirely the opposite. During the early years, the grading and improvement of the soil was one of the chief concerns. In certain areas the ground level was dropped ten to twelve feet, a major effort before the days of diesel-powered caterpillar tractors and backhoes. The original terminal moraine pond was enlarged to a lake, and excavations, in some places as much as seven feet, for the artificial brook were made at the same time the entire slope of the meadow was changed. Dams of glacial boulders were constructed and the course of the brook was designed to look as natural as possible. Then, in order to prevent undue loss of water, the entire creek bed was lined with the blue clay that was removed while excavating the foundation for the laboratory building.

In the spring of 1911, the Local Flora Section was started with a six-hundred-foot-long valley site of about two acres. Numerous beds for native plants and woodland conditions were provided for the other plants. The south wing of the Administration Building and the northeast wing of the greenhouse were also started at this time.

The water was first turned into the brook in May 1912. This feature was the particular joy of the Director, who was often heard to refer to it as "my brook," since it was constructed upon his insistence and against the advice and wishes of others.

That same year the Garden received 514 specimen trees and shrubs from the Arnold Arboretum, 375 of which had been gathered by Ernest Wilson (best known for his discovery of *Lilium regale* and some sixty rhododendrons) on his four exploratory trips to China. Hugo De Vries (the Dutch botanist who is credited with interpreting Mendel's laws of heredity and the development of the mutation theories) planted an American sweet gum tree *(Liquidambar styraciflua);* and the east side of the Mount Prospect Reservoir, measuring three acres, was given to the Garden.

Next came the Japanese Garden. A gift of Mr. Alfred T. White in 1914, this is an Oriental garden in the true sense, having been designed by a Japanese architect, Mr. Takeo Shiota, and embodying the Eastern idea of a place for contemplation rather than for activity. Its beauty is maintained with the use of rocks, which form a deep gorge in the hill bounding one side of this garden and the water that flows over these rocks, into the lake below.

The Rock Garden was opened in 1917. The rocks that provide the background to the plants are glacial boulders deposited during the last Ice Age by one of the continental ice sheets that terminated on Long Island, and were dug up during grading op-

erations on the grounds. They make up in authenticity and geo-
logical interest what they may lack in value for plant culture,
varying in size from small cobblestones to boulders six feet or
more in dimension. Twenty-eight of them bear bronze labels in-
dicating their type and age.

By the end of that decade, the Administration Building and
the conservatories were finished, thousands of trees were planted,
the construction on the water-lily pools was begun, and the Austrian pines *(Pinus nigra)* on the east side of the Japanese Garden
lake were planted.

The group of Australian cycads housed in the conservatories
are a case in point of the difficulties surrounding the stocking of
such an enterprise as the Garden. In 1914, Dr. Gager arranged,
through the curator of the Botanic Garden in Queensland, Australia, for an expedition to collect these plants. They were gathered, packed in large cases, and shipped. However, due to the
demands on shipping brought about by the First World War, they
were landed and transferred at Sydney, Port Said, and London,
for in each port their ship was commandeered for carrying troops.
After seven months of travel the cycads arrived in Brooklyn and
because of excellent packing plus their natural resistance to
drought, they were still alive and went on to grace the conservatory.

During the 1920s the Garden continued to grow. The Cherry
Walk of magnificent Japanese flowering cherries (*Prunus* 'Seki-
yama', also known as *P. serrulata* 'Kwanzan') were planted; one
hundred ginkgo trees *(Ginkgo biloba)* were planted on the Overlook at the south side of the Brooklyn Museum; the iron picket
fence that surrounds the Garden was installed, taking seventy
working days for completion; and the one-acre Cranford Rose
Garden was constructed and dedicated.

The decade of the 1930s again saw the planting of thousands
of trees including 1,392 trees and shrubs for the Japanese Garden
and the Osborne Section, given by the New York City Parks
Department; the building of ten pergolas in the Osborne Section;
the beginning and completion of the Wall Garden, some 385 feet
long; the dedication of the Herb Garden (including first prize for
the Knot Garden at the International Flower Show in 1938); and
the great hurricane of September 21, 1938, during which a forty-
year-old plane tree *(Platanus* × *acerifolia)* was blown off of Boulder Hill and fifty-five other trees were felled by the winds.

After the death of Dr. Gager in 1943, a well-known plant

physiologist, Dr. George Avery, became the Garden's second director on August 1, 1944. Little more than one month later the second hurricane of the century hit the Garden and uprooted more than four hundred trees, but this did nothing to dampen the enthusiasm about the new director's appointment.

After attending to some administrative details, including the organization of a pension fund for Garden employees, Dr. Avery ushered in a new postwar era of Garden expansion, and his stewardship has often been called the Golden Years of the Garden.

In 1945 a headline appeared in one of the newspapers of the day: "Botanic Garden outdraws Dodgers with 1,250,000 visitors annually," and many of these visitors came through the new Eastern Parkway Gate. Many were members of the Garden, but far more were "casuals" and the new director began to ponder the role of the Garden.

"Many botanic gardens," he wrote, "are great outdoor flower shows in spring and early summer, but this brief display can hardly justify the financial outlay for year-round care. It is important, therefore, that botanic gardens play a twelve month active and useful role in their communities." So he embarked on a campaign to bring the garden to public attention through classes, plant information by telephone, radio talks, and his brainchild, a new publication called *Plants & Gardens*.

Four handbooks, one for each season, were mailed to Garden members and in turn could be ordered from the Garden. This publication eventually enabled the Garden to be known throughout the English-speaking horticultural world, and it increased the membership by thousands.

New gardens were added in the 1950s including the Iris Garden and the Garden of Fragrance for the Blind. More trees and plants were added, notably a vast collection of rhododendrons at the base of the slope south of Mount Prospect Playground. And construction proceeded on a replica of the five-hundred-year-old Ryoanji Zen temple garden in Kyoto, Japan, a project completed in 1964.

Dr. Louis B. Martin became Director in September 1969 after Dr. Avery's retirement and served in that position until January 1972, when he left to become President of the Chicago Horticultural Society. It was during his brief tenure that the Garden Shop was created.

Elizabeth Scholtz had come to the Garden in 1960 as Assistant Curator of Instruction. She later became head of the adult education program and under her leadership the course enrollment grew from one thousand in 1960 to four thousand in 1971. In January 1972, Miss Scholtz became the first woman director of a major urban botanic garden in the United States.

Under her leadership the Ryoanji Garden was reopened; the Garden continued to arrange travel-study tours for members in many countries around the world; the irrigation system was renovated to allow the Garden to be independent of city water; volunteer Garden guides were trained; the original Shakespeare Garden south of the Children's Garden had become shaded by tall trees, and a new version was located opposite the Japanese Garden; and in 1978 the Garden was approved as an All-America Selections Display Garden.

On July 1, 1977, the Brooklyn Botanic Garden was legally separated from the Brooklyn Institute of Arts and Sciences. It is, at present, an independent not-for-profit corporation that is governed by a voluntary board of trustees. The Garden's grounds and buildings are owned by the City of New York and the Garden is in part supported by public funds through the Department of Cultural Affairs and the New York State Natural Heritage Trust. All other funds are raised from private sources.

In July of 1980, Donald E. Moore was appointed President of the Garden and Miss Scholtz became Vice-President.

Now the new conservatories were planned. Vast numbers of plants had to be moved in order to begin construction, including the removal by helicopter of the original *Malus* 'Red Jade' to the northwest part of the Osborne section. This tree was a parent tree that had been started from seed in 1934 and granted a plant patent in 1956.

On May 18, 1984, the ceremonial groundbreaking for the new conservatories was held; the actual building began on May 14, 1985. That same year one acre of land from the south slope of Mount Prospect Playground was given to the Garden, making a total of fifty-one acres.

In December 1988, the old and dying *Fraxinus pennsylvanica* was removed from the north end of the Rock Garden. On May 18 of that same year the new Steinhardt Conservatory was dedicated and a new era began for the Garden. As in any living garden, there is a continual cycle of change. (Because the Conservatory deals basically with plants grown under glass rather than those grown outdoors, its collection has not been included in this book.)

Now in July of 1990, Judith D. Zuk has been appointed the new President of a Garden that today has more than 22,000 members representing all fifty states and more than fifty-five other countries.

# CHAPTER TWO

# ANNUALS AND PERENNIALS

A number of crows cawed at each other from the top of a nearby tree. It was a beautiful early summer's day in June, although some might say that the air was a bit cool for Brooklyn that time of year. Three women had just passed through the turnstile of the Brooklyn Botanic Garden's entrance facing the rear of the Brooklyn Museum.

All three were elderly and loaded with paraphernalia that included various bags and purses, plus binoculars hung on cords around their necks. All three wore hats that were small, black, flat, and decorated with artificial fruits of one kind or another, and each carried her own brightly colored tapestried bag that held various items of crochet work, knitting needles, and balls of yarn.

They paused on the path that winds along the Herb Garden on the right and a bed of annuals on the left.

"Now that's pretty," said the first lady as she pointed to the flowers. She appeared to be the leader of the group.

"Whoever would have thought of putting red and purple together?" asked the second.

"You did when you crocheted your scarf," said the third.

"But that's yarn," said the second.

The bedding annuals they extolled were arranged along a three-foot-high raised bed fronted with native stone. Against a backdrop of witch hazels and various evergreens, the annuals were planted with a line of the taller *Perilla* 'Red-leaf' at the rear, with a mix of *Salvia splendens* 'Hotline Violet' and the deep blue of *Impatiens* 'Gem's Violet'. Here and there were sparks of red and orange from that Victorian favorite, the tassel flower, *Emilia javanica*. And spilling over the edge of the stones were creeping zinnias, *Sanvitalia procumbens* 'Mandarin Orange', their short-petaled and big-eyed daisylike flowers hovering just above the meandering eight-inch-high plants.

The confrontation of colors was partially relieved with the silver-gray of a dusty miller cultivar 'Silver Lace' *(Senecio cineraria)* and a clump of beautiful caladiums, *Caladium* 'White Queen'.

Finally, as if to prove the inaccuracy of the dictum "Less is more," a new combination appeared to the left of the bed, consisting of a deep purple ornamental pepper cultivar 'Midnight Special' surrounded by clusters of a pink-plumed cockscomb, *Celosia plumosa* 'Pink Castle'. The whole mix was alive with bees and skipper butterflies. The vibrant color scheme in this garden extended beyond the customary begonias and impatiens to include more unusual annuals. The Brooklyn Botanic Garden's annual borders demonstrate the striking effects that are possible when annuals are used creatively.

The ladies continued to walk and chat, stopping to listen to the soft coos of a mourning dove overhead, and stopped again to praise a bed of mixed red and white salvias, *Salvia* 'Hall of Fame Fireworks', planted in a mixed bed set in front of a line of Rocky Mountain junipers *(Juniperus scopulorum),* the blue-gray needles of the junipers and the brilliant hues of the salvia making a striking combination. Later in the season, the leadwort *(Ceratostigma plumbaginoides)* will provide a startling contrast with its piercing blue flowers. The gardener who thought of those unusual and striking color combinations for what the Garden calls the "Border Mound" is Douglas Dudgeon, a onetime member of the New York City Parks Department, who joined the staff of the Garden in 1985. Mr. Dudgeon is in charge of the Shakespeare Garden, the

Fragrance Garden, and the border at the Washington Avenue entrance.

He was walking along the path that leads past the Shakespeare Garden, carrying his cultivator over his shoulder with the aspect of a pilgrim on his way to the high Himalayas.

We told him of the three ladies and both their and our delight with that unusual combination of purples, pinks, and oranges. "When you plan a display, do you work it out beforehand?" we asked.

"Yes," he replied. "During the winter months I collect all the catalogs that feature bedding plants, then work out the designs on paper using crayons for color and at the same time noting the various heights of the plants."

The cultivator that he leaned on has had its four tines cut to half their length, then filed to make rounded tips. We had never seen one like it before.

"This is a great tool for working with shallow-rooted plants," he said, "especially for getting in behind the bushes and working with the soil in all these raised beds. I've never seen one offered for sale so I had to make my own." The shortened tines enable him to cultivate the soil in his annual beds without disturbing delicate roots.

Another gardener shares in the responsibilities for annual bedding plants beside Mr. Dudgeon. He is Bernard Currid, who is in charge of the Garden's annual and perennial borders, the Herb Garden, and the lily pools that front the administration buildings, now connected to the new Steinhardt Conservatory.

Mr. Currid, who we will meet later on when we discuss the Herb Garden, also cares for a long border that parallels the reflecting lily pools fronting the Administration Building and its new wing that leads to the conservatory. He points out that he changes the design every year. At no time is the plan for any of the borders left to chance. He has been at the Garden for over twenty-one years.

"We start with a basic idea for the borders, then in January, when the weather is too uncomfortable for too many hours out-of-doors, we sit down and we go through all the catalogs, and after completing a careful sketch of the layout, we order a whole slew of stuff, with this as the result.

"But there is more to a good annual border than the choice of plants. We cultivate and cultivate again. I just finished weeding this bed yesterday, and it takes me a whole day to do the job correctly." This particular border he pointed to fronts the lily pools and is 130 feet long. "I pull out every weed that I see. That's the big secret of such a planting: frequent cultivation and doing it well."

We paused before a particularly attractive combination of polka-dot plants growing in front of a bank of rose-colored ornamental grasses.

The polka-dot plant *(Hypoestes phyllostachya)* makes an excellent pot plant for the windowsill and has been used in houseplant collections for years. But here it serves as a most attractive and unusual border plant that forms mounds of foliage about one foot tall, and doing well in full sun and also partial shade. The particular cultivar is 'Pink Splash'.

The ornamental grass used in the background is a perennial that in Brooklyn is treated to a winter indoors. Known as *Pennisetum setaceum* 'Burgundy Giant', the leaves and the flower spikes are a rich deep rose color.

"All the books tell you it's better to put the taller plants at the back of a border," he said, "but in selected places I let them grow toward the front so they can artfully drape over the smaller plants. It adds an air of mystery to the border."

As Mr. Currid's experience shows, the rules of gardening are not sacrosanct, and gardeners need not be afraid to play with them. Part of the fun of gardening is in trying out new plants and new ideas. Flouting the conventional wisdom can produce beguiling results. And failed experiments in the flower garden can always be corrected next year. In the case of the larger plants falling over the shorter, reason says that the taller plants should be way at the back of the border. But by carefully selecting the quality of the plant allowed to fall about—in this case the graceful weeping blades of grass—the effect is both spontaneous and planned, hence mysterious.

## • SOME SEASONAL BEDDING PLANTS FOR SUN OR SHADE.

Surely all gardeners are familiar with plants such as wax begonias, impatiens, and geraniums. Here are some less common plants to consider for seasonal bedding. *Note:* Bedding plants are usually sold in three categories, a plan originally devised in England:

Hardy annuals (H) are plants that tolerate a reasonable degree of frost; even in the colder parts of the country, many of their seeds survive a winter outside and germinate in the spring. The alternate freezes and thaws of late February and March will not harm them, and in fact are often necessary for germination to occur.

Half-hardy annuals (HH) are usually damaged, set back, or killed by continued exposure to frost, but most will stand up to an occasional light freeze and are impervious to endless days of cool, wet weather, a common occurrence in the English climate.

Tender annuals and perennials used as annuals (T) come from the warmer parts of the world and need warm soil for germination. They are immediately killed by frost.

*Alcea rosea,* hollyhock. (H) Biennial grown as an annual, to 6 feet; tall spikes of large single or double flowers in shades of red, pink, rose, yellow, white. Full sun, in well-drained soil of average fertility. Good background plant; may need staking. Blooms first year from seed if started early indoors. This is the flower that children use in making dolls, and it is lovely in cottage gardens.

*Anchusa capensis,* bugloss, Cape forget-me-not. (HH) Biennial grown as annual; to 1½ feet; clusters of blue, pink, or white flowers. Full sun to partial shade. Grows best in cool weather. Cut back after first flowering for rebloom.

*Brassica oleracea,* Acephala Group, ornamental cabbage and kale. (H) Biennials grown as annuals; to 15 inches; heads of frilled leaves in red-violet and green, or green and white, with shades in between. Colorful accent in late summer and fall. Full sun, in any average garden soil. Direct-sow in summer. Holds up well in cool weather. Edible but tough to chew. Works well in a pot, and is being seen in more and more autumn gardens.

*Browallia speciosa.* (T) Perennials grown as an annual; to about 1 foot high; flowers to 2 inches wide, in shades of blue, violet, purple, white. Full sun to partial shade, in moist but well-drained soil of average fertility. Good for bedding, pots, or hanging baskets.

*Calendula officinalis,* pot marigold, marybud. (H) Annual, to 1½ feet; double daisylike flowers in shades of yellow, gold, and orange. Full sun, in any average garden soil. Grows best in cool weather, blooms from spring to fall. Easy to grow and excellent in pots. Found in BBG's Shakespeare Garden.

*Capsicum annuum,* ornamental pepper. (T) Annual, to 2½ feet; grown for its conical red, orange, yellow, or purple fruit. Full sun, in well-drained soil rich in organic matter. Set outdoors when danger of frost is past; grows best in warm weather. Fruit is edible but hot! Does well in pots. Doug Dudgeon paired a deep purple cultivar with a dusty pink celosia at BBG in the summer of 1989.

*Celosia cristata,* Plumosa Group, plumed celosia. (T) Annual, to 1 foot; feathery flower plumes in shades of red, rose, apricot, gold, salmon, cream. Full sun, in any average garden soil. Easy to grow, and the newer pastel shades mix well with other colors in the garden. Flowers dry well.

*Cheiranthus cheiri,* wallflower. (H) Short-lived perennial grown as an annual when started early indoors; to 2½ feet; fragrant orange, yellow, red, red-brown, or purple flowers. Full sun, in moist soil. Blooms in spring or summer, depending on variety, doing best in cool weather. Excellent in pots and rock walls. Found in BBG Fragrance Garden.

*Cleome hasslerana,* spider flower. (H) Annual, to 4 or more feet high; clusters of long-spined flowers in pink, rose, or white. Prefers full sun but tolerates some shade; any well-drained garden soil. Blooms all summer; tolerates dry weather. Striking background plant. Often self-sows.

*Coleus* × *hybridus.* (T) Perennial grown as annual; to slightly over 1 foot; small spikes of tiny flowers that are usually removed, as this plant is grown for the colorful foliage produced in various combinations of red, red-brown, green, pink, white. Full sun to partial shade, in any average garden soil. Easy to propagate from cuttings. Smaller varieties excellent as edging.

*Consolida ambigua (Delphinium ajacis),* rocket larkspur. (H) Annual, to 4 feet; spikes of blue, pink, or white flowers in late spring to early summer. Full sun, in fertile, moist but well-drained soil. Plants may need staking.

*Dianthus chinensis,* China pink. (HH) Annual, to 1 foot; grassy gray-green leaves; single, often fringed, flowers in shades of red, pink, and white, with mild clove fragrance. Full sun, in moist but well-drained soil.

*Digitalis purpurea* 'Foxy', foxglove. (H) Biennial grown as hardy annual, this variety blooming first year from seed; to 4 feet; spikes of tubular spotted-purple flowers, also available in other shades. Full sun to partial shade, in moist, well-drained soil. Grows best in cool, moist climates.

*Dolichos lablab,* hyacinth bean. (T) Perennial vine grown as annual, to 15 feet long; oval compound leaves; pealike rosy purple or white flowers. Full sun, in average garden soil. Needs trellis for support. Seedlings resent transplanting, so start out in individual peat pots.

*Euphorbia marginata,* snow-on-the-mountain. (HH) Annual, to about 3 feet tall; grown for showy white bracts surrounding small green-ish flowers. Full sun, in well-drained soil. Grows best in warm weather.

*Gypsophila elegans,* annual baby's breath. (HH) Annual, to about 2 feet; sprays of small white or pink flowers in summer. Full sun, in fertile, well-drained soil; prefers but does not require alkaline pH. Good for cutting, and excellent growing along the edge of a wall.

*Heliotropium arborescens,* heliotrope. (T) Annual, to about 2 feet; clusters of tiny vanilla-scented purple or violet flowers. Full sun, in moist, fertile soil. Grows best in cool weather. Found in Fragrance Garden.

*Hypoestes phyllostachya,* polka dot plant. (T) Perennial grown as annual, to about 1 foot; deep green leaves with pink dots and splashes. Full sun to partial shade. Nice in border or containers; makes a good houseplant. Blue flowers are inconspicuous. Bernard Currid combined this in a bed with flowering annuals and a *Pennisetum* cultivar for a striking effect.

*Ipomoea nil, I. purpurea, I. tricolor,* morning glory. (T, H) Annual vines to 8 feet, with saucer-shaped flowers in blue, pink, purple, deep red, or white. Full sun, in any average garden soil. Easy to grow from seed, but soak overnight before planting. Often self-sows.

*Kochia scoparia* Forma *trichophylla,* summer cypress. (HH) Annual bush to 3 feet; feathery green leaves resembling cypress foliage turn red in fall. Full sun, in well-drained soil tending toward dryness. Plant as accents in borders, for hedging, or in pots. Produces the effect of a small shrub in a single season.

*Lobularia maritima,* sweet alyssum. (H) Perennial grown as annual, to about 8 inches high; small spreading plants covered with tiny honey-scented flowers in white, pink, purple, or red. Full sun to partial shade, in moist but well-drained soil. Fine for edging, containers, rock gardens. Shear back spent flowers; blooms all summer until frost. May self-sow. Found in Fragrance Garden.

*Mirabilis jalapa,* four-o'clock. (T) Perennial grown as annual, to 2 feet; red, pink, orange, yellow, white, or striped flowers open in late afternoon. Full sun to partial shade, in well-drained soil. Tuberous roots can be dug and stored over winter, replanted next spring.

*Ocimum basilicum* 'Dark Opal', purple basil. (HH) Annual, to 1 foot; fragrant, deep reddish-purple leaves. Full sun, in any average garden soil. Handsome in flower gardens; edible, too. Pinch off flower stalks to encourage bushiness. Found in Fragrance Garden.

*Papaver rhoeas,* Shirley poppy. (H) Annual, to 2 feet; large single or double flowers in crimson, scarlet, pink, salmon, yellow, white. Full sun, in reasonably fertile, well-drained soil. Poppies do not transplant well, so sow *in situ* or start seeds in peat pots.

*Pelargonium* species, scented-leaved geraniums. (T) Perennials grown as annuals, to 2 feet; small pink or white flowers; small leaves with scent of rose, apple, nutmeg, ginger, peppermint, lemon, or other fragrances. Full sun, in good, well-drained garden soil with moderate moisture. Good container plants; can be brought indoors over winter.

*Pennisetum setaceum,* fountain grass. (T) Perennial ornamental grass grown as annual in cold areas. To 4 feet; narrow arching leaves; slender flower plumes of pinkish white in summer; variously colored cultivars available. Full sun, in well-drained soil of average fertility. If winters are cold, take plants indoors over winter.

*Perilla frutescens,* common perilla. (T) Perennial grown as annual, to 3 feet; deep reddish purple leaves with overlays of bronze. Full sun to partial shade. Good background plant for other annuals. Pinch off the small white flowers.

*Portulaca grandiflora,* rose moss. (HH) Annual, to 6 inches high, trailing habit; ruffly flowers in red, magenta, rose, pink, salmon, orange, yellow, white. Full sun in sandy, well-drained soil. Lovely in rock and wall gardens; best in hot, dry conditions. We found it growing in pockets in a stone wall by the BBG Herb Garden.

*Ricinus communis,* castor bean. (T) Annual, to 6 feet; huge palmate leaves to 3 feet across. Full sun, in well-drained soil. Striking as background or screening plant; very tropical-looking. *Warning:* Seeds are poisonous.

*Sanvitalia procumbens,* creeping zinnia. (HH) Annual, to 6 inches high, trailing habit; small dark-centered daisylike flowers of golden yellow or orange. Full sun, in light, well-drained soil. Withstands hot, humid weather.

*Torenia fournieri,* wishbone flower. (HH) Annual, to 1 foot; flowers similar to Johnny jump-ups, each combining blue, violet, and yellow. Partial shade, in moist, reasonably fertile soil. Lovely in borders receiving afternoon shade; it flourished in a shady part of an annual border at BBG.

*Verbena × hybrida,* garden verbena. (HH) Perennial grown as annual, to 1 foot; clusters of fragrant red, pink, lavender, purple, blue, yellow, or white flowers. Full sun, in any average garden soil. Remove spent flowers for bloom from midsummer to frost. Found in Fragrance Garden.

## CARING FOR ANNUALS THROUGH THE SEASON

As with many garden activities, getting a jump on the seasons is always important. When working with annuals, prepare the soil during the autumn before planting, or in early spring as soon as the soil is workable. If you plan to add compost and other organic matter, do so as early as possible to give it time to mellow before planting.

Start seeds of hardy and half-hardy annuals (and perennials that masquerade as annuals) indoors in late winter and start to harden off seedlings in April and May. Direct-sow hardy annuals as soon as the soil can be worked in spring.

In warm climates, start seeds of late spring- and summer-blooming annuals indoors in winter and start planting out in early spring. Direct-sow cold-tolerant flowers. In the warmest climates, set out bedding annuals in early spring.

Plant out pansies as soon as the soil is workable in spring.

In warm climates, sow hardy and half-hardy annuals (such as ageratum, sweet alyssum, bachelor's buttons, calendula, larkspur, candytuft, poppies, snapdragons, and sweet peas) in autumn, to bloom in winter and spring. Or sow in January for early spring flowers.

Plant tender annuals in late spring or early summer, when the danger of frost is past and the soil is warm. Harden off seedlings started indoors before moving them to the garden. In warm climates plant out tender annuals in mid-spring. In all climates, avoid planting in very hot weather.

In warm climates, direct-sow annuals in summer for fall flowers. Replace early annuals and spring bulbs with heat-tolerant flowers such as cosmos, marigolds, and portulaca, in early summer.

Thin direct-seeded annuals about a month before planting.

Water new plantings regularly until they become established.

Water established plants as needed during hot, dry weather. When soil feels dry one to two inches below the surface, it's time to water. Be sure to water deeply. Annuals in containers need to be watered every day—sometimes twice a day—in summer. Water hanging basket planters by putting ice cubes on top of the soil where they will slowly melt.

Fertilize annuals every few weeks to once a month, especially when in containers, during the growing season, using seaweed extract, fish emulsion, 5-10-5, or other all-purpose plant food.

Deadhead (remove fading or dead flowers) annuals to prolong bloom. Pinch back bushy plants like impatiens to get more flowers. Shear back small-leaved plants like sweet alyssum to get a bushier shape and more flowers. Shear once or twice during the growing season, then feed and water.

Keep the garden clean to help prevent pests and diseases. Keep beds and borders weeded and mulched. Cultivate often if no mulch is used. If disease occurs, remove the infected plants. At the first sign of pests, take appropriate measures. Spray with insecticidal soap. If you use pesticides, be extremely cautious and follow package directions carefully.

After the first frost, pull and discard all tender annuals; many others adapt to colder temperatures. In warm climates, pull them when they stop blooming in late fall.

Marigolds, nasturtiums, petunias, and some other annuals can be dug and potted up in fall for continued bloom indoors. Take cuttings of begonias, geraniums, and impatiens for winter flowers indoors.

## PERENNIAL BEDS AND BORDERS

One highlight of most public and private gardens is the perennial bed or border, an area designed to produce the same look year after year, and accomplishing this through the use of perennials with the addition of bulbs and annual bedding plants to provide further bursts of color and fill in the empty spots.

Although there is maintenance involved with perennials, it is far less than the yearly planting out of annuals. Outside of weeding, a perennial border can be enjoyed for many years with care reduced to deadheading spent flowers, and dividing crowded plants. By planting a skillful blend of many species and cultivars, blooming times may be staggered throughout the season and those perennials that fade after flowering, like poppies and iris, can be masked with temporary plantings of annuals.

Bulbs should also be given a chance in the perennial garden since many produce flowers not only in spring but the rest of the garden year. Nothing is quite as spectacular in the early summer garden as the bright yellow produced by a mass of lily leeks *(Allium moly)* or the tall stalks of summer-flowering hyacinths

*(Galtonia candicans)*. And when their leaves die back down, the empty spots can be filled with more bedding plants.

By mixing perennials, bulbs, and annuals, the garden can be a source of continual bloom from early spring to late fall, and in many areas of the country, on into winter.

There are many ways to combine flowers into pleasing beds and borders. Color schemes are one basis for designing a garden. You can build a garden from a monochromatic scheme (the all-white garden at Sissinghurst in England is probably the most famous example), from harmonious colors close to one another on a color wheel, from contrasting colors, or from polychromatic (multicolored) flowers judiciously mixed.

But there are other themes for gardens besides colors. A garden can revolve around the use of leaves rather than flowers, such as the popular gardens devoted to gray and silver foliage. Or they can be collections of plants from the same family, like a garden of ornamental grasses, a garden of various daisies, a garden exclusively of daylilies or hostas, or perhaps a garden completely of bulbs. Institutions such as the Brooklyn Botanic Garden sometimes create gardens of plants in the same botanic family (called systematic collections) to serve as a teaching tool. And don't forget specialties such as a Japanese garden, a garden of roses, a garden devoted to everlasting flowers, or a garden to produce cut flowers throughout the garden year, usually called a cutting garden. The BBG also has a wonderful garden of fragrant plants.

Another type of theme garden revolves around a famous person or a historical epoch. One such idea is to research the flowers that would be grown during colonial days and create the garden that George Washington would have had in his backyard. Another popular garden theme is plants mentioned in the Bible. A third, one which can be found in the BBG, is devoted to plants mentioned in the works of Shakespeare or otherwise grown during Elizabethan times.

## • *SOME OUTSTANDING PERENNIALS*

*Achillea* spp., yarrow. To 2 feet; finely cut foliage; flat-topped heads of small flowers in summer in yellow, gold, pink, red, white. Full sun, in any well-drained garden soil of average fertility. Good for cutting or drying. Divide in spring or fall.

*Aquilegia* spp., columbine. To 3 feet; compound leaves; gracefully spurred flowers in late spring to early summer, in blue, purple, pink, rose, red, yellow, white; in some hybrids the central cup is creamy white or yellow. Partial shade to full sun, in reasonably fertile, moist but well-drained soil. Divide in spring. Deadhead for continued bloom. Hummingbirds love columbines. Excellent as cut flowers. Can be planted in a Shakespeare garden.

*Anemone* × *hybrida,* Japanese anemone. To 4 feet; pink or white flowers in late summer and fall. Full sun to partial shade, in moist soil. Seldom needs division. Can be planted in a Shakespeare garden.

*Armeria maritima,* thrift, sea pink. To 10 inches; basal rosette of narrow leaves; round heads of small rose, pink, purple, or white flowers in early summer. Full sun, in well-drained, preferably sandy, soil.

*Artemisia ludoviciana* silver king artemisia, *A. schmidtiana* 'Silver Mound'. The silver king artemisia is upright, to 2 feet, with narrow silvery leaves; 'Silver Mound' is round, about 1½ feet tall and wide, with delicate, finely cut silver-green foliage. Full sun, in well-drained soil. Gray-green leaves beautifully set off pink or blue flowers. Divides easily in spring or fall.

*Aster novae-angliae, A. novi-belgii,* New England aster, Michaelmas daisy. To 4 feet; many-rayed daisylike flowers in shades of red, rose, pink, purple, blue, white, blooming in the fall. Full sun, in fertile, moist but well-drained soil. Many cultivars available. Divide every other year.

*Astilbe* spp. From 1½ to 4 feet; ferny leaves; feathery plumes of red, rose, pink, or white flowers in late spring or early summer. Partial shade, in moist, humusy soil. Divide every 3 years. Use 3 or more plants in a group for good effect.

*Aurinia saxatilis (Alyssum saxatile),* basket-of-gold. To 1 foot; grayish green leaves; covered with clusters of small golden yellow flowers in spring. Full sun, in well-drained soil of average fertility. Drainage is critical. Lovely at border's edge and along walls.

*Campanula* spp., bellflowers. From 8 inches to 3½ feet, depending on species; bell-shaped flowers of blue, violet, pink, or white in early summer. Full sun to partial shade, in moist but well-drained, fertile soil. Lovely in beds and borders and as a cut flower.

*Ceratostigma plumbaginoides,* leadwort. To 12 inches; clusters of deep blue flowers in late summer; oval leaves. Full sun, in well-drained soil of average fertility. Good ground cover.

*Chrysanthemum maximum,* shasta daisy. From 1 to 3½ feet; classic yellow-centered white daisies; bloom in summer. Full sun to partial shade, in fertile, moist but well-drained soil. Good as cut flower. Divide every other year.

*Chrysanthemum* × *morifolium,* hardy mum. From 8 inches to 4 feet;

many hybrids in a range of sizes, flower forms, and colors, but all are variations on the well-known garden or florist's mum; flowers in every color except blue, blooming in the fall. Full sun, in fertile, moist but well-drained soil. Pinch back until midsummer. Divide every spring. Mulch in cold climates, especially those without snow cover.

*Coreopsis* spp., tickseed. From 1 to 3 feet; single or double, golden yellow daisylike flowers in summer. Full sun, in well-drained soil of average fertility. Easy to grow; withstand drought. Good as cut flowers. Deadhead for continued bloom.

*Delphinium elatum.* To 6 feet; large spikes of blue, violet, purple, lavender, pink, or white flowers in summer, some with contrasting center called a "bee." Full sun, in moist but well-drained, very fertile soil. Does not grow well where summers are hot. Plant in back of the border.

*Dianthus* spp., garden pinks. From 6 inches to 1½ feet; grassy gray-green leaves; single or double flowers, often with fringed petals and clove fragrance, in shades of red, rose, pink, and white, blooming in late spring to early summer. Found in fragrance gardens.

*Dicentra spectabilis,* bleeding heart. To 2 feet; divided leaves; heart-shaped pink flowers on arching horizontal stems in mid-spring to early summer. Partial shade, in moist, humusy soil. An old garden favorite from Japan.

*Dictamnus albus,* gas plant. To 3 feet; glossy compound leaves and attractive and unusual pink or white flowers. Full sun, in well-drained but moist soil of good fertility. Choose location with care because once planted it resents moving. Common name comes from the volatile gas produced by its leaves; the gas can supposedly be ignited by a match on still summer evenings.

*Epimedium* spp. To 1 foot; heart-shaped leaves, sometimes ever-green; clusters of unusually shaped tubular flowers in early spring, in pink, yellow, orange, red, or white, depending on the species. Partial shade, in moist but well-drained fertile soil. Excellent in rock gardens, especially as ground cover. Transplants easily, and should be divided every few years.

*Eryngium* spp., sea holly. To 3 feet; in summer, rounded thistlelike flower heads appear, surrounded by spiny bracts, silvery or steel blue in color; spiny leaves. Full sun, in sandy, well-drained soil of moderate fertility, not too rich. Unusual and dramatic in the garden; can be planted in a Shakespeare garden.

*Filipendula* spp., meadowsweet. To 7 feet; fluffy heads of tiny pink or white flowers in summer, in some species resembling cotton candy; compound leaves. Full sun, but will succeed in partial shade with moist soil rich in organic matter. Plants eventually form a big clump. Does not do well in hot, dry summer weather.

*Gaillardia* × *grandiflora,* blanket flower. From 6 inches to 3 feet; red-and-yellow daisylike flowers in summer; slightly hairy leaves. Full sun, in well-drained soil of average fertility. Short-lived, rarely overwintering in wet soil. Center of crown dies back each year but new plants appear around the edges. Will often bloom from seed the first year.

*Geranium* spp., cranesbill, hardy geranium. From 6 inches to 1½ feet; flowers in rose, pink, lavender, blue, or white, in spring or early summer; lobed or divided leaves. Partial shade or full sun, in moist but well-drained soil. Dislikes intense summer sun. Striking grown against a wall. Leaves of some species turn red in the fall.

*Gypsophila paniculata,* perennial baby's breath. Branching plants to 3 feet; plants are covered with panicles of tiny, single or double white or pink flowers in summer. Full sun, in moist but well-drained soil, not too fertile, with neutral or slightly alkaline pH. Plants like rock walls. Very easy to grow but do not transplant well. Good for cutting and drying.

*Helleborus niger,* Christmas rose, *H. orientalis,* Lenten rose. *H. niger* grows to 1 foot high, with basal oblong leaves, often evergreen; flowers are white flushed with pink, blooming in late fall, winter, or early spring, depending on location. *H. orientalis,* the Lenten rose, grows to 1½ feet; oblong leaves; clusters of flowers, cream, green, pink, or purplish, in late winter or early spring; flowers are attractive from first bloom until seedpods open. Partial shade to shade, in moist but well-drained soil rich in organic matter. Remove old foliage in late winter or early spring. North of USDA Zone 6, mulch is necessary, especially where snow cover is lacking.

*Heuchera sanguinea,* coral bells. To 2½ feet high; tiny bell-shaped flowers, red, pink, or white, on long, slender stems, in spring and summer. Basal clumps of scalloped leaves. Full sun to partial shade, in moist but well-drained soil rich in organic matter. Excellent as edging in borders, in rock walls, and in rock gardens.

*Hibiscus moscheutos,* rose mallow. From 3 to 7 feet, depending on variety; huge ruffled flowers in summer, in shades of red, rose, pink, white. Full sun, in moist soil. Very tropical-looking. Can be grown in pots. Not hardy in the extreme northern U.S.

*Iberis sempervirens,* perennial candytuft. To 1 foot; clusters of small white flowers in spring; small narrow green leaves, usually evergreen. Full sun, in well-drained soil. Cut back after spring flowering.

*Iris* × *germanica,* bearded iris. From 8 inches to 3 feet; large flowers in many shades of purple, blue, pink, red-violet, yellow, orange, white, in early summer; narrow sword-shaped leaves. Full sun, in reasonably fertile, well-drained soil. Plant with fan of leaves pointing in the direction you want plant to grow. Divide after flowering. Can be planted in a Shakespeare garden.

*Iris sibirica,* Siberian iris. To 4 feet; long, slender grassy leaves; flowers in shades of violet, purple, or white, late spring to early summer. Full sun to partial shade, in moist, slightly acid soil rich in organic matter. Easy to grow and resistant to pests and disease.

*Lamium maculatum,* spotted dead nettle. To 1½ feet; whorls of small red-violet or white flowers in early summer; silvery green leaves. Can grow in full sun, in any well-drained soil of average fertility, but better in partial shade. Many cultivars available.

*Ligularia* spp. To 4 feet; round or kidney-shaped basal leaves with stout stems on plants that bear tall spires of yellow or orange daisylike flowers. Partial shade in evenly moist soil of good fertility. Cultivars 'Orange Queen' and 'Othello' have leaves up to 1 foot wide, those of 'Othello' with purple undersides. Plants wilt on hot days, even with plenty of water available, but quickly recover in late afternoon. Beautiful in bog gardens or at the edge of a pond.

*Monarda didyma,* bee balm. To 3 feet; terminal clusters of elongated flowers in shades of scarlet, rose, pink, or purple; fragrant leaves. Full sun to partial shade, in fertile, moist but well-drained soil. Prone to mildew in overly wet and shady spots. Plants are short-lived and should be divided at least every other year. Can be planted in a fragrance garden.

*Myosotis scorpioides,* perennial forget-me-not. To 1½ feet; Familiar small blue flowers with yellow, pink, or white eye, blooming in spring and summer. Partial shade, in moist, humusy soil. Beautiful in woodland gardens.

*Papaver orientale,* oriental poppy. To 3 or 4 feet; basal, toothed leaves; stems covered with silky hairs; large brilliant flowers in shades of scarlet, crimson, salmon, violet, and white, all having dark centers, blooming in early summer. Full sun, in well-drained soil of average fertility. Easy to grow; good for cutting—be sure to seal cut end over flame. Can be planted in a Shakespeare garden.

*Phlox subulata,* mountain pink, moss pink. To 6 inches; needlelike leaves, evergreen in warmer climates; covered with flowers in shades of rose, pink, purple, or white in spring. Full sun, in well-drained soil of average fertility. Nice for edging, ground cover, or in rock garden.

*Physostegia virginiana,* obedient plant. To about 4 feet; long, narrow leaves, spikes of light purple, rosy pink, or white flowers from late summer into fall. Full sun to partial shade, in moist but well-drained soil. Flowers will hold whatever position they are pushed into. Good for cutting.

*Platycodon grandiflorus,* balloon flower. To 3 feet; cup-shaped flowers of violet, blue, pink, or white look like hot-air balloons until they open. Full sun to partial shade, in light, well-drained, reasonably fertile soil. Roots are among the last in the garden to produce foliage, so mark their placement. Good for cutting.

*Primula × polyantha,* primrose. To 8 inches; basal rosette of long crisp leaves; clusters of flowers in shades of violet, rose, pink, red, yellow, white, in spring in the north, winter in the south. Partial shade, in fertile, moist but well-drained soil with acid pH. Plant in beds of spring flowers or in rock gardens. Can be planted in a Shakespeare garden.

*Pulmonaria officinalis,* blue lungwort, Jerusalem sage. To 1 foot; clusters of flowers in early spring, opening blue and turning pink with age. Oval leaves are spotted with white. Partial to full shade, in moist soil of average fertility. Nice bedding plants for shady spots. Can be planted in a Shakespeare garden.

*Rodgersia* spp. To 4 feet; large palmate leaves, sometimes with a bronze cast; clusters of small white flowers in summer. Full sun to partial shade, in moist, even boggy, soil rich in organic matter. Striking plants for wet places, nice next to stream or pond.

*Rudbeckia hirta* 'Gloriosa', gloriosa daisy. To 3 feet; coarse leaves covered with short hairs; large daisylike flowers with ray flowers in many shades of yellow and reddish-brown to burgundy. Full sun in any average garden soil. Easy to grow, these short-lived perennials will often bloom the first year from seed; they will self-sow. Very drought-tolerant. Can be transplanted while in bloom. Excellent as cut flowers.

*Sedum* spp., stonecrop. From 6 inches to 2 feet; fleshy oval leaves, green or deep red; terminal clusters of tiny red, pink, yellow, or white flowers in summer. Full sun to partial shade, in moist but well-drained soil of average fertility. *Sedum* 'Autumn Joy' is one of the top 10 perennials of all time.

*Sempervivum* spp., houseleek. Low-growing rosettes of succulent leaves, sometimes edged in red; flowers are small at tips of stems, but often unusual and quite beautiful. Plants spread by means of offsets. Full sun, in well-drained soil of average fertility. Useful in borders, walls, and rock gardens.

*Stachys byzantina,* lamb's ears. To 1½ feet; large oval leaves covered with soft white hairs; small purple flowers in summer on strong feltlike stems, excellent for drying. Full sun to partial shade, in well-drained, even dry, soil of average to poor fertility. Nicely complements pink and blue flowers in bed and borders.

*Thalictrum* spp., meadow rue. From 2 to 5 feet; branching plants with small compound leaves; fluffy clusters of small lavender, pink, or yellow flowers from spring into summer. Partial shade to full sun, in moist but well-drained soil rich in organic matter.

*Veronica* spp., speedwell. From 1 to 3 feet; narrow leaves; spikes of tiny blue or violet flowers in summer. Full sun to partial shade, in well-drained soil of average fertility. Deadhead for repeat bloom. Good for cutting.


## THE SHAKESPEARE GARDEN

"Now 'tis the spring, and weeds are shallow-rooted; suffer them now and they'll o'ergrow the garden," says Queen Margaret in *Henry VI,* Part II, and those sentiments are in good company both in the Shakespeare Garden and with its gardener, Doug Dudgeon. We visited in late May.

"I'm out here most of the year," he said, "even in winter, when I'm doing pruning and maintenance work. During the growing season I spend a great deal of my time weeding, as they are always popping up. Every day there's always a weed somewhere in the garden."

"Originally," he continued, "this garden was meant to contain plants found in the garden at Shakespeare's home at Stratford-on-Avon in the 1600s. The flowers used are plants either mentioned in the plays or actually growing in his original garden. We try to keep as close to the old-fashioned flowers as possible. This garden has been on this spot since 1979, when it was relocated from its first home down by the Children's Garden."

Today the garden holds some eighty species of plants. There are flowers from early March into October, although in late May and June the color is at its height.

Although perennials make up the major part of the garden, it does contain the common garden or salad nasturtium *(Tropaeolum majus);* pot marigolds *(Calendula officinalis),* used in the Middle Ages for both ulcers and toothaches; Scotch thistle *(Onopordum acanthium),* and the unusual and often overlooked St. Mary's thistle *(Silybum marianum).* This last plant is not grown for the small and pale thistlelike flowers, but instead for the unusual cut and spiny leaves that are speckled with white blotches. In Shakespeare's time this latter thistle was boiled as a potherb.

Yes, the lilies bloom, the poppies wave in the summer winds, and the sweet peas climb, but in among the more attractive flowers are plants like stinging nettle, *Urtica dioica,* which is said to have reached England by way of Caesar's soldiers who, according to legend, not having pants thick enough to withstand the cold British winters, were said to pluck nettles to rub over their limbs so they burned and smarted for the rest of the day. And would you believe that most of the chlorophyll used in commerce (it's an ingredient for certain medicines and has long been used to color foods and drugs) is generally obtained from nettles?

We asked Mr. Dudgeon if there was anything special about the soil or the care in this particular garden.

"No," he answered. "I just fertilize once in the spring with a 5–10–5 fertilizer, and the soil is basically the original clay, but over the years it's been continually mixed with compost and peat moss."

Brooklyn gets cold in the winter but only the low boxwood hedges *(Buxus sempervirens)* need protection against the low temperatures. In December the hedges are screened with burlap to prevent windburn.

We walked past the Shakespeare Garden at every opportunity all summer long. We saw the hummingbirds flock to the columbines *(Aquilegia vulgaris* and *A. canadensis)* and realized that even the common or orange daylily *(Hemerocallis fulva),* when in the company of Shakespeare's flowers, attains a new beauty. And we saw the peony *(Paeonia suffruticosa),* the oriental poppy *(Papaver orientale)* and the English rhubarb *(Rheum rhabarbarum),* this last plant reminding us of just how good a pie made with rhubarb and wild strawberries could be.


## PLANTS IN THE SHAKESPEARE GARDEN

NOTE: Not all the plants below would have been present in Shakespeare's original garden, but they have crept in over the years and are too familiar to visitors to be removed.

*Aconitum napellus,* aconite, monkshood
*Adiantum pedatum,* maidenhair fern
*Allium ampeloprasum,* leek

*Allium cepa*, onion
*Anemone japonica*, Japanese anemone
*Aquilegia canadensis* and *A. vulgaris*, columbine
*Artemisia absinthium*, wormwood
*Artemisia dracunculus*, French tarragon
*Aster ericoides*, heath aster
*Bellis perennis*, English daisy
*Buxus sempervirens*, boxwood
*Calendula officinalis*, marybud, pot marigold
*Carum carvi*, caraway
*Chamaemelum nobile*, chamomile
*Cnicus benedictus*, blessed thistle
*Coronilla varia*, vetch
*Crataegus* sp., hawthorn
*Crithmum maritimum*, samphire
*Cynara scolymus*, artichoke
*Cynoglossum officinale*, tongue of dog
*Cytisus scoparius*, broom
*Daucus carota* var. *sativus*, wild carrot, Queen Anne's lace
*Dennstaedtia punctilobula*, hay-scented fern
*Eranthis cilicica*, winter aconite
*Eryngium maritimum*, sea holly
*Foeniculum vulgare*, fennel
*Fragaria vesca*, strawberry
*Fritillaria imperialis*, crown imperial
*Fritillaria persica*, Persian fritillary
*Galanthus nivalis*, snowdrop
*Hedera helix*, ivy
*Hemerocallis fulva*, common daylily
*Hyssopus officinalis*, hyssop
*Ilex aquifolium*, English Holly
*Iris reticulata*
*Iris* × *germanica*, fleur-de-lis
*Jasminum nudiflorum*, jasmine
*Lamium maculatum*, dead nettle
*Lathyrus* sp., sweet pea
*Laurus nobilis*, bay, laurel
*Lavandula angustifolia*, lavender
*Lilium candidum*, lily
*Lonicera periclymenum*, honeysuckle
*Lychnis flos-cuculi*, crow flower
*Lythrum salicaria*, loosestrife

*Malus* spp., crab apple
*Mandragora officinarum*, mandrake
*Mentha spicata* and *M.* × *piperita*, mints
*Mespilus germanica*, medlar
*Myrtus communis*, myrtle
*Narcissus* spp., narcissus
*Onopordum acanthium*, Scotch thistle
*Origanum vulgare*, marjoram
*Paeonia suffruticosa*, peony
*Papaver orientale*, poppy
*Pinus sylvestris*, Scotch pine
*Poterium sanguisorba*, burnet
*Primula* sp., primrose
*Pulmonaria officinalis*, lungwort
*Quercus rubra*, oak
*Rosa eglanteria*, eglantine rose
    *R.* × *alba*, white rose
    *R. gallica*, red rose
    *R. moschata*, musk rose
*Ranunculus acris*, cuckoo buds
*Raphanus sativus*, radish
*Rheum rhaponticum*, rhubarb
*Rosmarinus officinalis*, rosemary
*Ruta graveolens*, rue
*Santolina chamaecyparissus*, lavender cotton
*Satureja montana*, savory
*Scilla hispanica*, wood hyacinth
*Sium sisarum*, skirret
*Taxus baccata* 'Repandens', yew
*Thymus vulgaris*, thyme
*Tropaeolum majus*, nasturtium
*Urtica dioica*, nettle
*Viola odorata*, violet
*Viola tricolor*, pansy
*Vitis vinifera*, grape

## THE FRAGRANCE GARDEN

The wonderful fragrance of flowers should be as important to the gardener as their colors. Just a small bed of richly scented flowers and leaves can be a real source of pleasure for the home.

ANNUALS AND PERENNIALS • 45

"Without charm there can be no fine literature, as there can be no perfect flower without fragrance," said Arthur Symons, and he knew of what he wrote. For who can imagine a rose without its sweet perfume or violets without their smell of spring?

Whether gathered from an herb garden or the garden proper, the petals of roses, calendulas, dianthus, and/or heliotrope can be added to a small potpourri to remind one of the glories of summers past while the snow is falling from the sky.

The Fragrance Garden is another one of Doug Dudgeon's responsibilities. It's an intimate garden with the plants in three-foot-high raised beds. Set into nooks are benches for people to sit on and watch the bees and butterflies come and go. The labels in this garden are carefully printed with the plant names in both type and braille.

Here the main emphasis is on the odor of the flowers and foliage; it can be sweet or sharp, depending on the chemical constitution of the plant. Actually a fragrance garden speaks to other senses as well as that of smell. The textures of the plants appeal to our tactile sense, and many are edible and reward our sense of taste. The BBG's Fragrance Garden is a heady amalgam of flowers and herbs.

We stopped before a large bed of *Iris × germanica* var. *florentina,* the source of orris, a powder made of its dried rhizomes and used extensively in the making of perfume. The plants' fans of leaves are trimmed after flowering to shorten them somewhat, and then, as summer progresses and the foliage withers from the top, they are cut back again.

"It's extra work but the leaves look so much better with this treatment. I divide the rhizomes directly after flowering," he said. (For more information on division, see Chapter Twelve, Gardening Techniques and Practices.)

Smaller plants grow in pockets between the stones in the wall.

"I transplant seedlings in a small parcel of earth and wedge them between the stones. You can wrap the roots in a layer of tissue or even a leaf. Soon the roots will take hold. If I start out with ten seedlings, I usually wind up with three that take.

"One of the problems with a fragrance garden," Mr. Dudgeon continues, "is that today's flowers are bred for size and color, and fragrance is often diminished." He finds that he must often seek out old varieties or species forms of plants instead of splashy new hybrids to get the best fragrance.

We pause before a teakwood garden bench set within an alcove with stone walls.

"This is a texture bed designed for the blind. This large agave *(Agave parryi)* spends the winters in the greenhouse, and in the summer I set it in the border, pot and all, but it's kept to the rear because the leaf tips are really sharp.

"And this marvelous hedge is not boxwood but Japanese holly *(Ilex crenata),*" he said, pointing to a low bushy plant with small deep green leaves that only reveal themselves as hollies when the leaves are held right up to the eye and the tiny serrated edges appear. "This plant comes in a number of cultivars and does very well here without the bother of winter protection."

The smells at this point were delightful. We paused before a group of plants meant to be touched, as the odor clings to the finger. There were mints, thymes, and scented geraniums in profusion. These plants were very popular in colonial times and were used not only to scent foods but to endow the handkerchief with a pleasant odor in order to help the average nose through what were often odoriferous times.

"This is clary sage *(Salvia sclarea),* and both its leaves and purple flowers have a very strong odor, and these are common chives *(Allium schoenoprasum)* [they smell mildly oniony] and lovage *(Levisticum officinale).* You can chew lovage stalks like gum, but the taste, a combination of licorice and parsley, is not something I would recommend." Lovage also grows quite large, and will overwhelm a small garden. Another plant in the Fragrance Garden is rosemary, whose needlelike leaves have a refreshing piney scent. The plant is not hardy this far north, but Mr. Dudgeon grows it anyway. "The rosemary *(Rosmarinus officinalis)* isn't fully hardy so it goes inside for the winter," he said. "Over here are garlic chives *(Allium tuberosum).* You can eat the starry white flowers and they have a mild garlic taste."

A huge black swallowtail butterfly flew across our path, aiming for a large fennel plant *(Foeniculum vulgare).* Both the mature butterflies and the caterpillars are fond of its delicate and lacelike anise-flavored foliage.

At one entrance to the Fragrance Garden is a large tree wisteria *(Wisteria floribunda).* Mr. Dudgeon is constantly trimming off the streamers.

"Almost every two weeks in the summer," he said, "I cut them off. I prune the vine in February, cutting back each stem to about two or three buds. These are the flower buds which will bloom in May."

• *A FEW FRAGRANT FLOWERS AND PLANTS*

Here are descriptions of a number of scented plants grown in the BBG Fragrance Garden.

*Allium schoenoprasum,* common chives. Perennial plant whose leaves are clipped for salads. An attractive garden plant.

*Allium tuberosum,* Chinese chives. Perennial whose leaves and flowers are used in salads. Also an attractive garden plant.

*Anethum graveolens,* dill. Cooking, pickling, and salad-flavoring herb grown as an annual.

*Antirrhinum majus,* snapdragon. Beautiful cutting flower with sweet blossoms, grown as annual.

*Artemisia abrotanum,* southernwood. Perennial subshrub with fragrant silvery green foliage.

*Cheiranthus cheiri,* wallflower. Very fragrant and colorful biennial. Can be grown as an annual if started early in the season; does not like hot summers.

*Chrysanthemum balsamita,* costmary. Fragrant foliage; leaves once used as Bible bookmarks.

*Dianthus* spp., carnations, pinks. Most species have fragrant blooms.

*Foeniculum vulgare,* fennel. Cooking herb with licorice odor.

*Galium odoratum,* sweet woodruff. Fragrant perennial with sweet-smelling flowers and foliage; dried for scent.

*Heliotropium arborescens,* heliotrope. Perennial grown as annual with very fragrant flowers with vanilla scent.

*Impatiens balsamina,* balsam. Very fragrant garden annual.

*Iris* × *germanica* var. *florentina.* Garden orris.

*Laurus nobilis,* bay leaf. Tree whose fragrant leaves have been used for cooking for centuries. Tub plant in north.

*Lavandula* spp., lavenders. Perennials whose flowers are dried for fragrance.

*Levisticum officinale,* lovage. Perennial herb with licorice odor to leaves.

*Lilium* spp., lilies. Most lilies have sweet fragrance.

*Lobularia maritima,* sweet alyssum. Sweet-smelling annual.

*Lonicera japonica,* honeysuckle. Sweet-smelling vine; can be invasive.

*Mentha* spp., mints. Peppermints, spearmints, Corsican mint, pennyroyal, all used for flavorings.

*Monarda didyma,* bee balm. Attractive garden perennial with fragrant leaves.

*Nicotiana alata,* flowering tobacco. Annual with sweet-smelling flowers.

*Origanum majorana,* sweet marjoram. Fragrant cooking herb.

*Pelargonium* spp., scented geraniums. Tender perennials grown for foliage, not flowers. Among the odors are pineapple, apple, mint, lemon, ginger, rose.

*Petunia* × *hybrida,* petunia. Sweet-smelling flower grown as annual. 'Blue Skies' is among the most fragrant varieties.

*Rosa gallica officinalis,* apothecary's rose. Crimson rose with especially sweet scent.

*Rosmarinus officinalis,* rosemary. Tender perennial whose refreshingly fragrant leaves are used for cooking.

*Salvia officinalis,* sage. Perennial with aromatic, rough-textured fragrant leaves used in cooking.

*Salvia sclarea,* clary sage. Biennial with strong-smelling leaves.

*Thymus vulgaris,* thyme. Perennial creeper with very fragrant leaves.

*Tropaeolum* spp., nasturtiums. Garden annual with fragrant flowers.

*Verbena* × *hybrida,* garden verbena. Sweet-smelling perennial usually grown as an annual.

*Wisteria sinensis,* common wisteria. Perennial vine with drooping clusters of fragrant pea-like blossoms of light purple or white.

## THE MONOCOT BORDER—
## ORNAMENTAL GRASSES AND RELATED PLANTS

A good botanic garden is also a teaching garden, and a part of what the Brooklyn Botanic Garden does is display plants in botanical families and groups.

"[A botanic garden] should be not only a place where different kinds of plants are exhibited, but where they are exhibited effectively, and not only for their own sake (botanically), but as materials for decorative planting and landscaping . . ." said Dr. Gager during his first year as director.

And nowhere in the Garden is that advice taken with more care than the Monocot Border. Here are plants from lilies to yuccas, on display in a border that shows not only their individual beauty but the fact that all are closely related plants.

Arvid "Slim" Zumwalt wears a number of hats at the Garden. He has been responsible for the Monocot Border, the Fern Grotto, the hosta beds, and the peony beds. He is also the man at the Garden who designs and constructs most of the horticultural and art exhibits, as well as beautifully made wooden stands that show off plants and sculptures to their best advantage. He has been at the Garden for eighteen years.

"I worked for a commercial greenhouse for three years," he said. "They grew acres of tomatoes and strawberries. The owner was an elderly Russian, and he'd hand you a packet of seeds and say, I want these by Easter, and at that time there wasn't the information around as today so you would be forced to experiment and you sure learned fast.

"Brooklyn has the only active systematic collection of monocots in the United States. Other public gardens have a scattering of monocots here and there, but this is the only one that I know of where they are all together."

The Monocot Border is an unusual collection of plants. Monocot is the short word for monocotyledon—one of the two primary divisions of flowering plants—whose seedlings have only one cotyledon (seed leaf). In this division are the grasses and sedges, bananas, lilies, bromeliads, irises, cannas, orchids, and the aroids, which include plants like philodendrons and Jack-in-the-pulpits. Plants belonging to this group lack the woody tissues necessary for the structural support of any sizable stem or trunk, so except for some palms, few are ever tall trees. Often the leaves have parallel veining and lack the complex net pattern of veins found in leaves of plants belonging to the dicots (dicotyledons) like maples or geraniums.

The border is a lazy S-shape measuring forty-five feet in length and ten feet in depth, and features an uncommon collection of plants, including many stands of ornamental grasses. It is located near a small stream.

We remarked that people who think that all the grasses look alike should see this collection of plants.

"It's quite extraordinary," said Mr. Zumwalt. "A landscape designer who saw this border showed an interest in maiden grass *(Miscanthus gracillimus),* so he bought a couple of clumps and called back to say that when spotlighted at night, people thought it was a fountain. More people should use them in the garden."

Among the plants in this border are the annual cloud grass *(Agrostis nebulosa);* the giant flowering onion *(Allium giganteum);* a number of daylilies, including a tall nocturnal species from China *(Hemerocallis altissima)* and the dwarf yellow daylily *(H. minor);* the blackberry lily *(Belamcanda chinensis);* a number of irises; and three yuccas, *Yucca filamentosa* or Adam's needle, *Y. flaccida* 'Ivory Tower', and *Y. glauca,* the soapweed.

The soil in the Monocot Border began as wet, soggy meadow, but as it turns out, many of the grasses love the extra water and because of it attain a good size. Here maiden grass, zebra grass *(Miscanthus sinensis* 'Zebrinus'), and variegated maiden grass *(M. sinensis* 'Variegatus') vary between six and ten feet in height. Then in the late summer and early fall, they put forth their taller plumes, silky feathers made of hundreds of individual blossoms glistening with metallic sheens, and giving this grouping of plants a beauty that lasts all winter long.

The ornamental grasses are not fussy when it comes to soil but should be divided in early spring before growth is too high.

Most of the grasses survive well into winter, and their autumn-colored blades add much beauty to the winter scene. It is best to cut down old growth in very early spring before new growth appears.

Included in the border are bamboos, gladioli, and huge mounds of Japanese iris *(Iris kaempferi).*

"Surprisingly enough," he continued, "the gladioli have over-wintered five years and the Japanese iris love it because of the extra water."

## SELECTED ORNAMENTAL GRASSES

Back at the turn of the century ornamental grasses were quite popular and were found in many large institutional and private gardens. Then their use fell into a decline until the late 1970s, when they were once again discovered.

The following plants are all a delight for the garden, all hardy to USDA Zone 5, never invasive, and as we mentioned before, very easy to care for.

Bulbous oat grass *(Arrhenatherum elatius* var. *bulbosum* 'Variegatum'), gets its name from bulbous stem bases that are really swollen nodes on the stem. These "bulbs" store water, making this grass especially effective in periods of drought. The variegated leaves grow about eighteen inches high, and unlike many grasses, these plants will adapt to light shade.

Quaking grass *(Briza media)* gets its name from the quivering and shaking that the spikelets exhibit in even the gentlest of breezes. The beautiful seed heads resemble puffed wheat. While the grass itself is nondescript, the blossoms are elegant in the garden and also useful in dried bouquets. Plants are easily naturalized and adapt to light shade.

Northern sea oats *(Chasmanthium latifolium)* is an especially lovely grass for the border or wild garden, not only because the flower heads are graceful and attractive but because it's another ornamental that will do well in partial shade, especially in the South. After the first frost the leaves and flowers both turn a rich tannish-brown and remain on the plant well into December.

Tufted hair grass *(Deschampsia caespitosa)* makes a mound of leaves that send up three-foot-high stems topped with lacy flower heads during midsummer. 'Goldstaub' has a decidedly yellow inflorescence while 'Tardifolia' blooms in late summer. Plants want full sun. *D. caespitosa vivipara* 'Fairy's Joke' is one of the few cultivars of any genus that truly deserves such a cute name. Instead of bearing the typical flowers that the grasses produce, these blossoms are tiny plantlets that appear on the outer edge of three-foot arching stems. Plants like full sun.

Giant wild blue rye *(Elymus racemosus)* has striking blue foliage to four feet. It's marvelous as an accent plant, especially good-looking when grown in combination with plants of a light green color. In order to produce the glaucous quality, once a year give the plants a handful of lime mixed in with the soil at the base of the plant. Full sun is necessary to maintain the color.

Blue fescue *(Festuca ovina glauca)* has bluish leaves that grow in very neat eight- to ten-inch mounds and are excellent when used as edges along paths, as very stylized ground covers, or spotted throughout rock gardens, as their blue color goes especially well with the colors of stone. Full sun is needed to hold the color. 'Sea Urchin' has spiky leaves.

Blue oat grass *(Helictotrichon sempervirens)* has bluish leaves that grow in 2-foot mounds. Like the fescues, the blue color of this is perfect for the rock garden plus the tall waving seed heads are also attractive. These grasses want full sun but are not happy where summers are extremely warm and only last at best a few years in the Deep South.

Japanese blood grass (*Imperata cylindrica* 'Rubra') grows about eighteen inches high and bears thin green leaves that turn a bright red in late summer. Especially valuable for late-season color when massed in the bed or border, this is also a good plant for the rock garden and naturalizing in the wild garden. If you live in an area with little or no snow, but typical USDA Zone 5 temperatures, be sure and mulch this grass. Plants prefer sun to light shade.

Eulalia grass *(Miscanthus sinensis)* grows in ten- to twelve-foot-high clumps of graceful leaves with beautiful silvery inflorescences in late summer and early fall. These are large clumping grasses effective as screens, living fences, or specimens in the landscape. It's difficult to believe that a grass purchased in a one-gallon container will, within a few years, form a clump three feet in diameter and up to seven feet high, but the *Miscanthus* will. These grasses all require full sun except for 'Variegata', which will do well in partial shade. 'Gracillimus' or maiden grass has graceful curved leaves to five feet. 'Zebrinus' has five- to six-foot leaves with light yellow horizontal bands, the bands appearing only after the weather warms, usually beginning the end of June. 'Variegata' bears variegated leaves, usually remaining about five feet tall.

Giant wind grass (*Molinia altissima* 'Windspiel'), usually listed simply as 'Windspiel' (windplay), is a magnificent grass with inflorescences on stalks to six feet that bend, never breaking, in the wind. They are great as specimen plants or naturalized. They need full sun.

Variegated purple moor grass (*Molinia caerulea* 'Variegata') forms a beautiful mound of variegated foliage with a variegated inflorescence, growing to two feet. Not only is this particular grass attractive in the summer; in the fall, the leaves turn a light tan, becoming a special accent in the garden. Plants prefer full sun but will adapt to light shade.

Switch grass *(Panicum virgatum)* is a native American grass growing to seven feet and producing an open and airy inflorescence like a granular fog. It's excellent when used as a specimen, to form an open screen, or for naturalizing. The cultivar 'Haense Herms' turns red in fall. These grasses need full sun. Switch grasses are slow to settle in, as much of their first-year growth is channeled into producing an extensive root system that penetrates deeply into the soil. This is the reason that panicums can survive prairie fires.

Fountain grass *(Pennisetum alopecuroides)* produces a thirty-inch mound of graceful leaves and a white feathery inflorescence like a narrow plume. *P. orientale* is adorned with pink plumes. It needs mulch in USDA 5. Plants need full sun.

Every old farmhouse garden, especially along the eastern seaboard, usually has old-fashioned ribbon grass *(Phalaris arundinacea* var. *picta)* growing somewhere amidst the old peonies and roses. The flowers are unimportant; the grass is grown for long, white striped leaves. This plant is excellent for naturalizing and holding banks but can be invasive in the garden proper. Full sun is best.

## THE HOSTA BED

Hostas seem to be the new stars on the popular plant horizon. There are over fifty species and cultivars of these members of the Lily family in the Hosta Bed, and since they are monocots, the bed is appropriately located across from the Monocot Border. These are valuable perennials, wonderful for shade gardens, and from the point of view of leaf variations, a diverse group of plants.

The first hostas came from Japan and China. There they were cultivated for centuries. The Japanese grow them both in pots and in gardens, and cut them up for stir-fry.

Cultural demands are few; hostas ask only a reasonable soil. Perfect mixes consist of loam, sand, and humus, one third each, but even clay soil can be used if commercial soil mixes or peat moss or even leaf litter are mixed in to increase the permeability of the soil. Fertilize in spring after growth has started, using a slow-release fertilizer.

Positioning varies from open, light, to medium shade, depending on the particular requirements of each variety.

Hostas can be dug with ease in the spring, but clumps can be moved throughout the garden year if enough soil is moved with them. They are one of the few perennials that can be moved in active flowering, without causing them even to droop.

The scapes (flowering stalks) should be removed after blooming to prevent seeds from forming. This is especially important since most seedlings will be inferior plants, usually unattractive either in leaf or flower.

Among the plants in the garden, *Hosta sieboldiana* is a favorite because it blooms in late summer and early fall, bearing nodding white flowers with a delightful honeylike fragrance.

Other excellent hostas found in the Garden include *Hosta* 'Blue Moon', which has blue leaves two inches wide and three inches long and becomes a flat clump some ten inches wide. It's excellent for a ground cover and in the rock garden, preferring shade or open shade; flowers are white, blooming in late summer.

'Blue Umbrellas' is much larger with foot-long leaves some ten inches wide, of a blue-green color, and is excellent for a background planting in a shade garden. Summer flowers are lavender edged in white. Unlike many other hostas, this plant adapts well to full sun.

'Sea Drift' has very attractive pleated leaves (called "piecrust" by the trade) with a prominent pattern of ribbing. Leaves are five inches wide and seven inches long of a rusty green color. Blossoms, appearing in midsummer, are lavender-pink. This is another plant that will adapt to full sun, though preferring light shade.

*Hosta fortunei* is an old war-horse of a hosta, having been around for decades. Old country gardens usually contain this plant. They make an excellent ground cover, forming mounds of medium green foliage with individual leaves about five inches wide and ten to twelve inches long. Pale purple flowers appear in June. 'Albomarginata' is a very pretty variegated form, the leaves edged with white.


## THE PEONY BED

About forty cultivars of *Paeonia lactiflora* are found in the Peony Bed. Big and blowsy flowers in whites, creams, rosy reds, pinks, and scarlets—colors never existing in the old-fashioned peonies found in Grandmother's floral border.

Peonies are very long-lived. Plants have been known to bloom for over one hundred years in the same spot. Since it's doubtful they will be moved, once in position, a good start is necessary.

New plants want a deep, sandy, rich soil, neutral or slightly acid, with plenty of humus and compost (well-rotted horse manure is exceptionally fine) plus a cup of bonemeal added to the soil around each plant. If your soil is too heavy, lighten it with the addition of sand or peat moss. Dig a hole at least eighteen inches deep and two feet wide for a new peony, and fill it in with the prepared soil well before planting time, giving the mix a chance to settle.

Be sure you set the plants at the same depth they were at the nursery, and use plenty of water in planting, muddying in the roots with a slurry of water and soil. Peonies planted too deeply will not bloom. Each spring scratch a cup or so of bonemeal or all-purpose fertilizer into the soil around the base of the plant.

Every so often a burgeoning peony branch will wilt and turn brown. This is caused by a fungus blight called botrytis. Quickly remove the diseased branch and burn it. Bordeaux mixture can be used in early spring to control blight.

Ants are very fond of the sweet sap produced by peony buds, but don't let them bother you. They do no harm. Just shake them off any flowers you want to cut and bring indoors.

If you do want to move and divide established plants, autumn is the best time. In order to flower, each division must have at least three eyes.

Peonies come in four distinct classes: single, Japanese, anemone, and double. Singles have five or more petals that surround a center of fertile stamens loaded with pollen. Japanese types have a single row of petals, but unlike the "single" class above, they surround enlarged stamens with little or no pollen, called staminodes. The anemone type is like the Japanese, but bears stamens that look like petals; they are called petaloid stamens, and they have no pollen. The doubles have so many petals that the center of the flower is usually covered.

There are hundreds of peony cultivars on the market today, but the following four, found in the Garden's plot, are excellent types.

*Paeonia* 'Festiva Maxima' has been a garden standby for generations, having been introduced to the garden world in 1851. It bears large pure white double flowers flecked with dots of crimson at the center of the base. The blossoms are very fragrant. 'Le Cygne', introduced in 1907 and thought by many gardeners to be one of the finest, bears very large pure white flowers. 'Bowl of Beauty' is a single peony that is large, pale pink, with petals surrounding upright creamy petaloid stamens. 'Scarlett O'Hara' is a new introduction, a single with bright red petals. 'Krinkled White' is a large-flowered Japanese type with pure white petals surrounding a golden center and looking for all the world like rumpled silk. All of the above plants are about thirty-six inches tall.

When cutting peonies for bouquets, take the buds that have just begun to open.

For tree peonies see chapter eight, Ornamental Shrubs and Vines.


## DAYLILIES IN THE GARDEN

Although there is no specific daylily bed at the Garden, plants are sited with the Peony Bed, the Hosta Bed, the Monocot Border, and various other places where a low-maintenance, long-blooming plant is needed.

Their botanical name is *Hemerocallis,* from *hemero* (Greek for beautiful) and *callis* (Greek for day—each individual blossom opens, matures, and withers in twenty-four hours). Daylilies were first described in a garden text published in 1629 as growing in boggy spots in what was then Germany; they had already reached England in 1575.

When settlers came to America from England and Europe, they brought some of their favorite flowers to brighten the colonial garden. But as a homesteader's time was at a premium, any plant that did make the trip had to be hardy and able to withstand a good deal of neglect—in essence, a beautiful weed.

Thus the common daylilies that line the rural roadsides of America are all escapees of early gardens. Impervious to the black macadam that often stops a few short inches from their roots, and seemingly unaffected by the chemical residues used to melt winter ice, they begin to bloom about the first of July when the summer is hottest.

They prefer full sun in the North and partial shade in the Deep South. Average garden soil will do, but as with most growing plants, the better the soil, the better the plant. Add humus and sand to heavy clay soil and humus and heavier soil to sand. Water once a week if the weather does not provide.

Plants may be left in one spot for many years, but once blooming starts to decline, it's time to divide. Propagation is by division in the spring or the fall. After replanting cut back the leaves to about eight inches from the crown, covering the crown with at least an inch of soil.

Among the cultivars recommended by the Garden are:

*Hemerocallis* 'Kazuq', a late bloomer that is almost a creamy white; in the Hosta Bed, 'Eenie Weenie', a short daylily with bright yellow blooms; 'Betty Woods', an early mid-season double flower of yellow-orange with a green throat; 'Antique Rose', a rose-pink ruffled flower blooming in midseason; 'Angel Fire', a scarlet-red that blooms in midseason; in the Peony Bed, 'Ed Murray', a mid-season flower of dark red with a green throat; 'Cairo Night', purple almost to black, blooming in early midseason; and a double-flowered form, *H. fulva* 'Kwanso'.

## CARING FOR PERENNIALS THROUGH THE YEAR

If you have mulched perennial beds and borders over winter, pull the mulch away in early to mid-spring.

Fertilize established plants in early to mid-spring—when new shoots appear—using compost, bonemeal, or 5–10–5 or other all-purpose fertilizers. The BBG cautions that bonemeal is expensive and its phosphate becomes available to plants only slowly. Be careful not to damage young roots when working the fertilizers into the soil.

Early spring is the best time to divide perennials that bloom in late spring, summer, and fall. Most plants take such disturbance in their stride since they are programmed to grow at this time of year. When danger of heavy frost is past, set out new perennial plants that can tolerate cool weather.

In warm climates, start hardening off seedlings of perennials started indoors over winter. Wait until mid-spring to harden off seedlings in cooler climates.

In warm climates, set out summer-blooming perennials in mid-spring. Then feed summer-blooming perennials in late spring. Heavy-feeding perennials can be fertilized in midsummer.

Mulching not only protects plants from the cold, it also insulates them against excessive heat and hot, dry summer weather in general. Keep beds and borders weeded if you haven't mulched them. Cultivate often, but be careful not to injure roots.

While the plants are still young, put stakes in place for tall-growing plants that will need them.

In early summer, sow seeds of summer perennials for bloom next year.

Water deeply during dry weather to prevent heat stress.

Deadhead throughout the growing season as flowers fade, to keep plants healthy and producing more flowers.

When plants are in bloom, notice those that are crowded and will need to be divided in fall or spring. Note on your garden plan all the plants that are ready for division.

In the fall, divide and transplant perennials that bloom in spring and early summer. Later bloomers can be divided in spring. Be sure to do any planting or transplanting at least a month before you expect your first serious frost, to give plants time to establish roots before the ground freezes. Many perennials can be planted in the fall. When new plants arrive from the nursery, plant them as soon as possible.

Cut back perennials to four or five inches before the ground freezes. In warm climates cut back when plants go dormant and the tops are no longer green. Clean up the garden, pulling weeds, removing stakes, and gathering up fallen leaves.

When the soil freezes, mulch the garden to prevent winter heaving.

Finally, winter is the time to update your garden plans and prepare seed and plant orders for the following spring.

# CHAPTER THREE

# THE
# ROSE
# GARDEN

There are over five thousand rosebushes of over one thousand varieties in the Brooklyn Botanic Garden, one of the most spectacular public rose collections in the country. Construction on the one-acre Cranford Rose Garden began in June of 1927 and was completed by November of that same year; two old roads from Brooklyn's past were found during the digging. The garden was dedicated in June 1928. Mr. and Mrs. Walter B. Cranford gave the money for the development, planting, and ongoing maintenance of this garden. The designer of the garden was Harold A. Caparn, a landscape architect.

The Oxford English Dictionary lists twenty-four entries for "rose," covering over three pages. Definitions beginning with "rose" run from the flower to a fever to the connection, usually brass, for a watering can to a type of stained-glass window in Gothic architecture. Add to this the over one hundred and fifty entries devoted to the rose in Bartlett's Familiar Quotations, plus the fact that over four thousand published songs make some reference to roses, and you begin to get some idea of the popularity of the rose.

The head gardener of the rose collection at BBG is Stephen Scanniello.

"It's a garden to show as many different kinds of roses as possible," he said. "In most rose gardens you will usually see many beds, each with a single variety of rose, but here the plan is to show as many roses as possible."

He made a grand gesture that included the entire garden.

"In the main section we have fifteen beds with an average of thirty rows per bed with beds of modern roses in the center and the old garden roses, and the species or wild roses about the garden's perimeter. And then to show the many ways of using climbing roses on archways, pergolas, lattice works, fences, on posts, on chains, in fact, all these techniques are illustrated here.

"I am also responsible for the small pool just to the rear of this garden. It's the only area in the rose garden that has a large number of one variety. There are approximately three sets of eleven arches, and in front of each arch is one variety of rose numbering from ten to twenty plants. Then the arches are covered with old ramblers and, around the pool, hybrid musk roses."

Mr. Scanniello has had six rose seasons at the Garden and has loved every minute of them. Except when doing research in the Garden's library or when trapped inside during inclement weather, he's either digging, weeding, or prepping the roses for winter, or carrying loads of compost or manure to the rose beds.

We asked him where he gets the plants.

"I go everywhere," he answered. "I go to whomever has the plants that I need. I have most of the roses offered by the big rose growers, but they all send me their new roses every spring. Now I go and look for roses that are rarer and harder to find, usually from the smaller nurseries. I even get them from Europe.

"When planting roses," Mr. Scanniello continued, "I start with good soil, at least two feet deep. That means that any clay is cut with humus and leaf litter or compost manure. I add rotted manure every year, spreading it about in the winter, when I have more time. Then, in addition to the manure, I use a granular 5–10–5 in spring and midsummer and on occasion I use foliar feeding."

He paused to frown at a Japanese beetle that landed on a nearby leaf.

"But I did try an old Native American way of adding one dead fish per bush, and it really worked."

"Minnow or gold?" we asked.

"Butterfish," he answered. "Someone brought me a bag of butterfish one day, so I experimented. And I notice that many gardeners have great luck with using liquid seaweed for a fertilizer with miniature roses."

Here is the procedure Mr. Scanniello follows when planting roses. He plants bare-root roses as soon as the soil can be worked in spring, while the plants are still dormant. In Brooklyn, he positions plants with the bud union one to two inches below the soil surface. (This is done in all climates where winter temperatures drop to o°F. or below; in warm climates plant with the bud union slightly above soil level.)

He soaks bare-root roses for twenty-four hours in a bucket of water before planting. Then he removes damaged canes and any canes smaller than the diameter of a pencil.

He advises digging the planting hole large enough to comfortably accommodate all roots (on the average, one to two feet across, and one to one and one-half feet deep). Loosen soil in the bottom of the hole; add a shovelful of compost or aged manure. Make a mound of soil in the bottom of the hole and spread the roots over and down the sides of the mound.

Fill in with soil, working it carefully around the roots with your fingers. When the hole is half filled, water to settle the soil. Fill the rest of the way with soil and water again. Rock the plant gently to settle it.

Mound soil around the base of the new plant to protect it. When the shoots begin to grow, gradually remove the soil mound.

Mr. Scanniello suggests putting supports for climbers in place before planting.

He waters regularly and deeply during dry weather (when the soil is dry to the touch about two inches below the surface, it's time to water). Water early in the day and be sure the leaves dry before nightfall—roses are very susceptible to fungus diseases.

An important practice in maintaining roses and encouraging them to rebloom is called deadheading—removing dead or dying blossoms. Mr. Scanniello and most other rose growers do this religiously. The best way is to cut the spent blossoms about a quarter-inch above the first leaf with five leaflets. If the bush is a rebloomer, the bud eye just below the cut will produce a new stem and new flowers. Dead flowers should be removed even if the rose blooms only once, as the bush then looks neater and does not expend energy in unneeded seed production.

We asked Mr. Scanniello about protecting roses over the winter.

"The only roses that we protect," he answered, "are the standards, or tree roses. These are carefully wrapped in salt hay and burlap. I do have a few roses that are borderline hardiness in USDA Zone 6, and I admit to babying them with ten to twelve inches of mulch, and one or two are completely covered with earth, then straw. But the roses are pretty much on their own, and if a plant doesn't survive, I replace it with another."

"There is scarcely any other plant," wrote Gertrude Jekyll, "which is attacked by so many or such persistent enemies as the rose. Strange to say, writers on rose culture, in enumerating these, invariably omit to mention the most potent enemy of all, and that is, adverse weather."

"When so many roses are grown so close together," said Mr. Scanniello, "there are problems with disease at this time, and black spot is the worst. We spray for it with fungicides and when it's very bad we spray every week, but when under control, less frequently."

Black spot causes variously sized circular patches of black to form, eventually causing the leaf to yellow and fall off. The best treatment is to remove the diseased leaves and keep debris cleaned up around the plants. It also helps to hose down the roses in the morning. The BBG recommends that gardeners contact their local county extension office for recommendations about pesticides and fungicides for roses.

Mildew is a fungus that does the same thing to rose leaves as it does to clothes left in a damp and musty closet. A white or gray powdery growth appears on the leaf surface, eventually causing the leaves to shrivel. Mild cases can be left alone, even though they are unsightly, but too much is too much and heavy infestations are best treated by removing badly infected leaves, watering carefully and increasing air circulation about the plants. Hosing down the plants with water also helps.

Canker is a fungus disease evidenced by dark spots forming on the cane, and soon all the growth above the canker dies. The infected area should be quickly removed by cutting below away from the diseased area.

SPECIES ROSES

There are about 150 species of roses found in the Northern Hemisphere, with flowers usually in tones of pink, although there are some whites, yellows, and reds. Most species blossoms have five petals. The pasture rose *(Rosa carolina)* and *Rosa multiflora* (this particular rose has become a weed in the Northeast because many people have planted them as living fences and seedlings have spread about) are well-known examples of species roses.

Other popular species roses include *Rosa moyesii,* a rose from western China with blood-red flowers followed by extraordinarily attractive brilliant red hips shaped like tiny bottles, and *R. eglanteria,* the sweetbriar rose, known in Shakespeare's time, and noted for its fragrant pink blossoms. Sweetbriar is one of the roses described by Matthias L'Obel in his book *Icones,* which contains accurate descriptions of cultivated roses at the end of the sixteenth century.

HYBRID TEAS

The year 1867 is considered the turning point in the history of rose cultivation, for it was then that 'La France', the first hybrid tea rose of great distinction, was introduced. Hybrid teas are today among the most popular of all roses in American gardens. The American Rose Society uses that year to mark the division between "old garden roses" and "modern roses." Like many classifications, it's an arbitrary division because there were hybrid teas before that date; many roses, for example, were needed to develop 'La France'.

Some of the popular hybrid tea cultivars are 'Peace', often called "the rose of the century," a beauty with yellow petals edged in pink; 'Helen Traubel', a pink-into-apricot blend; and 'Tropicana', a pure, fluorescent orange.

CLIMBING ROSES

Climbing roses fall into several classes, including climbing hybrid teas (a small group) and rambler roses. The plants have flexible canes and need support like lattice work or trellises, and the gardener must fasten the canes to the support; roses are not true vines and do not produce tendrils or actually twine about like sweet peas, morning glories, or clematis.

A few of the notable climbers in the Cranford Rose Garden are 'Blossomtime', a very fragrant rose of medium pink with thirty-five to forty petals, blooming in mid-season; 'Dortmund' (a *kordesii* climber named by Wilhelm Kordes, a well-known twentieth-century hybridizer), that bears brilliant single red blossoms with a white center; 'Golden Showers', with medium yellow double blossoms throughout the growing season; and 'Veilchenblau', a very old rose that is often found in abandoned gardens, its rootstock having been used for grafting and outliving its tender connection. The flowers are violet semi-doubles with a white center, and have a fragrance of green apples.

### SHRUB ROSES

Shrub roses grow as shrubs and often bloom throughout the season. They are hybrids, generally modern roses, and don't fit into any other category. They are of informal habit, with an average height and spread of about five feet.

Popular shrubs in the rose garden include 'Alchymist', a fragrant apricot double with sixty-five to seventy-five petals, and 'Constance Spry', named in honor of the English author, which has fragrant light pink double blossoms for early-season bloom.

### OLD GARDEN ROSES

The old garden roses comprise many erstwhile favorites including the moss roses (Gertrude Jekyll said of the moss rose that no other rose surpasses it in excellence of scent), albas, the Bourbon roses, noisettes, China roses, tea roses, Portland roses, hybrid perpetuals, and centifolias. This group of roses has found new popularity in the last few years and there are now special plant societies devoted to the collection of old garden roses—especially from cuttings taken from plants in cemeteries, where for years they survived continual cuttings by hand lawn mowers, but are now being destroyed by power mowers and weed eaters.

*Rosa gallica officinalis* is often called the Apothecary Rose, because an infusion made from the petals was used as a flavoring for other medicines and as a lotion for certain eye diseases. The blossoms are semi-double, bearing light crimson petals and showy yellow stamens, blooming once a year. *R. damascena,* the damask rose, was praised by Virgil and Ovid and was widely grown by Roman florists. It, too, has a long commercial history —its flowers were distilled to produce attar of roses.

*Rosa* × *alba,* a cross between *R. canina* (the dog rose) and possibly *R. damascena,* was long under cultivation in Italy and included in its stable the White Rose of York *(R.* × *alba* 'Semi

Plena'); is noted for adapting to shade better than many modern roses, has attractive hips, and is very fragrant. *R. canina* was termed the dog rose because the Romans believed its roots would aid in the treatment of hydrophobia.

The original cabbage or Provence rose, one of the centifolia roses, was *Rosa centifolia,* an important ingredient of attar of roses, and grown throughout the gardens of France in the Middle Ages. It was widely cultivated until it lost ground to the hybrid teas. It should not be confused with the Rose of Provins, for this flower was another common name for *R. gallica officinalis,* and was raised near the city of Provins, on the outskirts of Paris, and used in the perfume industry.

The original moss rose was a sport of the cabbage rose (*Rosa centifolia* 'Muscosa'), identified by the mossy look of the calyx and the pedicels, or flower stalks. Gertrude Jekyll notes that the "mossy calyx [has] its own delicious scent, of a more aromatic or cordial character."

The bourbon rose (*Rosa × borboniana*), a natural hybrid between a China and a damask rose, was discovered on the island of Bourbon—now called Reunion Island—off the coast of Madagascar, where farmers hedged their fields with China and damask roses.

## FLORIBUNDAS

Floribundas are a modern development; they resulted from crossing the hybrid teas and the polyanthas. Some of these are often used as greenhouse cut flowers. Included in the Garden's collection are 'Betty Prior', from 1935, having single medium pink flowers that bloom in mid-season with a repeat; 'Cathedral', an All-America Rose Selection (AARS) winner from 1976, with apricot-colored doubles that bloom in mid-season; and 'Saratoga', an AARS choice for 1964, bearing very fragrant white double blossoms for mid-season bloom.

## GRANDIFLORAS

The grandifloras are based on the cultivar 'Queen Elizabeth', developed in the 1950s. They are tall roses with clustered flowers and produce several individual stems on sturdy canes. Among the grandifloras in the collection are, of course, 'Queen Elizabeth', second only to 'Peace' as one of the best-known roses in cultivation, a fragrant double with medium pink petals that blooms mid-season with an excellent score for repeat blooming, and an AARS from 1955; 'Prominent', another AARS, this time in 1977, an orange double for all-season bloom; and 'White Lightnin', a very fragrant double with large white blossoms, blooming all season.

## MINIATURE ROSES

The miniature roses are possibly descended from one flower, *Rosa chinensis* 'Minima', and today number over six hundred cultivars. Miniature bush roses look exactly like their larger relatives but are less than eighteen inches high. If given enough light, they make excellent houseplants.

## LANDSCAPE ROSES

The new Meidiland or landscape roses originally came from France and are perfect as ground covers and for hedging in a small garden. Since they are reproduced by cuttings and usually grow on their own roots—unlike many other roses that are grafted—most of these are hardy to USDA Zone 4. Look for 'White Meidiland', bearing pure white double flowers that begin in June and repeat throughout the summer, with plants growing about two feet high and spreading to five feet; 'Bonica' has pink double flowers on plants eventually reaching five feet in height with a five-foot spread, but they can be trimmed to a desired height; 'Scarlet Meidiland' flowers with vivid scarlet blooms that last up to two weeks on the bush, and one week as cut flowers; plants grow to a height of three feet with a five-foot spread.

Tree or standard roses, like those found in elegant English gardens or in *Alice in Wonderland,* are produced by budding cultivars on a tall understock, one and one-half to six feet above the ground. They need much winter protection in areas colder than USDA Zone 7.

## FAVORITE ROSES

When asked about his favorite roses Mr. Scanniello replied:

"One is 'Electron', a hybrid tea that has All-America status from the 1970s. This is a good pink rose, with fragrant blossoms on long stems and foliage that remains green in the heat of summer.

"A good climber is 'New Dawn', interesting also because it was the world's first patented plant back in 1930. The flowers are fragrant light pink semi-doubles that bloom in mid-season and have a good repeat bloom. 'Don Juan' is another excellent trellis rose that bears deep red double flowers that are very fragrant, blooming all season.

"For a floribunda try 'Apricot Nectar', an All-America rose selection for 1966, bearing double flowers with apricot-pink petals that are yellow at the base; or 'Iceberg', a pure white rose known as 'Schneewittchen' in Germany and a Royal National Rose Society Gold Medal winner in 1958. The flowers are doubles with thirty petals that bloom early to mid-season, followed by a repeat bloom for the rest of the season."

We walked through the Cranford Rose Garden on many golden afternoons and talked about the beauty of the flowers. When passing certain of the hybrid teas, you could almost hear the Talking Rose from *Through the Looking Glass* commenting, "It's the fresh air that does it, wonderfully fine air it is, out here."

## • A SELECTION OF ROSES TO GROW

There are many fine roses suitable for American gardens. This table lists just a few of them.

### HYBRID TEAS

'Charlotte Armstrong'. Fragrant, deep pink blossoms; dark green foliage.

'Chrysler Imperial'. Large, fragrant, crimson flowers; medium-sized plants.

'Color Magic'. Ivory-to-pink blossoms, slightly fragrant; dark green foliage; to 4 feet.

'Dainty Bess'. Single fragrant soft pink flowers with dark stamens; vigorous plants to 4 feet.

'Fragrant Cloud'. Strong, classic tea rose fragrance, coral-red flowers; glossy deep green leaves.

'Garden Party'. Fragrant ivory blossoms flushed with pale pink; glossy foliage.

'Miss All-American Beauty'. Fragrant, deep pink flowers; medium green leaves; vigorous plants to 5 feet.

'Mr. Lincoln'. Rich, deep red flowers, very fragrant; glossy dark green foliage; vigorous plants to 5½ feet.

'Paradise'. Fragrant mauve flowers edged with red; glossy, deep green leaves; vigorous plants to 4½ feet.

'Peace'. Large double fragrant yellow flowers edged with soft pink, which deepens in color as the flowers age; deep green leaves; to 6 feet. One of the most popular roses in the world.

'Royal Highness'. Large, very fragrant, pastel pink blossoms; dark green foliage; prone to diseases.

'Sutter's Gold'. Yellow flowers veined and overlaid with golden orange; fruity fragrance; deep green foliage; to 4½ feet.

'Tropicana'. Fragrant bright red-orange blossoms; deep green foliage; vigorous plants to 6 feet.

'White Masterpiece'. Very large, lightly fragrant white flowers; green leaves.

## GRANDIFLORAS

Upright, bushy plants with flowers very similar to hybrid teas.

'Comanche'. Slightly fragrant red-orange flowers; medium green foliage; vigorous plants to 5 feet.

'Elizabeth Scholtz'. Fragrant flowers, deep yellow and orange flushed with red, color deepening as flowers age; vigorous plants to 4 feet.

'Montezuma'. Slightly fragrant coral blossoms; glossy medium green foliage; vigorous plants to 5 feet.

'Pink Parfait'. Slightly fragrant pink flowers; medium green foliage; vigorous plants to 4½ feet.

'Prominent'. Slightly fragrant orange-red flowers; dark green foliage.

'Queen Elizabeth'. Fragrant clear pink blossoms; glossy deep green leaves; vigorous plants to 7 feet.

'Tournament of Roses'. Coral-pink blossoms, slightly fragrant; glossy dark green foliage.

## FLORIBUNDAS

These plants have abundant clusters of flowers smaller than hybrid teas and grandifloras. Floribundas bloom for a long time and are wonderful when massed.

'Eutin'. Deep red blossoms; glossy deep green leaves; vigorous plants to 3 feet.

'Evening Star'. Slightly fragrant white flowers; deep green leaves; to 3½ feet.

'Poulsen's Pearl'. Fragrant, light pink single blossoms; medium green leaves; to 3 feet.

'Redgold'. Slightly fragrant yellow flowers edged with red; medium green leaves; vigorous plants.

'Sea Pearl'. Light pink blossoms; deep green foliage; vigorous plants to 3½ feet.

'Showbiz'. Slightly fragrant, medium red blossoms; glossy deep green leaves; vigorous plants.

'Trumpeter'. Slightly fragrant, orange-red flowers; glossy deep green leaves; to 4½ feet.

## HYBRID MUSK ROSES

A group of fragrant hybrids with a shrubby growth habit. They bloom heavily in early summer and intermittently thereafter.

'Ballerina'. Lightly scented single light pink flowers shading to white in the center; to 4 feet.

'Buff Beauty'. Fragrant apricot-yellow blossoms; deep green foliage; to 5 feet.

'Cornelia'. Highly fragrant small flowers, apricot-pink at first, maturing to soft pink; bronzy green foliage; to 5 feet. Can be grown as a hedge.

'Penelope'. Very fragrant, white and yellow flowers; glossy, deep-green leaves; colorful hips; to 6 feet.

## HYBRID RUGOSA ROSES

Hardy shrubs with spicy-scented flowers; plants are very thorny but can tolerate difficult conditions and a range of soils. Most produce large ornamental hips.

'Belle Poitevine'. Deep rose pink flowers; medium green leaves.

'Roseraie de l'Hay'. Strongly fragrant crimson blossoms deepening toward purple as they mature; bright green leaves; to 8 feet.

'Sarah Van Fleet'. Very fragrant rosy pink flowers; leaves are bronzy green when young; to 8 feet.

'Schneezwerg'. Slightly fragrant white flowers; light green foliage; dense shrub to 5 feet.

## POLYANTHAS

These low-growing plants produce clusters of small flowers; they may bloom all summer and are lovely grown as edgings, or in front of taller shrubs.

'China Doll'. Slightly fragrant medium pink flowers; medium green leaves; to 1½ feet.

'The Fairy'. Warm pink flowers; medium green leaves; low, spreading habit. This rose has been known to bloom from early summer until frost.

'Happy'. Bright rosy red flowers; deep green leaves; to 15 inches.

'Margo Koster'. Slightly fragrant, coral-pink flowers; medium green leaves; to 1 foot.

## MODERN SHRUB ROSES

These roses are generally easy to care for and bloom repeatedly. The taller varieties can be trained as climbers.

'Alchymist'. Fragrant apricot blossoms; glossy deep green leaves; to 12 feet. Can be trained on a trellis.

'Bonica'. Soft pink flowers; glossy deep green foliage; ornamental red hips; to 5 feet. Can be grown as a hedge.

'Constance Spry'. Large, fragrant, clear pink flowers, many petalled like peonies; deep green foliage; to 7 feet.

'Goldbusch'. Fragrant yellow blossoms; light green leaves; to 5 feet.

'Maigold'. Fragrant, deep yellow flowers; glossy, medium green leaves; to 5 feet.

'Westerland'. Fragrant, apricot blossoms; deep green leaves; to 6 feet.

## OLD GARDEN ROSES

Large-flowered and wonderfully fragrant, these are the roses of perfumers and painters. The full flowers have many petals, the canes are very thorny, and the shrubs are vigorous. Albas, centifolias, damasks, damask perpetuals, gallicas, hybrid perpetuals, and moss roses all need a winter cold period in order to grow well. Bourbons, Chinas, teas, and noisettes generally do better in warm climates.

'Alfred de Dalmas'. Moss rose with soft pink flowers that lighten to creamy white as they age; pale green leaves; to 4 feet.

'Belle de Crecy'. Gallica rose with pinkish purple flowers; deep green foliage, few thorns; to 5 feet.

'Boule de Neige'. Bourbon rose with pure white blossoms; glossy, deep green leaves; to 5 feet.

'Celestial'. An alba rose with light pink flowers; silvery green foliage; to 6 feet.

'Celsiana'. A damask rose with semidouble, clear pink flowers; silver-green foliage; to 5 feet.

'Charles de Mills'. Gallica rose with deep purple-red flowers, a mix of crimson and plum; deep green foliage, few thorns; to 5 feet.

'Comte de Chambord'. Damask perpetual rose with warm pink flowers; silver-green foliage; to 4 feet.

'Empress Josephine'. Gallica rose with lightly fragrant, rose-pink blossoms; deep green foliage; to 3 feet.

'Fantin-Latour'. Hybrid China rose with soft, warm pink flowers deepening to shell pink in the center; bright green foliage; to 6 feet.

'General Kleber'. Moss rose with light pink flowers; medium green leaves; to 5 feet.

'Louise Odier'. Bourbon rose with warm pink flowers; deep green foliage; to 6 feet.

'Tour de Malakoff'. Centifolia with mauve-pink flowers shaded with deeper purple; medium green leaves; to 7 feet. Plants need some support but can be trained as climbers.

'Variegata di Bologna'. Bourbon rose with red and white striped flowers; light green leaves, few thorns; to 7 feet.

'William Lobb'. Moss rose with flowers of deep pinkish lavender; deep green leaves, to 6 or more feet.

## Species Roses

These are the roses that occur in nature throughout the world.

*Rosa banksiae* 'Lutea'. The banksia rose is small, double, yellow, slightly fragrant, and flowers very early in the season; light green leaves; to 30 feet. This is a rose for southern properties only, not hardy in the north.

*R. carolina*. Small single pink flowers, fragrant; glossy medium green leaves; to 6 feet. Spreads by means of suckers.

*R. eglanteria*. The sweetbriar rose has small, single pink blossoms; glossy medium green leaves; to 10 feet.

*R. foetida* 'Bicolor'. The Austrian copper briar is a cultivar of a species rose that has unpleasant-smelling flowers (the exception that proves the rule). Single blooms are a bright copper red inside and golden yellow on the reverse; leaves are medium green; to 6 feet.

*R. moyesii*. Small, single red flowers; small, medium to deep green leaves; to 10 feet or more. This rose is grown as much for the brilliant red jug-shaped hips as for the flowers. 'Geranium' has redder flowers, and is more compact, growing to 8 feet with a 7-foot spread.

*R. palustris*. The swamp rose bears small, single, medium pink blossoms; light to medium green leaves; to 12 or more feet tall. Needs wet, even swampy soil.

*R. rugosa*. Very fragrant, single mauve-pink flowers; glossy, deep green leaves; large, red, edible hips, rich in vitamin C; to 5 feet. Spreads and can be grown as a hedge. Tolerates sandy soil.

*R. wichuraiana*. Small, fragrant, single white flowers; glossy, deep green leaves; to 20 feet. Grow as a climber or trail as a ground cover.

### CLIMBERS AND RAMBLERS

These repeat bloomers can be trained on pillars, trellises, arbors, fences, rock walls, and other supports.

'Belvedere'. Rambler; small, double, soft pink blossoms; to 30 feet.

'Blaze'. Climber; lightly fragrant, rich red blossoms; medium green leaves; to 9 feet.

'Blossomtime'. Climber; fragrant, medium pink flowers; medium green foliage; to 9 feet.

'Dortmund'. Climber; fragrant red flowers with white centers; glossy, deep green foliage; to 12 feet.

'Dr. J. H. Nicolas'. Climber; highly fragrant, medium pink blossoms; deep green foliage; to 10 feet.

'Handel'. Climber; slightly fragrant, cream-colored blossoms edged with pink; glossy, medium green foliage; to 15 feet.

'Leontine Gervais'. Rambler; coppery pink blossoms; glossy, medium green foliage; to 20 feet.

'New Dawn'. Climber; fragrant, light pink blossoms; glossy, medium green foliage; to 15 feet.

'Paul's Himalayan Musk'. Rambler; highly fragrant, pale pink flowers; glossy, medium green foliage; to 30 feet; not hardy in the north.

### MINIATURES

Miniature roses can be grown in containers, as edgings in the garden, or in beds of their own. Watch out for spider mites when growing indoors. Outdoors, in areas with cold winters, mulch with hilled-up soil or straw, especially where there is no snow cover. Trim dead tips in spring.

'Beauty Secret'. Highly fragrant, medium red blossoms; medium green leaves; to 1½ feet.

'Centerpiece'. Velvety, medium to deep red blossoms; deep green foliage; to 16 inches.

'Cupcake'. Medium pink flowers; medium green leaves; to 15 inches.

'Green Ice'. Slightly fragrant white flowers turn greenish as they mature; glossy, medium green leaves; to 8 inches. Good for hanging baskets.

'Holy Toledo'. Slightly fragrant orange flowers with gold at the base; glossy deep green foliage; to 1½ feet.

'Jean Kenneally'. Slightly fragrant apricot blossoms; medium green leaves; to 2 or 2½ feet.

'Lavender Lace'. Slightly fragrant mauve flowers; medium green leaves; to 1 foot.

'Minnie Pearl'. Light pink blossoms; medium green foliage; to 2 feet.

'Pacesetter'. Fragrant white blossoms; deep green foliage; to 18 inches.

'Rainbow's End'. Yellow blossoms flushed with scarlet at the edges; glossy, deep green foliage; to 1½ feet.

'Red Beauty'. Slightly fragrant deep red flowers; glossy deep green leaves; to 1 foot.

'Starina'. Orange-red blossoms; deep green leaves; to 16 inches.

# CHAPTER FOUR

# THE
# HERB
# GARDEN

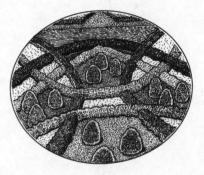

Many gardeners tend to think of an herb garden as a place of narrow winding paths liberally spiked with gravel, cleverly edged with on-side bricks, with soil both baked and hard, the whole affair shimmering with heat waves from a strident sun above. Oh, the odors of the plants are wonderful, but the imagination demands a retreat for a cold drink and relief from the heat.

The Herb Garden at Brooklyn Botanic Garden is far from being the typical herbal spread. An August afternoon will confront the visitor with spectacular islands of plants.

The garden is a rough rectangle with one long straight side facing north, paralleling the back of the Brooklyn Museum and screened by trees and the iron fence that surrounds the entire Brooklyn Botanic Garden. The other long side is convex, a low stone wall with the entrance to the left. The left side is bounded by a slope and a center set of wide and stately steps that lead up to a rise that again overlooks the Museum. Here there are dark tree trunks and a sense of age. At the right end of the garden is another low stone wall. In the center is the knot garden.

This particular garden clearly shows that herbs can be used in an almost unlimited number of ways—in vegetable gardens where basil, parsley, and chives are not only attractive to see, pleasant to smell, but great in food and salads; in flower gardens where the bright red of blooming bee balm, the graceful and lacy leaves of fennel, or the lovely flowers and soft fragrance of lavender are most welcome; or finally as ground covers or between steppingstones where the many types of creeping thymes or fragrant chamomile are so practical to grow.

Herbs are easy, too. Their soil demands are few, wanting only a well-drained spot, usually in full sun. In fact, the very properties of taste and smell that make them so attractive often become less intense in direct proportion to any improvement in the soil. For more ease of care, group perennial herbs together so their roots can remain undisturbed when you weed or till the soil. Grow perennial herbs like other perennial plants, and annuals just like other annuals.

Most of the plants here are in island beds and narrow borders. One particular large grouping consists of fennel *(Foeniculum vulgare)*, purple perilla *(Perilla frutescens* 'Atropurpurea'), joe-pye weed *(Eupatorium purpureum)*, and cut-leaf teasel *(Dipsacus laciniatus)*, all in full bloom and all magnificent. And all have, or once had, uses in the world of trade: fennel makes a delicious tea and marvelous flavoring for food; perilla is grown in Japan for the oil-bearing seeds; Joe-pye weed was once used to treat kidney problems; and teasels were used to raise the nap on woolen cloth—this use explains their preponderance around abandoned textile mills.

"There are over three hundred different kinds of herbs here," said Bernard Currid, the curator of these beds since 1968, "most of them being hardy, although some have to be taken in for the winter or we take cuttings or buy seed if they don't self-sow. The castor bean, for example, will self-sow in the New York area, but if you really want a big plant, you have to start them early."

We commented on the attractive bed of coltsfoot, *Tussilago farfara*, over by the steps and asked if it had to be contained.

"No," he answered. "I started it there because it looks so attractive and I keep it in check by frequent cultivation. It is also planted in an island bed by itself."

He paused for a moment to crush a Japanese beetle and then said, "That's the secret of keeping things in check. Hard work at the right time."

We stopped to examine some living fossils, the horsetails.

"Those horsetails, *Equisetum hyemale,* are there because to me an herb is a plant for use, and that includes fragrance, medicine, folklore, or even scrubbing pots and pans." The plant's old common name, scouring rush, describes one of its traditional uses.

We asked about keeping horseradish in check.

"Well," he answered with a smile, "I originally had it in a natural setting, but now it is set within a bottomless wooden box about eighteen by eighteen inches square and a foot deep."

A baby rabbit actually looked up from a hole in the Elizabethan Knot Garden, and almost seemed to be checking up on Mr. Currid.

"They were all born in that hedge," he said, "generations of them. Hundreds of people walk by and never know the rabbits are there."

Knot gardens have a long and colorful history beginning three thousand years ago in ancient Sumer, a region of lower Babylonia. There carved designs were created that used intricate patterns of entwined snakes. Soon such designs appeared throughout the Middle East and found their way into the decorative arts, including carpets, such rugs reaching Europe by the fifteenth century. The earliest documentation of gardens using such designs was in a book published in 1499, *Hypnerotomachia Poliphili,* or *The Dream of Poliphilus.* The book was attributed to a Dominican friar and included woodcut illustrations of elaborate flower beds and topiary gardens laid out in complicated, interlocking designs.

Knot gardens became extremely fashionable, especially as they indicated that the owners had means far beyond those of average people—since even then, when labor was usually too cheap to note, these gardens took immense effort to maintain.

Thomas Hill's book *The Profitable Arte of Gardening,* published in 1568, presents an elaborate diagram of interwoven lines, called "A proper Knotte to be cast in the quarter of a garden, or otherwise as there is sufficient roomth," set in a "lawn" of either thyme or hyssop.

Each knot garden was usually framed within a square or rectangle with the design being traced in low-clipped hedges of evergreen herbs and small shrubs; usually, tinted stones, pottery shards, colored sands and other types of earth were neatly set between the hedges.

"Our knot garden is a copy of the original by Thomas Hill," said Mr. Currid, "but it's been modified slightly because the original was just too intricate."

The knot garden must be meticulously groomed to maintain its neat, intricate shape. We asked when it was trimmed.

"Frequently," he answered. "Probably every week. Anybody who wants something like this will have to work at it. This bed has been here about ten years. And you can see by the height that I often cut it back very hard."

Patterns for such gardens need not be too complicated and can be derived from anything from published designs in various garden books to one derived from a tooled leather design on an antique book or the diagrams of various knots found in any current manual on sailing.

The BBG's Knot Garden uses dwarf red Japanese barberry and little-leaf Japanese barberry (*Berberis thunbergii* 'Crimson Pygmy' and 'Minor') and three boxwoods, Kingsville dwarf box, variegated box, and dwarf edging box (*Buxus sempervirens* 'Compacta', 'Argenteo-variegata', and 'Suffruticosa').

Other plants especially suited for such gardens are: yellow pot marjoram (*Origanum vulgare* 'Aureum'); lavender cotton *(Santolina chamaecyparissus);* lamb's-ear *(Stachys byzantina);* Allwood pink *(Dianthus* × *allwoodii);* parsley *(Petroselinum crispum);* and a number of the creeping thymes (*Thymus* spp.).

As we walked along, Mr. Currid provided a running commentary:

"This is the American native plant pokeweed, *Phytolacca americana,* a weed to most people, although the English use the plant in the back of larger borders. The angelica, *Angelica archangelica,* is a biennial that provides stems for candying and leaves for a vegetable, and attractive bloom; it self-sows. The caraway, *Carum carvi,* also self-sows, and this annual larkspur, *Consolida ambiqua,* self-sows too, and as it dies back the perilla will cover it up. Over here is a supposed cure for malaria, sweet wormwood, *Artemisia annua,* and the Madagascar periwinkle, *Catharanthus roseus,* is not only a beautiful plant but is being used in the treatment of some forms of leukemia.

One of the few flowers in this garden that is little known as a treatment (although Native Americans once used it), that has no other economic use, and lacks any fragrance is the brilliant red cardinal flower *(Lobelia cardinalis)*. From an aesthetic point of view, it belongs in every collection, and in the Herb Garden its glories are unexcelled.

"There's a good reason for its success," said Mr. Currid, "and that's water. This area is a bog area since I trenched it down about a foot or more and lined it with plastic sheeting. Then I added this rock."

He pointed to a rock about two feet high—but this was not an ordinary piece of rock. The crevices and channels that were part of its surface made it look like a mountain range in miniature.

"We had a rock Penjing exhibit here some years ago [these were rocks, single or in small groupings, arranged in trays to depict miniature landscapes, often emphasizing the majesty of high mountains] and I asked if we could have it after the exhibit was over. The original source of water is over here on the other side of the walkway so I ran a copper tubing underground and finally up a cleft in the rock, filling up the cleft with cement to match the stone's color. The water trickles down to provide refreshment for moisture-loving herbs."

It was obvious as we walked around with Mr. Currid that success with gardening is often as simple as choosing plants to fit the conditions that you have in your own backyard.

Here in early spring the primroses, *Primula veris,* bloom. The corolla of the flower was once used as a sedative and for treating insomnia. The sweet flag, *Acorus calamus,* does beautifully, too. Nearby parsnips, *Pastinaca sativa,* send up small yellow-green flowers on a plant that, while not a true herb, is considered by many to be one. Leeks, *Allium ampeloprasum* (the national emblem of Wales), and monk's rhubarb, *Rumex alpinus,* abound in a combination planting that only the most imaginative would ever think of. This last plant looks like a regular rhubarb without heavy stems and bears very showy panicles of flowers; its young leaves were once used as salad greens.

A fig tree, *Ficus carica,* stands to one side. Figs don't normally survive this far north. But in the winter Mr. Currid bends it down flat to the ground and covers the trunk and stems with a six-inch layer of leaves and salt hay, just pulling it back up in spring; it survives and bears figs.

"This can be done for several years until the stem gets too woody," he explains. "Then cut it back hard."

It's planted under a ginkgo tree, *Ginkgo biloba,* and the leaf combination is very attractive.

The ginkgo, we learned, is the last representative of a class of plants that flourished in Mesozoic times, when dinosaurs ruled the earth. It's an elegant tree for city planting, adapting well to polluted air. But its ripe "fruit" has an unfortunate smell resembling rancid fat, so the planting of male trees is suggested. The fan-shaped leaves, which resemble maidenhair fern, are so attractive that it's a beautiful tree for most gardens.

"That's another secret of good gardening," said Mr. Currid. "Combining the textures and structures of the many different leaves that grace a plant because the flower is but one part of the story."

Russian sage, *Perovskia atriplicifolia,* has sage-scented leaves, but it is the lovely sprays of lavender-blue flowers in summer and fall that have led it on its way to becoming one of the "pop plants" of the 1990s. It has been in the Herb Garden since before 1968, long before the plant became popular.

"The lavender (*Lavandula angustifolia* 'Hidcote') was spectacular this year," continued Mr. Currid, "but these particular plants have a problem since they are by a wall and people love to sit here. So to discourage them, I made a two-by-two-inch hump of cement and soil mix along the edge of the top, filled it with a thin layer of soil, and plant *Portulaca grandiflora* in it every summer. It's related to the other portulaca called purslane, *P. oleracea,* an old-fashioned salad herb that is rich in vitamin C. I know I should be a purist and go in strictly for herbs that have a use, but this gives us a chance for more fun."

Nearby stand tall tripods made of bamboo stakes and entwined with hop vines, *Humulus lupulus,* their whole flowers used to both flavor and preserve beer. They once were also used when dried as a pillow stuffing to treat insomnia. The tripods are a marvelous way to display this handsome plant.

Ahead of us a bed of balloon flowers, *Platycodon grandiflorus,* was in full bloom, and nearby we spotted a bed of Egyptian walking or top onions, *Allium cepa.* The balloon flowers were once used by Chinese herbalists to help expel mucous from the respiratory tract. The top onions form small bulbils on the top of tall flowering stalks that eventually bend over with their weight. The little bulbils root into the earth, becoming the next crop of onions—hence the common name "walking."

We left Mr. Currid a few minutes later. His work in the Herb Garden was over for the day. With one last stoop in a bed of perilla for the removal of a troublesome weed or two, he left to attend the water lilies that grow in the pools opposite the new conservatory. The rabbits in the Knot Garden seem to look after him with fondness.

## • SOME HERBS TO GROW

*Note:* Most herbs originally found their way to gardens either because of a use in the treatment of illness or as a flavoring agent, usually to mask the smell and taste of food kept before the days of refrigeration. Do not experiment with herbal remedies unless you are assured by good medical authority that there is no danger involved.

Since most gardeners are already familiar with the most common culinary herbs, such as parsley, basil, spearmint, and oregano, we have focused here on more unusual plants to consider for herb gardens.

*Achillea millefolium,* yarrow. Perennial to 3 feet; ferny leaves; flat-topped heads of tiny white flowers. Various medicinal uses including "opening the pores and purifying the blood." Excellent in dried arrangements and long a traditional dye plant. Full sun, well-drained soil; adapts to dry soil but dislikes a soggy spot. Pretty in the perennial garden, and a number of cultivars are available. You may divide every other year in spring or fall.

*Acorus calamus,* sweet flag. Perennial to 3 feet; leaves resemble cattails; 2-inch spadix of tiny greenish-yellow flowers juts out from the stem. Once used to cure flatulence and colic. The rhizome is used for perfume in hair tonic. Sun or partial shade in marshy soil or with rhizome under water. Propagate by division in spring or fall.

*Allium tuberosum,* garlic chives. Perennial to 1½ feet; narrow flat, garlic-flavored leaves; clusters of fragrant star-shaped white flowers. Used in cooking; edible blossoms excellent and exotic in salads. Full sun; any average garden soil. Propagate by seed.

*Aloe barbadensis (Aloe vera),* medicinal aloe. Tender perennial usually grown as houseplant; to 2 feet; narrow fleshy leaves, light green, sometimes spotted; tubular orange-red or yellow flowers. Jellylike sap is healing and soothing for minor burns and abrasions. Full sun (or sunny windowsill); can summer outdoors in well-drained soil of reasonable fertility; will take shade. Propagate by offsets.

*Aloysia triphylla,* lemon verbena. Tender deciduous woody shrub to 15 feet (shorter when container-grown), with lemon-scented, lanceolate leaves and spikes of tiny tubular, lavender flowers. Use dried leaves in teas, potpourris, and sachets. Full sun; summer outdoors in fertile moist garden soil.

*Angelica archangelica,* angelica. Biennial to 8 feet; round, hollow, branched stems resemble celery. Magical qualities have been ascribed to this plant; tea made with it is used to treat digestive problems. Stems can be eaten as vegetable or candied (licoricelike taste). Partial shade; moist but well-drained soil. Grow from seed.

*Anthriscus cerefolium,* chervil. Hardy annual to 2 feet; light green compound leaves resembling parsley; umbels of tiny white flowers. Once used to cleanse the blood. Best used as a cooking herb to flavor egg dishes; one of the *fines herbes.* Partial shade; moist, humusy soil. Grow from seed.

*Artemisia dracunculus,* French tarragon. Perennial to 2 feet; narrow pointed aromatic leaves; sometimes small panicles of tiny whitish green flowers. A classic kitchen herb; the licoricelike flavor of fresh leaves mellows and sweetens when leaves are dried. Full sun to partial shade; moist but well-drained, fertile soil. Divide every 2 to 3 years; mulch where winters are cold. Propagate from cuttings or by division. Do not confuse with inferior Russian tarragon, *A. dracunculus* var. *inodora,* which is more robust and weedy.

*Ballota nigra,* black horehound. Perennial to 3 feet; deeply scalloped lance-shaped leaves on square stems; small purple or white tubular flowers. Once used as an antispasmodic. Full sun in poor soil. Propagate by division.

*Baptisia australis,* blue false indigo, Indian rattle. Perennial to 3 feet; attractive leaves with 3 leaflets; pretty pealike blue flowers followed by large black pea pods. Once used to color linsey-woolsey, but color proved to be not fast; many investors lost big money. Full sun to partial shade; moderate soil. Excellent as a substitute for a shrub, but dies down to ground in winter. Propagate by division or by seed.

*Berberis thunbergii* 'Crimson Pygmy', dwarf red Japanese barberry. Small-leaved shrub to 3 feet; spiny branches; brilliant autumn color. Berries once used to make throat gargle and as a mild purgative, also used for dye. Full sun to partial shade; fertile, moist, well-drained soil. Nice in a knot garden—easily trained and takes pruning well. Propagate by division.

*Borago officinalis,* borage. Annual to 2 feet. Leaves and stems covered with fine bristles; pretty sky blue star-shaped flowers. Flavor similar to cucumbers, and used to flavor alcoholic beverages; young leaves good in salad. Full sun; fertile, moist but well-drained soil. Propagate by seed; self-sows.

*Buxus sempervirens* 'Suffruticosa', dwarf edging box. Perennial shrub to 3 feet; small glossy dark green leaves with distinctive scent. Although poisonous, it was once used to purify the blood and for rheumatism. Used as a low hedge in knot gardens. Full sun to partial shade; average garden soil; likes lime (or a mulch of marble chips). Takes clipping well; water thoroughly before pruning in hot weather. Propagate by cuttings.

*Calendula officinalis,* pot marigold. Branching annual to 1½ feet; oblong leaves and golden yellow or orange ray flowers all summer. A variety of traditional herbal uses including: skin ointments; as a dye; as a saffron substitute. Flowers dry well. Full sun; well-drained soil of average fertility; does well in pots. Propagate by seed.

*Carum carvi,* caraway. Biennial, sometimes annual, to 2 feet; hollow stems, finely cut leaves, flat-topped umbels of tiny white flowers. Seeds once used as a stimulant and in children's ailments. Now used as flavoring and in seedcakes. Full sun and good garden soil. Propagate by seed.

*Chamaemelum nobile,* Roman chamomile. Perennial to 9 inches; single or double white daisylike flowers; feathery threadlike leaves; scent similar to apples. Infusion or tea excellent for upset stomach; in rinse for blond hair; in potpourris. Can be used to make a chamomile lawn by clipping plants before flowering. Full sun to partial shade; light, dry soil. Propagate by seed.

*Chrysanthemum cinerariifolium,* pyrethrum. Perennial to 2 feet; divided ferny leaves and daisylike flowers with white rays and yellow centers. Source of pyrethrin, a natural pesticide. Full sun to partial shade; well-drained soil with reasonable fertility. Divide every year or so to maintain vigor.

*Chrysanthemum parthenium,* feverfew. Biennial or perennial to 3 feet; lobed leaves like garden chrysanthemums; small daisylike flowers with white rays and yellow centers. Although described as having a nauseating taste, it was once used for headaches and "hysterical conditions." Full sun to partial shade; well-drained but average soil. Propagate by seed.

*Coriandrum sativum,* coriander. Hardy annual to 2 feet; branching stems, divided leaves similar to Italian parsley; flat umbels of tiny white-to-pinkish flowers. Once used to relieve flatulence. Now used in cooking; the strongly flavored leaves are essential in many Chinese, Mexican, and Indian dishes. Full sun in light, well-drained, good garden soil. Propagate by seeds.

*Crocus sativus,* saffron crocus. Fall-blooming bulbs with grasslike leaves; crocus flowers have red-orange stigmas which are the source of saffron. Stigmas and styles are collected (35,000 flowers yield 8 ounces of saffron); infusion used to flavor and color a variety of foods, particularly in Spanish and Indian cuisines. Full sun to partial shade; light, well-drained soil. Lift and divide corms every 2 or 3 years; takes several years to flower from seed.

*Elettaria cardamomum,* cardamom. Tender perennial to 6 feet or more; long narrow dark green leaves and trailing racemes of little white flowers. Seeds once used as treatment for flatulence. Now used in cooking. Partial shade; rich, moist soil. Bring indoors over winter.

*Equisetum hyemale,* scouring rush. Perennial to 5 feet; jointed, ridged stems with fanciful tops, minuscule leaves. High silica content makes stems useful in scouring metal or wood. Full sun to partial shade; almost any soil, including water. Excellent in pot sunk in pool. Divide in spring. *Warning:* Can be invasive.

*Eupatorium purpureum,* joe-pye weed. Perennial to 10 feet; toothed leaves and large terminal clusters of purplish flowers. Roots once had medicinal uses including treatment of kidney problems. Full sun to partial shade; moist, fertile soil. Grows wild throughout much of North America. Large and striking in perennial border.

*Foeniculum vulgare,* fennel. Perennial, usually grown as annual, to 4 feet or more; feathery deep green or, in one form, bronze-colored foliage; umbels of tiny yellow flowers. Anise-flavored leaves and seeds used in cooking and in teas to settle stomach. Full sun; well-drained soil; hardy only to 10° F. May self-sow. The bronze form is especially attractive in the garden.

*Galium odoratum,* sweet woodruff. Perennial ground cover to 8 inches; whorls of hay-scented, deep green leaves; small white fragrant flowers in late spring. Used to flavor May wine, in teas, in potpourris. Shade; humusy, moist but well-drained soil. Propagate by division or by seed.

*Gaultheria procumbens,* wintergreen. Perennial ground cover to 4 inches; small shiny evergreen leaves, little white flowers followed by red berries. Leaves used for tea; oils used to flavor gum and candy (teaberry). Partial shade; humusy, moist soil with acid pH. Propagate by division.

*Genista tinctoria,* woadwaxen, dyer's greenweed. Shrub to 3 feet; small shiny leaves; pealike yellow flowers. Flower heads used for yellow-green dye. Full sun; well-drained average soil. Propagate by seed or cuttings.

*Glycyrrhiza glabra,* licorice. Perennial to 7 feet; yellow-green pinnate leaves; purple pealike flowers. Root is widely used as a flavoring and in cough medications. Full sun to partial shade; moist, fertile soil. Roots are dug and divided in late fall when tops are dry.

*Humulus lupulus,* common hop. Perennial vine to 25 feet or more; heart-shaped leaves; white flowers on separate male and female plants.

Used in beer and as a sedative. Decorative when trained on a post or trellis. Full sun; deep, well-drained, humusy soil. Dies back to ground in winter. Propagate by seeds.

*Hyssopus officinale,* hyssop. Perennial to 3 feet; spikes of small blue-violet flowers, narrow leaves on woody stems. Strong, bitter mint flavor; 'Alba' has white flowers. Leaves used in poultices for bruises and wounds, and in teas: "A decoction of hyssope made with figges, water, honey and rue and drunken, helpeth the old cough." Full sun to partial shade; light, well-drained soil. Attracts bees and butterflies; nice in flower gardens.

*Indigofera tinctoria,* indigo. Tender perennial to 5 feet; purple, pink, or white pealike flowers. Source of blue dye much valued during colonial times. Full sun; fertile, moist, well-drained soil. Bring indoors over winter.

*Inula helenium,* elecampane. Perennial to 6 feet; coarse, toothed leaves and large golden daisylike flowers. Root is used to treat coughs and sore throats. Full sun to partial shade; moist, moderately fertile soil.

*Laurus nobilis,* bay laurel. Tender tree; glossy deep green leaves; 5 to 6 feet tall when grown in a pot. Aromatic dried leaves used in cooking and to soothe upset stomach; oil used to treat rheumatism. Full sun to partial shade; well-drained, reasonably fertile soil. Hardy only to 10° F and not hardy at the Brooklyn Botanic Garden; bring indoors for winter except in warm climates. Propagate by cuttings.

*Lavandula angustifolia,* lavender. Shrubby perennial to 2½ feet; narrow gray-green leaves; spikes of small lavender to purple flowers on ends of slender, waving stems. Flowers used in perfumes, bath oils, soaps, potpourris, and sachets; oil used on bruises, sore muscles. Full sun; light, well-drained soil. Hardy to −10° F. Harvest for drying before the flowers fully open. Propagate by seed.

*Levisticum officinale,* lovage. Perennial to 6 feet; ribbed hollow stems resemble celery, as does flavor; compound umbels of small greenish-yellow flowers. Various medical uses: "The seed thereof warmeth the stomachke, helpeth digestion. . . ." Leaves have earthy celery flavor and are used in soups and stews. Full sun to partial shade; fertile, moist, well-drained soil. Attractive in perennial border. Propagate by seed.

*Marrubium vulgare,* white horehound. Branching perennial to 3 feet; woolly stems and leaves; whorls of white flowers. Bitter, *bitter* cough tonic—one of the five bitter herbs ordered to be eaten at Passover. Also used in ale and in candy. Full sun; sandy, well-drained soil. Propagate by seed.

*Matricaria recutita,* German chamomile. Annual to 20 inches; feathery threadlike leaves; white daisylike flowers; scent similar to apples.

Used for upset stomach, as a rinse for blond hair, and in potpourris. Full sun to partial shade; well-drained, sandy soil. Propagate by seed.

*Melissa officinalis,* lemon balm. Branching perennial to 2 feet; toothed, lemon-scented leaves; inconspicuous white flowers in summer. Used in cooking or dried in potpourris. Full sun to partial shade; well-drained soil of average fertility. Propagate by seed or division.

*Mentha pulegium,* European pennyroyal. Low-growing perennial; small rounded leaves; mauve blossoms; strong mint scent. Fresh leaves used as insect repellent. Partial shade; moist, fertile soil. Excellent for growing between rocks in pathways. Propagate by cuttings. Not hardy at BBG; new plants started there each year.

*Mentha requienii,* Corsican mint. Low-growing perennial; tiny leaves; small mauve flowers; strong peppermint scent. Original flavoring in creme de menthe. Light shade; fairly dry, average soil. Beautiful in rock gardens and between paving stones. Needs mulching where winters are extremely cold. Propagate by cuttings.

*Mentha suaveolens,* apple mint. Perennial to 3 feet; rounded hairy leaves; small white or pink flowers; fruity applelike scent and flavor. Used in cooking. Full sun to partial shade; moist, fertile soil. The cultivar 'Variegata' known as pineapple mint. Propagate by cuttings. *Warning:* Very invasive.

*Monarda didyma,* bee balm. Annual, biennial, or perennial to 4 feet; distinctive scarlet flowers on square stems. Cultivars in shades of pink, red, purple, and white. Used as tea to soothe a variety of ailments. Used in cooking for citrus quality. Full sun to partial shade; moist, fertile soil containing organic matter. Divide every 3 years, as older plants fade away.

*Myrrhis odorata,* sweet cicely. Perennial to 3 feet; ferny leaves and clusters of tiny white flowers. Leaves and roots used in cooking; flavor resembles celery with anise highlights; in years past a "splendid tonic for young girls." Partial shade; moist, well-drained soil with added organic matter. Propagate by division or by seed.

*Nepeta cataria,* catnip. Perennial to 3 feet; toothed grayish green leaves; boring white flowers in August. Used in tea, in olden times, to promote perspiration, and so loved by cats that they become "frolicsome, amorous, and full of battle." Full sun to partial shade; sandy, well-drained soil. *N. × faassenii* is a hybrid to 24 inches with wrinkled leaves and decorative violet flowers. Propagate by division or by seed.

*Origanum majorana,* sweet marjoram. Tender perennial to 1 foot; small rounded leaves, tiny white or pink flowers with distinctive knot-shaped buds; grown as annual in the north. The volatile oil, *oleum majoranae,* is used externally for bruises and sprains. A classic in the kitchen, especially for stuffings and sauces. Full sun; light, well-drained soil. Propagate by seed.

*Perilla frutescens* 'Crispa'. Tender perennial grown as annual to 3 feet; deep reddish-purple leaves with bronze tones, with frilled edges. Grown in Japan for the oil-bearing seeds; used in U.S. as attractive bedding plant. Full sun to partial shade; reasonably fertile garden soil. Propagate by seed.

*Pimpinella anisum*, anise. Annual to 2 feet; feathery leaves on long stems; flat umbels of yellow-white flowers. Once used in cough medicines. The licorice-flavored seeds are now used in foods, confections, liqueurs, and as an aid to digestion. Full sun; light, well-drained, average soil. Propagate by seed.

*Podophyllum peltatum*, May apple. Perennial to 1 foot; large round lobed leaves sit on stems like umbrellas; white pendulous flowers; oval yellow fruit. Once used medicinally, but is quite toxic and can cause violent reactions. Partial shade; moist, fertile soil. Attractive growing in wildwood banks. *Warning:* Plant and seeds are poisonous; only the ripe fruits are edible.

*Poterium sanguisorba*, garden burnet. Perennial to 3 feet; small deep green rounded and toothed leaves; small pinkish purple flowers. Once used to treat hemorrhages. Leaves have cucumberlike flavor; used in salads. Full sun to partial shade; well-drained soil of average fertility. Nice edging plant in the garden. Propagate by seed.

*Rheum rhabarbarum*, rhubarb. Perennial to 3 feet; huge leaves on thick fleshy red or green stems; tall panicles of white flowers followed by flat, winged fruits. Once used as a laxative. Leaf stalks are used in pies and sauces. Full sun; deeply dug, well-drained and reasonably fertile soil. Propagate by division. *Warning:* Leafy part of leaves are poisonous.

*Rosmarinus officinalis*, rosemary. Tender evergreen shrub to 4 feet; deep green needlelike leaves, piney scent; small light blue flowers; hardy only to 10° F (not hardy at BBG), so bring indoors for the winter. Once used as a headache cure and, combined with borax, to treat baldness; oil still used for aching joints. A classic culinary herb used in the kitchen for centuries. Good subject for topiary. Full sun; well-drained average garden soil. Propagate by seed or cuttings.

*Ruta graveolens*, rue. Evergreen perennial to 3 feet; pinnate leaves with oblong rounded bluish-green segments; small yellow to yellow-green flowers. An attractive garden plant both grouped and as an edging. Full sun; well-drained soil with neutral pH. Propagate by seed or cuttings. Mulch with salt hay in winter. *Warning:* Oil in leaves can cause toxic reaction; some people have skin reactions.

*Salvia elegans*, pineapple sage. Tender perennial used as annual, to 3 feet; ovate leaves smell of pineapple; bright red tubular flowers. Used in kitchen. Full sun; well-drained, fertile soil. Propagate by seed.

*Salvia sclarea,* clary sage. Biennial to 5 feet; oblong heart-shaped leaves; hooded bracts cover blue, lavender, or white flowers in spikes. Once used for stomach complaints and the mucilage of the seeds in eyewash; also for clary wine. Whole plant has a strong, pungent smell. Attractive in gardens. Full sun; well-drained soil of average fertility. Propagate by seed.

*Santolina chamaecyparissus,* lavender cotton. Perennial to 2 feet; tiny silvery leaves; small heads of minuscule yellow flowers. Once used for treating worms in children. Popular when dried for wreaths and arrangements. Full sun; well-drained but average soil. Propagate by seed or cuttings.

*Satureja hortensis,* summer savory. Annual to 1½ feet; narrow gray-green leaves; small white to pink flowers. Once used as a medicinal additive lending an aromatic quality. Good in stews and soups. Full sun; well-drained but average soil. Propagate by seed.

*Satureja montana,* winter savory. Perennial to 1 foot; narrow shiny deep green leaves; small white to pink flowers. Rub leaves on insect bites. Used in the kitchen, but has a coarser flavor than summer savory. Full sun; light, well-drained average garden soil. Propagate by seeds or cuttings.

*Stachys officinalis,* betony. Perennial to 3 feet; toothed hairy green leaves; tubular red-violet flowers in short spikes on top of stem. Once employed as a tonic but now only used for external applications as a poultice. Very ornamental in the garden. Full sun to partial shade; moist but well-drained soil of average fertility. Propagate by seed or division.

*Tanacetum vulgare,* tansy. Perennial to 4 feet; tiny yellow flowers, like daisies without the petals, carried in small clusters on tops of stems; ferny, aromatic, pine-scented leaves. Once used to treat hysteria; now an attractive garden perennial. Full sun to partial shade; well-drained soil of average fertility. Propagate by division or seed.

*Teucrium chamaedrys,* germander. Perennial to 2 feet; purple to red-violet flowers in whorls near tops of stems; dark, glossy, green toothed leaves. Used medicinally for intermittent fevers and gout. Excellent for a low hedge, as it responds to trimming; good in knot gardens. Full sun to partial shade; well-drained soil of average fertility. Propagate by cuttings, as seeds germinate slowly.

*Thymus citriodorus,* lemon thyme. Perennial to 1 foot; small shiny dark green lemon-scented leaves; little pink flowers. Used in tea and to season foods. Full sun to partial shade; light well-drained soil of average fertility. Not hardy in far north. Propagate by cuttings.

*Tussilago farfara,* coltsfoot. Perennial to 8 inches; large, toothed leaves shaped something like a horse's hoof; bright yellow, daisylike flowers appear before leaves, often first flower of spring. Classic herbal remedy for coughs, and dried leaves were smoked for pulmonary complaints, but little used today. Attractive ground cover for wild garden. Full sun to partial shade; moist soil of average fertility. Propagate by cuttings. *Warning:* can be invasive, so contain plants.

*Valeriana officinalis,* valerian. Perennial to 5 feet; toothed deep green leaves; panicles of small pink flowers. Used by herbalists to allay pain and promote sleep. Attractive in the garden, but plant has pungent scent. Full sun to partial shade; moist, fertile soil rich in organic matter. Propagate by division.

*Vetiveria zizanioides,* vetiver, khus-khus. Tender perennial to 8 feet; an ornamental grass with straight stems and 3-foot leaves. Sweet-scented roots traditionally used for woven handicrafts, and distilled oil used for perfume and toilet waters. Full sun; moist, fertile soil. Must winter indoors where frost occurs. Propagate by division.

*Viola odorata,* sweet violet. Spreading perennial to 6 inches; heart-shaped leaves and fragrant purple to violet flowers. Leaves have antiseptic qualities. Flowers used in potpourris and as perfume ingredient; also as candied violets. Partial shade; moist, fertile soil rich in organic matter. Not hardy in extreme northern and southern U.S. Propagate by division or by seed. *Warning:* Spreads quickly by runners and can be invasive.

# CHAPTER FIVE

# NATIVE PLANTS AND WILDFLOWERS

On a clear and fine morning in early June it is difficult to realize that a continual battle for life is occurring in all gardens, and it is doubly difficult when the garden is an elegant perennial border, manicured to beat the band and full of butterflies and humming-birds. But at the same time, spiders pursue their prey, wasps sting, ladybugs travel about in search of aphids, the hawk pursues the rabbit, the cat pursues the mouse.

But in the BBG's Wild Garden—especially with its civilized pathways lined with low log fences that we are cautioned not to leave—we ramble through seemingly uncontrolled and bursting growth of wildflowers in profusion—and it's easier to accept the concept of "Nature, red in tooth and claw."

Wild gardens are exceptional for a number of reasons, chiefly because they need less fussing and maintenance than their more cultured counterparts. If finding time for gardening is a problem, one of the best ways to reduce the number of hours you spend working in the garden is to grow plants that naturally flourish in the sort of conditions present on your property. The different environments found in the Local Flora Section of the BBG offer some examples of the different types of wild gardens that are possible.

The Local Flora Section of the Garden was started in 1911 and was meant to hold only those plants that occur wild within approximately one hundred miles of New York City—European imports like the dandelion, buttercup, burdock, chickweed, and other interlopers were not intentionally grown in this era.

In 1942, Henry K. Svenson wrote the following in the *Brooklyn Botanic Garden Record*: "Our section occupies about two acres on the southern slope of the terminal glacial moraine which runs the length of Long Island, and possibly a fragment of the 'flat woods' of the outwash plain which extends southward to the ocean and which gave the English name of Flatbush to the Dutch village previously known as Midwout (Middlewoods). As early as the Battle of Long Island, which took place in 1776 on these same hills, the trees had been cut down; but fragments of the forest, still found to the westward, in Queens County, show a vegetation much richer than that of the other parts of Long Island."

The last trace of original vegetation disappeared from the Garden long ago, and all plants have been brought in from the outside, either by collection, purchase, or gift. Before the garden was established in 1910, a border mound had been constructed along Flatbush Avenue, and this border mound now cuts off much of the noise of traffic and the distracting sights of that thoroughfare.

Outside of an existing native black cherry tree *(Prunus serotina)* of unknown age, the oldest planting in this garden is a stand of mountain laurel *(Kalmia latifolia),* set out sometime in 1912. The original builders were so dedicated to the establishment of wild plants that they actually brought in sand from the New Jersey pine barrens and Long Island (until it was realized that quartz sand purchased from local dealers produced almost as good results).

Jacqueline Fazio began her reign over the Local Flora Section in 1980. Her first two years were spent in cleaning up the Local Flora Section; its charming wooden gates with their two open bronze fretworks of a moccasin flower, a Canadian lily, a Jack-in-the-pulpit, and a large orb-weaving spider (designed by artist Eva Melady), had been closed to the public for many years.

"Originally," she said, "Local Flora was to be based on the systematic arrangement of the plants, but that didn't work because a number of plants from the same families did not require the same environment. So in 1931, long before it was the popular thing to do, the Garden devised the present format that puts plants in ecological zones rather than systematizing them. Their habitats are determined by topography, rock formation (which influences alkalinity or acidity of the soil), moisture, drainage, and light."

There are eight different zones within Local Flora. Each is home to a number of native American plants that are so beautiful or interesting that they belong in any garden devoted to wildflowers (or for that matter, often in the perennial border), as long as their specific requirements are met.

The Serpentine Rock area is often associated with that characteristic rock and its dull green color (said to resemble a serpent's skin). These areas are low in available calcium and are relatively infertile, but they support a number of localized plant species including various ferns, flowering dogwood (Cornus florida), and the trumpet creeper vine (Campsis radicans), its blossoms continually beckoning to hummingbirds.

The Dry Meadow is a treeless plain dominated by grasses, interspersed with a number of spring- and autumn-flowering perennials. Here the bee balm (Monarda didyma), whose common name of balm means the plant is a member of the mint family, flaunts its scarlet blossoms and is visited by endless groups of delighted bees; white snakeroot (Eupatorium rugosum) whose common name is derived from the belief that the root would cure snakebite, bears fluffy heads of tiny white flowers; and spotted joe-pye weed (Eupatorium maculatum), with its tall-stemmed clusters of light purple flowers, makes a striking contrast to the goldenrods (Solidago spp.). Goldenrods are often ignored by gardeners because most people believe them to be the cause of hay fever, but they are really innocent of the charge—the real culprit is the common ragweed (Ambrosia spp.), which often grows near goldenrod.

The Kettle Pond represents a depression that resulted from the melting of a partially buried ice mass left by a glacier ten thousand years ago. When such depressions fill with water, they support a large variety of plant and animal life. Turtleheads (Che-

*lone glabra)*, with flowers that closely resemble their reptilian namesake, and boneset *(Eupatorium perfoliatum)*, so named because opposite leaves are joined around the stem and were once thought to be helpful in the setting of broken bones, bloom around the edge of the pond, while cattails *(Typha latifolia)* and arrowheads *(Sagittaria latifolia)* grow directly in the water.

The Wet Meadow is a low-lying, treeless area in full sun in which some moisture always is evident in the soil. The great blue lobelia *(Lobelia siphilitica)*, which came by its species name because the plant was once thought to be a cure for syphilis, and its relative, the brilliant scarlet cardinal flower *(Lobelia cardinalis)*, are both at home in this spot.

The Bog is a continually wet and spongy area similar to a swamp. In nature, the Bog's bottom consists of accumulations of peat, which in turn is composed of sphagnum moss that originally grows on floating pads on the water's surface and contributes to the peat as it decays. Here the growing medium is extremely acid and the common plants include bog rosemary *(Andromeda polifolia)*, a great favorite for smaller rock gardens; cranberry *(Vaccinium* spp.); meadowsweet *(Spiraea latifolia)*, with its clusters of tiny pink flowers resembling wads of cotton candy; and the pitcher plant *(Sarracenia purpurea)*, not only attractive for its tubular trumpet-shaped leaves, in which insects are trapped and digested, but also for its unusual greenish purple nodding flowers.

The Pine Barrens area has a shallow sandy soil with high acidity and low fertility and resembles the barrens of New Jersey and Long Island. The flora include pitch pines, hollies, and shrubby members of the Heath Family plus a number of rare and endangered plants. Sand myrtle *(Leiophyllum buxifolium)*, a native evergreen shrub that is excellent for garden borders and perfect for the rock garden, blooms, along with prickly pear *(Opuntia humifusa)* and the beautiful pine barren sandwort *(Minuartia caroliniana*, also known as *Arenaria caroliniana*.

The Limestone Area has rock formations that give the soil alkaline rather than acid properties, and the structure of the stone provides a foothold for the rare walking fern *(Camptosorus rhizophyllus)* and the charming American columbine *(Aquilegia canadensis)*.

The Border Mound builders never realized just how valuable their efforts would be to the Local Flora Section and the entire Garden. They had no way of knowing just how noisy automobile traffic could be. This earthen bank with its various plantings is now absolutely necessary to muffle the sounds of contemporary traffic along Flatbush Avenue. The bank points out a practical way to control this problem in other noisy areas of both the city and the suburbs. A border mound next to the road might even help to control the heavy sound of trucks on back-country roads. Asters *(Aster* spp.) and black-eyed Susans *(Rudbeckia hirta)* bloom here along with a number of shrubs and trees including the eastern white pine *(Pinus strobus)* and the Canadian hemlock *(Tsuga canadensis).*

Finally, the Woodlands of the Local Flora Section consist of two types of forest found in the vicinity of New York City.

The first is the deciduous tree grove, where maples, beeches, and oaks grow together with an understory of shrubs and wildflowers. Underneath the interlacing branches, three of the most beautiful species of spring flowers, trilliums *(Trillium* spp.), hepaticas *(Hepatica* spp.) and wood anemones *(Anemone quinquefolia),* among others, awaken to the warming sunshine of March and April.

The second woodland area is the evergreen forest, consisting of hemlocks, red cedar *(Juniperus virginiana),* and white pine. Among the flowers found here are horsebalm *(Collinsonia canadensis),* partridgeberry *(Mitchella repens),* pokeweed *(Phytolacca americana),* and false Solomon's seal *(Smilacina racemosa).*

We asked Ms. Fazio about fertilizing in such a wild garden.

"I don't," she answered. "Everything here is pretty much on its own. Basically I'm treating wild plants as they should be treated, starting out with soil that is correctly prepared, a year or two of help with careful watering while they settle in, and then pretty much leaving them alone. The only thing I've done is to help out the cherry tree because it's so old, using a soil auger and packing the holes with fertilizer and peat moss, and the original mountain laurel *(Kalmia latifolia)* has benefited from iron chelates added to the soil.

"There is no master plan. I have a general map of the area, and when I get a plant suited to the Dry Meadow, for example, I just try to find a spot that is environmentally correct."

We stopped on the path that runs between the Wet Meadow and the Pine Barrens to discuss the problems of poison ivy and the use of jewelweed *(Impatiens capensis)* in its treatment. "The plant's juice," she said, "really doesn't stop the rash from spreading, but it does cut down on the itching, and that itch is often instrumental in the spread of the rash." We also admired a large clump of horsemint *(Monarda punctata)*, with its yellow flowers dotted with purple and capped with bracts brushed with white. "It's found in the pine barrens of New Jersey," she said, "because it likes a sandy, well-drained soil. Although it can be invasive, it's beautiful when bunched together . . ."

A number of glittering thread-waisted wasps, with body colors of blue and orange streaked with metallic green, bobbed about in the air above the blossoms. One buzzed by.

". . . and the insects are predatory ichneumon wasps, as attractive in their own way as butterflies and producing larvae that attack many insect pests.

"It's a common perception of most people that everything blooms in May and June and then it's over for another year. Here we are in mid-August on a very hot day and we're surrounded by flowers."

And we were. But rather than standing in front of a stately spring border with its controlled mounds of flowers, we were instead surrounded by jumbles of leaves and large dashes of color, almost like being within a very large and very beautiful impressionist painting.

By using various combinations of native American wildflowers, plants that bloom not only in the spring but on into the heat of summer and the shorter days of autumn, Ms. Fazio works with flowers until the cold nights of early winter put a cap on all of nature's bloom.

We pointed to a Japanese beetle and asked if there were insect problems.

"Plenty, but who cares? One of the beauties of a wild garden is the lack of concern for insect problems. As for that beetle, I hope it's having a good time. Here, for example, is Jerusalem artichoke *(Helianthus tuberosus)*, growing and flowering even though it has a continual fight with aphids. My biggest problem here is rabbits, especially with transplants."

Wild gardens are not meant to be manicured in the same way that formal gardens are. Here amid the confusion of leaf and flower, the occasional weed is lost in a sea of green. And because of the layered plan of such a garden, with a profusion of plants at different heights, the damage by insects is not as noticeable. Then, too, the majority of plants in such gardens are tough Americans, plants that have not been endlessly hybridized and eventually weakened like many of the perennials found at today's nursery centers.

The Jerusalem artichoke is an American native. The common name has nothing to do with Jerusalem but is a corruption of the Italian *girasole,* which means "turning to the sun," a practice common to all sunflowers. Here in the Garden it was growing beautifully in the company of a huge stand of joe-pye weed, the purple of one in kindly confrontation with the bright yellow of the other.

Ahead in the Dry Meadow was a beautiful white flower.

"That's the flowering spurge *(Euphorbia corollata),* sometimes called the tramp's spurge, or, of all things, wild hippo. And here are wild roses, in this case *Rosa virginiana;* not only are the flowers beautiful but they are followed by very large red hips that the birds are especially fond of."

And that is also part of the charm of a wild garden. The birds and insects are busy all day long.

Ahead of us was a concentration of prickly pear *(Opuntia humifusa),* and just a few feet away, turtleheads and great blue lobelias bloomed in elegant combination with jewelweed.

We paused at the gate and looked up to see a Virginia creeper *(Parthenocissus quinquefolia)* rambling through the branches of a white birch *(Betula papyrifera)* and thought of Aldo Leopold's remark in *A Sand County Almanac:* "There are some who can live without wild things, and some who cannot." In this particular part of the Garden, there are plenty of wild things for those who care.

## A PLACE FOR YOUR WILD GARDEN

Wildflowers are never quite as grandiose as the plants found in a typical garden or herbaceous border; they need a more intimate setting. And a wildflower garden should not involve massive amounts of earth moving: You can't create a bog in the middle of Death Valley, and you shouldn't try. It is also foolish, if you live on the Outer Banks of North Carolina, to attempt to create the kind of woodland garden found near the rockbound coasts of Maine, or if you live in southern California, to attempt to grow and maintain a collection of wildflowers from the prairies. While it's true that money can accomplish almost anything, in these days of dwindling resources it is sometimes an immoral proposition to try. It's often amazing how we can continue to believe that the grass is greener next door or in the next state.

Often the most beautiful plants to grow are those found growing naturally in one's own climatic area.

If you have decided to grow wildflowers, first walk around your property and answer for yourself the following questions:

1. *Is your property or climate wet or dry?* If you are in a dry area of the country, remember you will have to water well at least once a week unless you specifically choose flowers that stand up to dry conditions, like yuccas or black-eyed Susans. Another idea is to check the plants found native to your own area, as these plants are more conditioned to local weather conditions. If your land is low bottomland, or on a flood plain, or the local water table is high, perhaps the wisest choice would be to select plants that like wet feet.

2. *Is there proper drainage?* Many plants have root systems that rot if they are exposed to too much water. So the condition of your soil and its drainage are very important matters to consider. If the soil seems impossible at best, as far as drainage is concerned, perhaps a garden in raised beds will be the answer, since here the content of the soil is entirely up to you. By properly placing such raised-bed systems, it is possible to provide the cultural requirements for many different types of plants. Without raised beds you will probably do best with bog plants, which can thrive in continually wet conditions.

3. *Is there sun or shade?* Many wildflowers bloom in the first flush of the spring sun before the trees overhead begin to leaf out, so it's obvious that a number of plants will adapt to life in the shade. Others demand full sun in order to perform. Here is a case in which a small map of your property showing the varying amounts of sun and shade can be extremely valuable.

4. *Are there any natural features that will work to your benefit?* We've always been amazed by people and developers who, before they begin to build one or more new homes, completely clear the land of any individuality it ever had, from the smallest tree to the largest rock. It's amazing how many beautiful gardens have been built around the humble beginnings of one or more trees or one or more boulders. So check your property for such landmarks that would be useful centerpieces for a wild garden.

5. *What kind of soil do you have?* While some plants do well in clay, others will quickly perish in the same spot. For most woodland wildflowers, for example, the soil should be well laced with humus or leaf litter to a depth of at least six inches. A mulch (see page 240) is helpful, and if you are in USDA Zone 6 or north, the

entire bed will benefit from the protection offered by a layer of evergreen branches or a carpet of leaves, especially if winter snows are undependable.

## COLLECTING WILDFLOWERS

Never disturb any endangered or protected plants unless they stand in the way of a developer's machinery. Each plant that disappears from the wild represents a weakening and impoverishment of the natural world; we are losing plant species at an alarming rate, depriving ourselves not only of their beauty, but also of their gene pool, which could someday provide breeders with resistance to a terrible pest, or a cure for some as yet unknown disease. And never buy wildflowers from nurseries that have no conscience about the environment. As in any type of business, there are unscrupulous people involved in supplying rare native plants to homeowners by ripping them out of the woods and fields, potting them up, and offering them for sale. So beware the cheap deal. It takes six to seven years for a trillium to be mature enough to flower. That means the nursery must care for seedlings year after year, and that means hours of investment. Does it make sense that the final plant is available for $2.98? Hardly! Here common sense should be your guide.

On the other hand, the beauties of a wild garden that develops over the years can sometimes be bound up with the memories associated with gathering the plants, as long as the plants are not protected and are on private land and gathered with permission. Each one tugs at the mind until you suddenly recall the spring day that you collected that violet in the back of a friend's woodland, or the walking fern from a friend's collection of rarities, or a plant that you have raised from seed provided by one of the many wildflower societies here in America.

## • AMERICAN NATIVE PLANTS TO GROW

### FERNS

*Dennstaedtia punctilobula,* hay-scented fern. To 2 feet; fragrant light green fronds, finely divided, about 8 inches wide. Full sun to shade, in any reasonable garden soil. Tends to spread but excellent for planting a bank.

*Onoclea sensibilis,* sensitive fern. To 2 feet; there are two kinds of fronds: fertile fronds are narrow, with a cluster of sporangia at the top, while sterile fronds have wider, coarser leaves. Sun to partial shade, in moist soil. Spreads quickly in good, moist soil. Fertile leaves remain for the winter garden and are excellent in dried bouquets.

*Osmunda cinnamomea,* cinnamon fern. To 5 feet, with fronds up to 10 inches wide. Fertile fronds, borne separately, are light brown (like cinnamon). Partial shade, in moist soil. The young fiddleheads (or croziers) of this fern are edible.

*Osmunda regalis,* royal fern. To 4 feet, fronds often 1 foot wide; croziers are reddish-brown. Partial shade, in wet soil. Good in bog gardens or next to a pool or stream. If planting in average garden soil, plant should be in a tub and its roots kept constantly wet. The fibrous roots are used as a medium for growing orchids and bromeliads.

### PLANTS FOR DRY MEADOWS

*Asclepias tuberosa,* butterfly weed. To 3 feet; terminal clusters of bright orange flowers, attractive to butterflies, in summer. Full sun, in average or dry garden soil. Easy to grow and easy to start from seed. Young plants best for transplanting.

*Aster novae-angliae,* New England aster. To 5 feet; purple flowers in fall have many slender rays and golden centers. Pink and rose cultivars also available. Full sun, in moderately fertile, well-drained soil. Divide every other year. Easy to grow. Many subtle variations in flower color, especially in the wild.

*Eupatorium rugosum,* white snakeroot. To 4 feet high; clusters of fluffy white flowers in late summer and early fall. Open to partial shade, doing well in a woodsy setting, with a well-drained soil of average fertility. Easy to grow. *Warning:* Cows that eat this plant produce poisonous milk.

*Monarda punctata,* horsemint. To 3 feet; short-lived perennial, often grown as annual, with terminal clusters of small, unusual yellow and purple flowers in summer. Full sun, in well-drained, sandy soil of average fertility. Also does well in seaside gardens.

*Rudbeckia hirta,* black-eyed Susan. To 3 feet; golden yellow daisies with dark brown centers. Full sun, in well-drained soil of average fertility. Drought resistant. Also does well in seaside gardens.

*Solidago* spp., goldenrod. To 5 feet; fluffy clusters of tiny golden yellow flowers. Full sun to partial shade in well-drained soil of average fertility. Difficult to identify many wild species as they interbreed with ease. Many garden cultivars available.

*Vernonia altissima,* ironweed. To 10 feet; branched heads of purple flowers in summer. Full sun to partial shade, in well-drained soil of average fertility. Excellent for the back of the wild border.

## PLANTS FOR WET MEADOWS

*Chelone glabra,* white turtlehead. To 3 feet; short spikes of white to pale pink flowers in late summer to fall, shaped like a turtle's head. Full sun to partial shade in moist soil, preferably with an acid pH. When spring growth reaches 6 inches, nip off the tender tips for bushy plants with more flowers.

*Gentiana andrewsii,* bottle gentian. To 1 foot; pale green leaves and clusters of tubular blue flowers that never fully open, blooming in late summer to fall. Full sun to partial shade (shade needed in southern gardens), in moist soil with plenty of organic matter. Easier to grow than other gentians.

*Hibiscus moscheutos,* rose mallow. To 8 feet; large ruffled flowers or pink, red, or white in summer. Full sun, in moist or wet soil, but tolerant of drier soils as well. *H. moscheutos* susbsp. *palustris,* the sea hollyhock, is the southern member of the genus.

*Lobelia cardinalis,* cardinal flower. To 6 feet; spikes of brilliant scarlet flowers in summer. Partial shade to full sun, in moist soil. Add extra peat moss (moistened) when planting. In the north, wet but mulched soil is necessary for the winter. Hummingbirds love this plant.

*Mertensia virginica,* Virginia bluebell. To 2 feet; clusters of small bell-shaped blue to purple flowers in spring. Full sun to partial shade in good organic garden soil with adequate moisture; add humus when planting; best with plenty of sun in spring. Often self-sows with ease.

*Sisyrinchium angustifolium,* blue-eyed grass. To 10 inches; grassy blue-green leaves; small starry blue flowers (members of the Iris Family), with yellow centers. Full sun, in moist, or even wet, soil. Easy to grow. Remove round seed heads for continued bloom.

## PLANTS FOR A BOG

*Andromeda polifolia,* bog rosemary. To 2 feet; low shrub of creeping habit; small evergreen leaves and small white or pinkish flowers in spring. Full sun to partial shade, and although preferring moist soil will grow in drier conditions. Excellent in rock gardens.

*Caltha palustris,* marsh marigold. To 3 feet; heart-shaped leaves, rich yellow flowers resemble buttercups, appearing in spring. Full sun in early spring followed by partial shade in summer, in wet boggy soil, or directly in water. Add plenty of humus when planting.

*Sarracenia purpurea,* pitcher plant. To 1½ feet; tubular, pitcher-shaped red-veined leaves with fluted edges, half-filled with water, in which insects fall, drown and are digested, providing nutrients to the plant; unusual flowers with downturned waxy petals. Full sun to partial shade in boggy conditions.

*Saururus cernuus*, lizard-tail. To 2 feet; vaguely heart-shaped leaves; long, curved spikes of tiny, very fragrant white flowers in summer. Full sun to partial shade, in boggy conditions. *Warning:* Very invasive and very hard to get rid of.

## PLANTS FOR A POND

*Nelumbo lutea*, American lotus. Plate-sized leaves that are held up out of the water; pale yellow flowers followed by interesting seedpods, good for drying. Full sun. Plants do well in shallow water and small pools but need 3 or 4 inches of water above the crown. Mix well-rotted manure in soil before planting and, if growing in pots, divide every few years. Will overwinter if roots are protected from ice.

*Nuphar luteum* spp. *macrophylla*, spatterdock. Large oval leaves, 1 foot wide, float on water; globe-shaped yellow flowers, blooming all summer. Full sun. Too invasive for a small pond, but excellent in a large pond or a small lake. Needs at least 2 feet of water depth.

*Nymphaea odorata*, fragrant water lily. Floating leaves to 10 inches across; fragrant white flowers to 5 inches across, open during the day. Can be grown in a 6-inch flowerpot in a small pool, with at least 1 foot of water above the crown. Will overwinter if roots are protected from ice.

*Orontium aquaticum*, golden club. Blue-green leaves, 6 to 12 inches long; curving spathe of yellow flowers. Full sun to partial shade. Plant roots in at least 1 foot of water.

*Typha latifolia*, cattail. To 6 feet; unmistakable brown club-shaped inflorescence; long sword-shaped leaves. Full sun to partial shade, along the edge of ponds or in pots for smaller pools. *Warning:* Can become invasive in earth-bottomed ponds.

## PLANTS FOR THE WOODLAND

*Aquilegia canadensis*, American columbine. To 2 feet; basal rosette of scalloped leaves; graceful flowers with yellow sepals and red spurs, in spring to midsummer. Full sun to partial shade, in well-drained soil of average fertility. Will seed about, eventually forming a small colony.

*Aruncus dioicus*, goat's-beard. To 7 feet; compound, feathery leaves; large panicles of tiny white flowers in summer. Full sun to partial shade, in moist, humusy soil. Flowers can be dried.

*Asarum canadense*, wild ginger. To 6 inches; heart-shaped leaves and inconspicuous brown inflorescences shaped like tiny jugs, in spring.

Partial shade, in fertile soil rich in organic matter. Will spread and can be used as ground cover.

*Collinsonia canadensis,* horsebalm. To 5 feet; branching plant with toothed leaves and long clusters of yellow lemon-scented flowers in summer. Partial shade, in moist soil of average fertility, but appreciates additional organic matter when planted.

*Dicentra eximia,* fringed bleeding heart. To 2 feet; bushy plant with finely divided foliage and elongated, heart-shaped deep pink flowers in summer, sometimes blooming into fall. Partial shade, in moist but well-drained soil of average fertility. Make sure it never lacks for moisture.

*Epigaea repens,* trailing arbutus. Creeping evergreen plant with deep green leathery leaves and fragrant white to light pink flowers; one of the first flowers in spring. Partial shade, in acid soil of average to poor fertility. On endangered list in many states; does not move well, so buy nursery-propagated plants.

*Geranium maculatum,* wild geranium. To 20 inches; branching plant with finely cut lobed leaves and violet flowers in late spring. Full sun to partial shade, in moist, fertile soil rich in organic matter. Looks best when set out in groups of at least 6 plants.

*Goodyera pubescens,* rattlesnake plantain. In bloom, to 15 inches; basal rosette of small evergreen leaves with delicate tracing of criss-crossed veins; upright stem topped with a small cluster of tiny white waxy flowers in summer; member of orchid family. Full sun to partial shade, in dry soil of average fertility and acid pH.

*H. acutiloba,* sharp-lobed hepatica. To 9 inches tall; pointed, three-lobed basal leathery evergreen leaves; charming bluish white flowers in early spring. Partial shade, in neutral or slightly acid, well-drained soil. Often found under oak trees.

*Lilium superbum,* Turk's-cap lily. To 8 feet; orange lilies spotted with purple, in summer, often as many as 30 flowers on one stem. Full sun to partial shade, in moist acid soil.

*Mitchella repens,* partridgeberry. Low creeping plant with small, rounded evergreen leaves; pairs of tiny fragrant trumpetlike flowers of white or pale pink; bright red berries in fall and winter. Partial shade in moist, acid, woodsy soil. Use lots of peat moss when planting, and mulch with pine needles.

*Oxalis acetosella,* wood sorrel. To 6 inches; cloverlike leaves and small white flowers veined with pink, in spring and early summer. Partial shade in slightly acid, well-drained, humusy soil. Only for cool areas; in the south, grow *O. violacea.*

*Phlox stolonifera,* creeping phlox. To 10 inches; oval leaves with bright pink flowers on upright stems, blooming in late spring. Cultivars also available in shades of rose, lavender, blue, and white. Full sun to open shade with a well-drained, humusy soil on the acid side.

*Phytolacca americana,* pokeweed. To 12 feet; long leaves and clusters of white or pinkish flowers on cerise stems, followed by shiny black berries in summer. Full sun to partial shade in any average soil. Will seed about, so this is only for the wild garden; loved by birds. *Warning:* Whole plant is poisonous to humans, especially when mature.

*Podophyllum peltatum,* May apple. To 2 feet; large, palmate leaves like woodland umbrellas; nodding white flower blooming in late spring, followed by yellow berry. Partial shade in moist soil with some humus. Excellent used as a ground cover for a woodland slope but foliage dies back in midsummer. *Warning:* The whole plant is poisonous except for the ripe fruit.

*Polygonatum biflorum,* small Solomon's-seal. To 3 feet; pointed oval leaves on curved stems; tubular, creamy, paired white flowers in spring. Partial shade, in moist, humusy soil. Plants often resent transplanting, so be patient. Excellent woodland ground covers. Name comes from seallike scars on underground stems where former branches originated.

*Smilacina racemosa,* false Solomon's-seal. To 3 feet; oval leaves on arching stems; clusters of small white starry flowers followed by red berries in the fall. Partial shade, in moist soil with an acid pH. Needs extra humus when planted and extra water during dry summers.

*Trillium grandiflorum,* giant white trillium. To 14 inches; tall rounded and pointed leaves in threes; white tri-petaled flowers in late spring. Partial shade in well-drained, acid, humusy soil, with extra organic matter. Never pick! The only food the flower's roots receive is from the season's one set of leaves. A beautiful flower for the woodland garden.

### PLANTS FOR THE SUN

*Echinacea purpurea,* purple coneflower. To 3 feet; coarsely toothed leaves; rose-purple daisylike flowers with copper-brown discs, blooming in summer. Full sun in well-drained, sandy soil of average fertility. Drought tolerant. Excellent at the edge of a woodland or in front of low shrubs and bushes. Easy to grow. (Although this plant is not native to the Brooklyn area, it is included in the Local Flora Section because it is such a supurb native American plant.)

*Opuntia humifusa,* prickly pear. Cactus, to 3 feet; with the large, flat, bristled pads typical of opuntias; yellow flowers in summer, followed by purplish fruit. Full sun, in well-drained, sandy soil. Not reliably hardy in colder parts of USDA Zone 5 and north.

*Viola pedata,* bird's-foot violet. To 6 inches; palmately lobed leaves;

deep blue flowers on slender, upright stems throughout spring. Full sun, in moist but well-drained acid soil of average fertility. If such soil is lacking in your garden, make a small raised bed using stones to contain this violet. In addition to their decorative flowers, most violets also produce self-pollinated (cleistogamous) flowers that produce nothing except seed and are usually not noticed by most gardeners; that's why the plants spread so rapidly and can become pests in the garden. The bird's-foot does not produce such flowers, so if you want more, let some violets go to seed.

*Yucca filamentosa,* Adam's needle. To 3 feet with basal rosette making a 2-foot circle; long stiff sword-shaped leaves are evergreen, with threads dangling from the margins; tall spikes of bell-shaped creamy white flowers in midsummer. Full sun, in well-dried, reasonably fertile soil. Seedpods are useful in dried arrangements. Hardy in both the northern and southern U.S.

# CHAPTER SIX

# THE
## ROCK
## GARDEN

Reginald Farrer was English. He was a garden writer, plant explorer, and gardener, who had a profound influence on the plants and planting of the Edwardian era just before World War I. Farrer did more to popularize the growing of alpine and rock garden flora than anyone else. It is said that at elegant and sophisticated dinners where conversation was usually about the doings of the royal family and scandal about the upper classes, everyone turned to talk of edelweiss, meconopsis, drainage, and compost when Mr. Farrer walked into the room.

The first rock gardens described in old books were usually built around existing rock outcrops, but since the early 1700s most such gardens have been constructed by piling up introduced stones. England's first such rock garden was built at the Chelsea Physic Garden in 1772, when Sir Joseph Banks, on returning from Iceland, brought with him slabs of lava. Repairs on the Tower of London were being made at the same time, and the old castoff stones were also brought to the grounds. There, mixed with broken brick, this collection of assorted detritus became a trend-setting garden.

When the rock garden came to America, though, the English viewed it as a "colonial" garden, not quite sophisticated enough (or rich enough with old money) to really support such a gardening style. How wrong they were.

Construction of the Rock Garden at the Brooklyn Botanic Garden began in the spring of 1916 and was completed in 1917, making it the first rock garden of any considerable size to be constructed in a public garden or park in the United States. Although the people at the Garden can surely not take credit for being the first to introduce rock gardening to Americans, they were right there at the forefront.

In 1931, Montague Free, for many years one of the Garden's outstanding horticulturists, wrote the following about the Rock Garden construction:

"The rocks used . . . are, for the most part, glacial boulders which were uncovered in the course of grading operations on other parts of the grounds. These boulders are very unprepossessing material for the construction of a rock garden, their rounded contours almost prohibiting any natural and artistic effects from being obtained. Their hard, impervious surfaces are far from ideal from the standpoint of the cultural requirements of the alpine plants, which revel in rocks of a rough, porous nature that will hold moisture and to which their roots may cling. In spite of these disadvantages, one is cheered by overhearing visitors commenting on the "wildness" and natural appearance of the garden. In order to provide quarters for plants that delight in rock crevices, a number of the larger boulders were split and the fissures filled with suitable soil. The fact that in 1918 over six hundred species and varieties were found in the garden, many of them alpines considered very intractable in this part of the country, is testimony that the difficulties of cultivation have, in part, been overcome. The number of species represented [in 1931] is almost eight hundred in spite of losses due to vandalism, carelessness on the part of visitors, and lack of adaptability to our conditions on the part of some of the alpines."

A "moraine garden" was constructed in 1917. "Moraine" is the term for the masses of small rocks and debris deposited at a mountain's feet by glacial action. This one was made by removing the existing soil of a small area to a depth of eighteen inches and replacing it with a mix of five parts of three-quarter-inch crushed stone, one part of sand, and one part of leaf mold. Like Julius Caesar's enemy Cassius, this mix has "a lean and hungry look," but it accomplishes three things necessary in rock gardening, especially in areas of sparse snowfall, yet enduring wet and cold winters:

1. It provides perfect drainage.

2. It encourages the plant roots to penetrate to a depth that is cool and moist, impervious to the heat above.

3. It insures that the plants' top growth will ripen, enabling them to better withstand the vagaries of a Brooklyn winter.

Here the more difficult species of the rock jasmine (*Androsace* spp.), the rockfoils (*Saxifraga* spp.), the woodruffs (*Asperula* spp.) and alpine primroses (*Primula* spp.) grow with great abandon.

"The general idea in making the garden," wrote Mr. Free, "was that of representing a boulder-strewn slope. This design, of necessity, was modified in places to provide proper cultural conditions as to drainage, depth of soil, and shade. . . . [Since] easy accessibility to the plants was of greater importance than maintaining intact the idea of a stony slope, our garden is well provided with walks and trails. These are made of broken flagstone, laid informally, and, in the case of the small trails, with a stepping-stone effect.

"In placing the rocks one can be guided by the views of those who assume that the plants which the rock garden contains are all important and that the arrangement of rocks is of little consequence, except insofar as it contributes towards the well-being of the plants; or, one may take the point of view, which is perhaps the better one, that the arrangement of the rocks should be as natural, as pleasing, and as artistic as possible, consistent with providing suitable accommodations for the plants that the garden is to contain. Anyone contemplating the construction of a rock garden would be well advised to study rock arrangement as it occurs in Nature and be guided, in part at least, by Nature's methods."

The key here is "natural." After all, shouldn't the plants be the thing, not the rocks? (Even though, during the heyday of the rock garden, many Victorian gardeners became so fascinated with the idea of building such a garden that they actually constructed huge mounds of stone, usually topped with a fountain or a nymph in some stage of distress or undress, and only at the finish did the plants come into play—but always to take a back seat to the rock itself.)

A final consideration in the plan should be convenience of viewing. Although the average gardener will not experience the crush of visitors that the Brooklyn Botanic Garden often has, the idea of making accessible trails for visitors is too often ignored, even in the smallest of backyards.

## MORE ABOUT THE SOIL

The beautiful plants that often thrive on a mountaintop must have special conditions to exist in the valley below, and the prime requirement in rock gardening—and usually in most other types of gardening as well—is to provide the plants with perfect drainage: They resent stagnant water at their roots! In designing and building a rock garden, the aim should be for perfect drainage using a sandy, porous soil.

If your particular garden spot is hampered by heavy soil that you are at odds about how to improve, think about building a small raised bed either of landscape timbers or, preferably, layers of fieldstone, then filling it with the prescribed soil.

The problem the gardener often confronts when dealing with alpine plants is their initial success in poorly drained soil. Early in the season they appear to prosper—but with the arrival of a typical American summer, the problems begin. If rainfall is lacking, the plants can be watered in the evening. But when the heat and the humidity both rise, to be followed by torrential outbursts of rain, the trouble begins. The ground around the plant's crown remains wet, the leaves do not dry quickly, and the eventual result is rot.

An excellent soil mix can be made of three parts of good loam mixed with one part of sharp sand (sharp sand is builder's sand—not to be confused with beach sand, which is not to be used, as it is laced with salt and so rounded from erosion that it easily packs together). This is then again mixed with two parts of humus, two parts of crushed stone or gravel, and one-half part of crushed limestone or old mortar—this last because most rock plants prefer a bit of lime in their diet.

The mixture should be at least fourteen inches deep, but if at all possible, even deeper. A raised bed of two to three feet in height filled with this mix will give you a garden that will flourish beyond your wildest dreams.

When the plants are all installed, a top dressing of crushed stone will help to keep the surface of the ground cool and provide a ventilated aspect for the plant's crown.

## THE ROCK GARDEN TODAY

The first creature that we met upon entering the Rock Garden at BBG was one of the ubiquitous rabbits. This particular rabbit was calmly sitting on top of a boulder labeled "Manhattan Schist of the Ordovician Age"—a boulder which was transported to this spot by a continental glacier during the last ice age.

A graveled path winds its way along the bottom of a low valley with gentle inclines on either side. The Rock Garden was originally designed to be a boulder-strewn slope, and that original impression remains today except for the change in appearance caused by the age of the various trees and shrubs that spring up here and there around the stones and boulders. Today the garden is undergoing a major renovation that includes building a dry streambed and bringing in many more rocks to expand the plantings.

It was a very hot day at the end of July, with temperatures in the garden's shade well above 90°F. Usually rock gardens in midsummer are not too interesting but all around us daylilies, hostas, and anemones were in bloom, along with Astilbe *(Astilbe chinensis),* Caucasian daphne *(Daphne caucasica),* and *Minuartia juniperina.*

William Giambalvo is the present gardener in charge. He began at the Rock Garden in 1987 and since then has been busy cleaning it up in preparation for the major renovation that is now underway, and updating the nomenclature of the plants under his charge. Only a few new plants have been added, and those are his personal favorites. They include the dwarf chrysanthemum *(Chrysanthemum weyrichii)* in both the pink and the white varieties; *Gentiana acaulis* var. *clusii,* with tufted foliage and three-inch stems bearing large open trumpets of azure blue speckled with green inside; campanulas; hybrid birch; *Platycodon grandiflorus* 'Apoyama', a Japanese balloon flower; and *Ramonda myconi,* this last a native of the Pyrenees with five-lobed flowers of rich lavender-blue, and prized by most collectors.

"One of my goals," he said, "is to get more summer- and

fall-blooming flowers in the garden. After all, springtime in any rock garden is usually a carpet of color, but in the summer and the fall there is not as much blooming."

We approached a huge clump of Japanese anemones (Anemone × hybrida), in full bloom, the plants covered with flowers. Behind it was a two-foot-high bush clematis from China (Clematis heracleifolia var. davidiana), covered with light blue fragrant flowers, while to the left stood a hardy fuchsia (Fuchsia magellanica), also about two feet tall.

"That fuchsia will flower the next year and the reason is the microclimate it occupies. We have a number of plants in the Garden that survive when they are not supposed to, and it's usually because of a microclimate."

Dictionaries define microclimates as the "climate of a small area," but it's amazing just how small the area can be. Often one plant will survive a debilitating winter because the worst of the weather is deflected by one large rock ten feet away, or because the plant is situated on a rise, and cold air flows down and around it before much damage can be done. Finding microclimates is one of the more exciting possibilities open to the adventuresome gardener.

"I belong to the American Rock Garden Society and am astounded by the variety their seed exchanges offer every year. It's an exciting and inexpensive way to enlarge a collection of plants."

We commented on the neatness of the beds.

"It's the rock mulch," he said. "We use three-eighths-inch bluestone gravel, and it's especially good because it cuts down on weeds but retains moisture, yet the form and the color are in keeping with a rock garden plan.

"But pine needles are also an excellent mulch. They allow water and air circulation, and look especially attractive with the rock surfaces and the dwarf conifers in the collection. And I also use wood chips since they also have a natural look to them.

"And every week I get out and weed because persistence is one of the secrets of having a great garden."

We stopped in front of a bed of baby's breath (Gypsophila spp.) and balloon flowers (Platycodon grandiflorus), the baby's breath tumbling over and about the rocks while the unopened buds of the balloon flowers seemed to hover above, looking for all the world like their nicknames.

Above the rock was a clump of the China pink (Dianthus chinensis 'Telstar') skirting about the base of a dwarf conifer, in this case a white pine (*Pinus strobus* 'Contorta'). Ahead of us what looked to be a million bees were swarming around a large summer sweet *(Clethra alnifolia),* its rich perfume scenting the hot summer air.

"We've removed around one hundred trees and shrubs, in some cases to open up the garden and expand the vistas." And he added, "It's important to have a garden such as this to provide ideas for the many visitors."

Other trees and shrubs were removed for various reasons; some were dead or dying, some were overgrown, and some were inappropriate for a rock garden. But woody plants are vital components of this garden. Mr. Giambalvo believes that a well-placed dwarf shrub is an important element of a rock garden, providing structure and offering year-round interest.

He stooped again to cut back the leggy stems of a Virginia spiderwort *(Tradescantia virginiana)* that first made its appearance back in the 1920s with no record of its ever before being planted there.

"Theoretically, they say, it should have been uprooted, because it was not meant to be in this garden, but it fits in so beautifully in its self-chosen position that no one has had the heart to banish it."


## SEASONAL BLOOM IN THE ROCK GARDEN

In 1930 the Garden published a thirty-three-page guide to the plants in its Rock Garden. The guide showed that there was something of interest in bloom in the Rock Garden during every month of the year, unlike other perennial borders and theme gardens at the BBG. Over the years many of the plants disappeared, but Mr. Giambalvo is aiming to once again extend the blooming season in the Rock Garden so it will have flowers most of the year.

Since it's a challenge for most of us to have flowers blooming in the early and late months of the year, here is a rundown of plants found in the BBG Rock Garden in 1930 from January through April, and October through December. The names of the plants have been updated.

JANUARY: In January the pale lilac blossoms of the Palestinian iris *(Iris vartanii)* displayed themselves during the first two weeks. During cold spells the plants were covered (in 1930, until February 20) until the weather moderated, then flowers were again produced, and continued until about the middle of March. January usually saw some open flowers on the alpine heath *(Erica carnea)*.

FEBRUARY: During the later part of February some of the mountain crocuses began to bloom—notably *Crocus korolkowii* and *C. vitellinus*. Snowdrops *(Galanthus* spp.) also were expected to exhibit their nodding white blooms, along with the cheerful yellow of those of the winter aconite *(Eranthis × tubergenii)*, which has much larger flowers than those of the more common species, *E. hyemalis*.

MARCH: In March the bulbous plants were augmented by *Narcissus cyclamineus*, very distinctive, with its completely reflexed perianth; the Siberian squill *(Scilla sibirica)*; the grape hyacinth *(Muscari azureum)*; several species of *Iris*, and quite a few crocuses.

These bulbous irises, coming as they do at a time when outdoor flowers are scarce, are altogether charming. Several species in the Rock Garden were *Iris histrio*, *I. vartanii*, and *I. reticulata*, the latter described as the best of the easily grown spring-flowering bulbous irises. Its flowers of rich blue-purple and gold have a delightful violet fragrance.

Many species and varieties of crocus were opening their flowers to the sun in March.

The nonbulbous plants were represented by *Helleborus foetidus*, a dowdy, homely relative of the exquisite Christmas rose *(H. niger)*, which unfortunately did not thrive at BBG. A real star of the Rock Garden in March was *Draba aizoides*, with its bright yellow flowers.

APRIL: Although April found the 1930 Rock Garden still somewhat bare, there were enough plants in bloom to give an inkling of the plethora to follow. Considerably over fifty species and varieties were expected to display their flowers during this month, including, of course, some holdovers from March. Bulbous plants were still much to the fore including grape hyacinths *(Muscari botryoides, M. racemosum*, and *M. elegans)*; a few tulip species, of which the most notable is *Tulipa kaufmanniana*, sometimes called the water-lily tulip; narcissus; glory-of-the-snow *(Chionodoxa* species and varieties). Glory-of-the-snow are eminently satisfactory rock garden plants. They thrive and increase with practically no care. Their flowers of various shades of blue, with some pink and some white forms, are cheerful and welcome, and they lend themselves admirably to association with dwarf carpeting plants.

Narcissus was represented in April by the charming angel's tears daffodil *(Narcissus triandrus)*, from Spain and Portugal, and the petticoat daffodil *(N. bulbocodium)*, from southern France to Morocco. Both of these are of borderline hardiness at BBG, but they came through the winter of 1929 very successfully and survived for some years.

There was a miniature replica of the trumpet daffodils that was seen in the Rock Garden, but it wasn't permanent. This is *Narcissus asturiensis (N. minimus)*, which grows only three inches high.

Nonbulbous plants began to give a better account of themselves in April. The Himalayan primrose *(Primula denticulata)* produced its lavender flowers in dense globular heads, and various forms of the auricula primrose *(P. auricula)* displayed their umbels of sweetly scented blossoms.

Two native bleeding hearts—*Dicentra eximia* from western New York and the mountains of Virginia, and *D. formosa* from the Pacific Coast—came into bloom toward the end of the month. Both species grow well in shade and are tolerant of sunshine. There were colonies of these plants, from self-sown seed, all over the Rock Garden, and bleeding hearts again grace the Rock Garden today.

Toward the middle of the month, the Pasqueflower *(Anemone pulsatilla)* displayed its rich purple flowers with their masses of yellow stamens. Each flower is surounded by a lacy ruff of gray-green, hairy bracts. Its achenes with long feathery styles are much in evidence after the blossoms have fallen, and serve to prolong the period of its attractiveness.

Other plants noted in April were *Trollius laxus; Hepatica americana; Draba aizoides* and *D. cuspidata; Arabis caucasica (A. albida); Bergenia* spp.; Siberian bugloss *(Brunnera macrophylla); Epimedium alpinum* var. *rubrum;* and *Euphorbia myrsinites.*

OCTOBER: In October bulbous plants were again found in the Rock Garden in considerable force.

Several species were varieties of the meadow saffron, sometimes incorrectly called "autumn crocus." In their finer forms these flowers do resemble Brobdingnagian crocuses, although in reality they belong in the Lily Family, while crocuses are affiliated with the irises. *Colchicum speciosum* and its varieties are considered the most desirable of the meadow-saffrons. The species form has flowers of clear rosy pink, 'Album' is pure white, and 'Atrorubens' is ruby violet with a white throat. Some of the species have curious tessellated flowers of purple and lilac, as in *C. variegatum*, which blooms in September. The commonest species is *C. autumnale*, of which there are several forms, including a white one, 'Album'. We bless these meadow saffrons in the fall when their cheery blossoms brighten up the Rock Garden, but in the spring, when their coarse, heavy foliage dominates the scene, we are tempted to wish them elsewhere.

Autumn crocuses were also part of the fall display. Their colors, in general, range from white to purple. The showiest and most desirable species is *Crocus speciosus*, with flowers of bright blue. There are several varieties of this species, of which the following were grown in the Rock Garden in 1930: 'Albus', var. *Aitchisonii*, and 'Globosus'. The pale lilac flowers of the Cilician crocus or *C. kotschyanus (C. zonatus)*, also display their fragile-looking perianths along with those of the bright lilac saffron crocus *(C. sativus)*. Forms of the last named species are grown commercially for the production of saffron used in coloring cakes and other foods. The use of stigmas and the upper part of the styles as a source of saffron has been known since the time of Homer.

NOVEMBER: With the exception of some of the autumn crocuses, which continued blooming into November, blossoming was limited to stray flowers on those persistent species that commenced their efforts months before. If the weather was not too cold and boisterous, a fair display was made by such plants as the harebell *(Campanula rotundifolia), Daphne cneorum, Callirhoe involucrata, Petrorhagia (Tunica) saxifraga,* and *Dicentra eximia.*

A hardy perennial, which was comparatively new at the time, *Chrysanthemum zawadskii (koreanum),* held its white flowers, tinged with pink as they aged, well into November. This species, however, is better suited for the perennial border than the rock garden.

DECEMBER: He who maintains that the rock garden is attractive even in December might be rated as an incurable optimist, but nevertheless a real rock garden enthusiast can find joy in dwarf evergreens, including various conifers, and also *Sedum, Sempervivum,* and *Iberis,* which keep their foliage all winter. The bright red berries of the rockspray *(Cotoneaster)* also offer color in December. A few flowers still remained in the Rock Garden, usually limited to a few species of *Crocus* that had the temerity to continue opening their flowers in spite of the season. Among these tardy bloomers were *C. ochroleucus,* with creamy flowers tinged with yellow at the throat; *C. salzmannii,* which sent up its dark lilac flowers in succession as though it had no intention whatever of stopping; *C. asturicus,* and *C. longiflorus,* with lilac-colored flowers. The latter was the showiest of this ambitious quartet.

And so the Rock Garden year came to an end, not in a blaze of glory, it is true, but with the promise of good things to come —for the flower buds on the alpine heath *(Erica carnea)* were already plainly visible and ready to open as soon as the weatherman gave them the slightest encouragement.

## • PLANTS FOR A ROCK GARDEN

*Anacyclus depressus,* Mt. Atlas daisy. Prostrate plant with hairy, finely divided leaves and white daisylike flowers; ray flowers are red on the undersides, closing at night. Blooms from spring into summer. Deadhead spent blooms. Full sun. Easily propagated by seed. Needs winter protection in extreme northern U.S. Elegant planted at the edge of walls and in pots for the alpine house. Must have well-drained soil; the slightest threat of standing in wet soil will rot these plants.

*Androsace sarmentosa.* To 8 inches; basal rosette of hairy green leaves; clusters of very pretty rose-pink flowers. Full sun; needs watering during a dry season.

*Anemone pulsatilla (Pulsatilla vulgaris),* Pasqueflower. To 1 foot; divided basal leaves, fuzzy stems; bell-shaped flowers of violet blue or reddish purple, outside covered with silky hairs, in spring. Plants appreciate a bit of lime in the soil. Fluffy seed heads are also attractive.

*Aquilegia flabellata (A. akitensis),* Japanese columbine. To 1½ feet; basal rosette of scalloped leaves; graceful flower with lilac blue sepals and strongly hooked spurs of lilac, petals tipped with yellow, in spring to midsummer. Full sun to partial shade. Easily increased by seed, but plants hybridize with ease. Deadhead spent flowers. Cultivar 'Alba' has white flowers.

*Arabis albida,* rock cress. To 8 inches; clusters of white flowers above glossy dark green leaves in spring. Full sun. Appreciates some water during growing season.

*Arisarum proboscideum,* mouse plant. To 6 inches; arrowhead leaves; the hood (spathe) around the flower extends upward to 6 inches above the flower and looks like a mousetail sticking up through the leaves. Partial shade and humus in the soil.

*Aster alpinus,* alpine aster. To 10 inches; dark green leaves are lance-shaped; violet daisy flowers with yellow centers, blooming in spring and early summer. Plants eventually form clumps. Sun to partial shade, fertile soil, and additional water during sparse rainfall. Deadhead for continued bloom.

*Astilbe chinensis.* To 1 foot; feathery plumes of purple-pink flowers in late summer; basal mound of divided, ferny foliage. Partial shade and moist, fertile soil. 'Pumila' is the plant usually offered.

*Aubrieta deltoidea,* false rock cress. Trailing mound-forming evergreen plants, 2 to 3 inches high; 4-petaled violet-blue flowers cover the foliage in spring. 'Dr. Mules' is an attractive cultivar usually offered. Full sun to partial shade in any porous soil. Cut back the plants after flowering to maintain shape. Excellent on walls.

*Campanula carpatica,* Carpathian harebell, tussock bellflower. To 1 foot; small, toothed leaves; upturned bell-shaped violet blue flowers in midsummer. Full sun. A number of cultivars including white and a lovely blue 'Blue Moonlight'. Excellent for growing on walls.

*Carlina acaulis,* stemless carline thistle. To 9 inches; flat clusters of lobed gray-green leaves with spines; large white silvery bracts surround reddish brown disk flowers, relatively stemless, in late spring. Full sun. Dried flowers were once used as hygrometers as the bracts close together in damp air.

*Chiastophyllum oppositifolium (Cotyledon simplicifolia).* Rosettes of evergreen light green succulent leaves turn reddish in sun; 6-inch sprays of tiny golden flowers on arching stems in summer. Full sun to light shade but needs some moisture. Excellent in crevices of walls or stones.

*Chrysanthemum weyrichii,* dwarf chrysanthemum. To 1 foot tall; lower leaves palmate, upper leaves lobed; daisylike blossoms with white ray flowers turning pink with age, and yellow centers; blooms in late September. From Hokkaido in Japan. Full sun. Plants make excellent ground covers.

*Chrysogonum virginianum,* goldenstar, green and gold. To 10 inches; toothed deep green leaves; 5-petaled golden yellow flowers resemble single marigolds; blooms in late spring to early summer. Partial shade. An American native and an excellent ground cover.

*Codonopsis clematidea,* bonnet bellflower. To 18 inches, but usually sprawling over and under other plants; oval leaves; bell-like flowers, pale blue without, bands of purple, bright yellow, dark brown, and blue veins within. Foliage has foxy but inoffensive smell. Full sun in acid soil. Plant on top of wall. Mulch below USDA Zone 6.

*Cyclamen hederifolium,* hardy cyclamen. To 4 inches; deep green heart-shaped leaves marbled with silver; small rose-pink to white nodding flowers of great beauty and charm in late summer. Partial shade; plenty of humus in the soil. Plant tubers in midsummer.

*Dianthus alpinus,* alpine pink. To 6 inches; narrow thin leaves; tufted plants are covered with small pink, red-pink, or speckled white flowers in late spring; fragrant flowers loved by butterflies, especially swallowtails. Full sun and excellent for the scree bed, where they slowly carpet an area.

*Dodecatheon pulchellum,* shooting star. To 10 inches; long leathery leaves; clusters of magenta-to-lavender flowers with reflexed petals and yellow centers in late spring. Partial shade with moist soil. 'Album' has white flowers. Plants go dormant in late summer.

*Doronicum cordatum,* leopard's bane. To 16 inches; toothed leaves; daisy flowers of yellow with many slender rays, blooming in spring. Full sun to partial shade.

*Draba* spp., Russian mustard. Tufted perennials, most under 10 inches; deep green rosettes; 4-petaled fragrant flowers of yellow, rose, or white bloom in early spring, often through the snow. Full sun. Excellent for the scree bed and also in pots for the alpine house. They tend to self-sowing.

*Dryas octopetala,* mountain avens. Low creeping plants with small evergreen leaves, deep green on top and silvery beneath; flowers are white, resembling small anemones, on 6-inch stems. Full sun. They make excellent ground covers.

*Edraianthus pumilio (Wahlenbergia pumilio),* grassy bells. To 3 inches tall; tufted plants with grassy leaves; violet-blue flowers in spring carpet the ground with sparkling color. Full sun. Excellent for the scree bed.

*Epimedium grandiflorum,* barrenwort. To 1 foot; heart-shaped evergreen leaves are bronzy when young, then turn green; flowers are yellow, shaped like a biretta (with 3 projections) and 4 spurs, blooming in spring. Partial shade in moist soil with plenty of additional humus. Excellent ground cover. Can be transplanted even while blooming.

*Erigeron karvinskianus (E. mucronatus),* fleabane. To 1 foot; long thin leaves; lovely pale pink and white blossoms on twiggy growth, flowering for months beginning in late spring, and flowering the first year from seed. Full sun. Beautiful in masses, especially on the tops of walls.

*Erinus alpinus.* To 4 inches; small toothed deep green leaves; clusters of small lilac-mauve flowers, blooming in spring. Full sun and poor soil, growing in cracks in walls and the barest minimum of earth. Short-lived perennial but easily reproduced from seed. 'Albus' is white. Easy to grow.

*Genista sylvestris* var. *pungens,* broom. To 6 inches; small shrub with spiny stems, narrow leaves; terminal racemes of bright yellow flowers in spring. Full sun. Plants form neat mounds and make excellent ground covers.

*Geranium dalmaticum*. To 6 inches; medium green lobed leaves; clusters of pretty 5-petaled rose pink or white flowers in late spring. Full sun in cooler climates but partial shade where summers are very hot.

*Gypsophila repens,* creeping baby's breath. To 8 inches; small lance-shaped leaves; masses of tiny white flowers in summer. Full sun. Beautiful when clambering over the edge of a wall.

*Hacquetia epipactis.* To 6 inches; palmately lobed leaves; tiny yellow flowers are surrounded by apple-green bracts, blooming in very early spring. Partial shade and moist soil. More interesting than beautiful.

*Helianthemum nummularium,* rock rose. To 1 foot; small evergreen leaves; 5-petaled yellow, red, orange, pink, or white flowers on gracefully curved stems, blooming in summer. Full sun, doing well in poor soil. Cut plants back after blooming is over.

*Hypericum olympicum,* olympic St. John's-wort. To 1 foot; subshrub with gray-green oval leaves; bright yellow flowers with prominent stamens, blooming in late spring and summer. Full sun.

*Iberis sempervirens,* edging candytuft. To 12 inches; subshrub with narrow leaves; small 4-petaled white flowers (turning a bit pink with age), with two petals longer than the rest, bloom in racemes that lengthen with age, in late spring. Trim the plants back after flowering. Excellent tumbling over walls and stones.

*Lamium maculatum* 'Aureum', spotted dead nettle. To 1½ feet; oval leaves of a golden color are spotted with white; pink flowers are relatively unimportant. Partial shade and moist soil. Not invasive like other nettles but will spread about in time.

*Leontopodium alpinum,* edelweiss. To 1 foot; narrow, felty leaves; clusters of small yellow flowers surrounded by white woolly bracts, blooming in early summer. Full sun. This is the legendary flower that was said to send young men to their doom as they fell over cliffs while picking it.

*Ophiopogon planiscapus* 'Arabicus', black mondo grass. To 6 inches; slow-growing clumps of evergreen straplike leaves turn purple-black with age; flowers are pink, followed by blue pea-sized fruits. Full sun. Needs protection north of USDA Zone 6. Elegant color point for the rock garden.

*Pachysandra procumbens,* Allegheny pachysandra. To 1 foot; toothed oval leaves with light green tracings on dark green background; flowers are purplish brown with conspicuous white filaments on spikes. An excellent ground cover in partial shade.

*Papaver burseri,* alpine poppy. To 10 inches; pinnate leaves in basal rosette; 4-petaled fragrant poppies usually white but also in orange and yellow. Full sun. Short-lived perennials, but seed about. Taproot very long, so it resists transplanting.

*Penstemon rupicola,* cliff penstemon. Low shrub to 4 inches; small evergreen leaves have a whitish bloom; rosy red flowers in summer. Not reliably hardy north of USDA Zone 6.

*Polygonum affine* 'Donald Lowndes', Himalayan fleeceflower. To 1 foot; mat-forming narrow dark green evergreen leaves turning bronze in fall; terminal spikes of tiny rosy red flowers in late summer to fall. Full sun. Slightly invasive, so keep at one end of the garden.

*Primula auricula,* auricula primrose. To 8 inches; basal rosette of leathery evergreen leaves, often covered with "meal" (a white, powdery substance); terminal clusters of flowers originally in yellow, but now available in many colors, blooming in spring. Full sun to partial shade; gritty soil on the alkaline side. Beautiful when grown in rock crevices and walls.

*Saponaria ocymoides,* rock soapwort. To 8 inches; trailing, with lance-shaped leaves; clusters of pink flowers cover the plant in late spring to early summer. Full sun. Especially tolerant of poor soil.

*Sedum* spp., stonecrop. From 6 inches to 2 feet; fleshy oval leaves, green or deep red, most species evergreen, and rooting as they move along; terminal clusters of tiny red, pink, yellow, or white flowers in summer. Full sun to partial shade. Most make excellent ground covers, as they are quite fine when in bloom. They will grow in very little soil. *Sedum album* is somewhat invasive but grows beautifully in walls, bearing many white flowers; *S. ewersii* has prostrate growth with pink flower heads in summer; *S. spathulifolium* has purple-gray leaves and bright yellow flowers in summer; *S. spurium* has dark green leaves and rich red flowers.

*Sempervivum* spp., houseleek. Low-growing rosettes of succulent leaves, sometimes edged with red; flowers in red, yellow, purple, or white usually appear clustered on top of spikes; many species are monocarpic. Spread by offsets. Full sun. The common name comes from *S. tectorum,* which in Europe often grows on tiled roofs without the benefit of much in the way of soil.

*Silene schafta,* moss campion. To 6 inches; small light green leaves; 5-petaled rose or purple flowers cover the plants from summer to fall. Full sun to partial shade. This species is best grown from seed.

*Solidago virgaurea* subsp. *alpestris,* European goldenrod. To 14 inches; oblong leaves; dense clusters of tiny golden yellow flower heads in late summer to fall. Full sun to partial shade. 'Nana' blooms in June to July.

*Trollius acaulis,* globeflower. To 10 inches; lobed, divided leaves; deep yellow-orange flowers like buttercups in spring. Full sun to partial shade. Unlike their larger relatives, these globeflowers are flat-petaled.

*Veronica repens,* creeping speedwell. To 4 inches; small shiny leaves; pale blue flowers in spring. Full sun. Many species grow along the edges of roads and "speed you well"; in Ireland speedwell was once sewn on clothes to keep the wearer from accident.

*Viola cornuta,* horned violet. To 8 inches; oval toothed leaves; spurred blossoms of red, yellow, apricot, purple, or white flower in late spring to summer. Partial shade. A tendency to spread but if kept to their own, worth the trouble.


## DWARF CONIFERS, SHRUBS, AND FERNS FOR ROCK GARDENS

The following plants are also desirable for the rock garden. They are either small conifers that remain evergreen, shrublike in character and becoming an important accent when mixed with the smaller plants usually found in such a collection, or they are ferns, especially notable for their leaf texture.

For the culture of dwarf conifers it should be noted that there is no need to add peat to garden soil unless it is extremely sandy, and also no need to use fertilizer on them. As with any other shrub, make sure the roots come in contact with the new soil, and water well after planting.

Many plants purchased today are grown in containers, then held over from season to season by the nursery. If any of your new plants are severely potbound, make several vertical cuts into the rootball before planting to encourage the growth of new roots in the surrounding soil. If the soil in the container is largely artificial (made from various mixes) and the plant is to go into entirely different soil, some of the container soil should be removed from the rootball before planting.

It should also be noted that moving many conifers is not difficult as long as the operation is carried out before the high heat of summer. The root pruning done while transplanting makes for a slower-growing plant.

A number of the heaths and heathers are fine plants for the rock garden. See chapter eight, Ornamental Shrubs and Vines, for a discussion of these plants.

Unless otherwise noted, the following plants will do well in full sun to partial shade, with the bit of shade being especially welcome in the South or the Far West.

*Chamaecyparis obtusa* 'Nana'. An extremely slow-growing dwarf Hinoki cypress that forms an irregular globe shape and grows 8 to 10 inches high in ten years—never much larger. The foliage is dark green and forms small cups that grow in tiers on the stubby stems. One of the best dwarf plants for the small rock or conifer garden. If possible, protect from heavy snows. Hardy to USDA Zone 5.

*Juniperus communis* var. *depressa*, ground juniper. A low ever-green shrub with sharp needles of blue-green and thin bark that shreds with ease. Usually about 3 feet high and will tumble over walls and rocks. 'Depressa Aurea' starts out the year with a vivid gold-yellow foliage that slowly turns to bronze-yellow and then bronze as the summer passes. It will reach 30 inches in ten years. Hardy to USDA Zone 4.

*Picea glauca* var. *conica*, dwarf Alberta spruce. First discovered in the wilds of Alberta in 1904, this is one of the more popular evergreen trees for the rock garden. It naturally forms a dense, conical bush about 3 feet high and 2 feet across in twenty years' time. Hardy to USDA Zone 4.

*Berberis thunbergii* 'Atropurpurea Nana'. A deciduous, com-pact shrub reaching a height of about 2 feet and bearing beautiful purple foliage in spring, followed by orange-yellow flowers. Will do well in average garden soil and may be pruned.

*Cotoneaster horizontalis,* rockspray or waterfall cotoneaster. A deciduous shrub with branches overlaid in a herringbone pattern and covered with small, oval, shiny green leaves; small pink flow-ers in late spring are followed in the fall by bright red berries. A young plant will grow against a bank, remaining only inches off the ground and, if planted on the edges of rocks, will pour over them like a waterfall. Hardy in USDA Zone 5.

*Cytisus* spp., broom. Evergreen whiplike branches bear tiny leaves; pealike blossoms in spring cover entire plant. Plants are not hardy below USDA Zone 5, and even there need protection from bitter winter winds. Excellent planted against a bank or set in a cluster of rock. *Cytisus* × *praecox,* Warminster broom, bears pale yellow flowers, eventually reaching a height of 10 feet, but can be pruned. *C.* × *praecox* 'Luteus' is a dwarf form not more than 1 foot high and bearing yellow flowers; *C* × *kewensis* has a semi-prostrate form, is usually under 1 foot in height, with a

2-foot spread, and is covered with creamy yellow flowers in spring.

*Gaultheria procumbens,* wintergreen, teaberry. A creeping plant with shiny evergreen leaves that were once the source of commercial wintergreen (plant now used is *Betula lenta*); drooping, waxy, bell-like flowers, usually hidden by the leaves, are followed by bright red berries. Soil should be acid, moist, and lightly shaded. USDA Zone 4.

*Tsuga canadensis* 'Cole's Prostrate'. An evergreen prostrate tree that actually hugs the ground (or rock), following its contours, and, with a rippled flow, sweeps over and then under the edge of a rock or bank. It prefers some shade and will not do well in hot sun or an exceptionally dry position. Average growth is 3 inches a year. If it is staked up for a few years, it will form a short trunk, then spill down like a small waterfall.

*Potentilla fruticosa* 'Mandshurica'. A deciduous shrub with many featherlike leaves and white flowers in late summer to fall. This particular cultivar usually spreads, but it is less than 18 inches tall and can be pruned to keep it within bounds.

*Spiraea bullata,* dwarf spiraea. A dense and compact deciduous shrub with small dark green leaves; deep pink flower heads are rose at first but lighten with maturity, blooming in summer. Plants will seed about, but seedlings are easily removed. Plant can be pruned to keep it within bounds.

# CHAPTER SEVEN

# JAPANESE GARDENS AND BONSAI

Once we walked through the Japanese Garden on an afternoon in mid-December. The air was cold, about 22°F. Most of the pond was frozen, yet one small section close to the Torii (a gateway to heaven constructed at the entrance or close to a nearby shrine), remained clear of ice, and a number of ducks had crammed themselves into that open water with the look of commuters on a rush-hour subway train. Underneath the cover of ice, the hazy forms of bright orange and spotted goldfish made serpentine curves in slow motion much like cold worms might look if climbing a winter hill.

The only colors before us were the light browns of the ducks, the diluted greens of the pine needles glowing through their coats of snow, and the lacquered red of the Torii. All the rest was the white of a very large sheet of paper. The Garden was beautiful, yet not one flower was in bloom. It was unmistakably Japanese.

The Brooklyn Botanic Garden's Japanese Garden incorporates traditional elements of Japanese garden design. To really appreciate the beauty of any Japanese garden, it is important to understand the philosophy behind it.

Japanese lands have always been crowded, and almost every available acre in Japan is taken up with farming and/or with places to live. The relatively small land area of Japan and the size of its population has been reflected in three religious philosophies: Shinto, Buddhism, and Zen.

Shinto existed before the seventh century and taught that man was a part of nature, not above it, and that part included not only the beasts of wood and field but also the foundations of nature itself: rocks, water, and plants. Later, when Japan adopted much of the Chinese civilization, it imported Buddhism, a philosophy that not only embraced nature but taught that the spirit of one's departed could combine with nature.

Finally Zen, a form of Buddhism that arose in India and came to Japan in the fourteenth century, taught that only by self-knowledge and introspection could mankind find truth. It was the Zen monk and artist Sesshu (1420–1506) who withdrew to a rural temple where he studied the placement of stones, especially those with flat tops, in a garden.

Thus nature is an integral part of any Japanese garden. In Japan one stone in the center of a bed of raked gravel can represent a ship at sea. Every pattern in a bamboo fence has a name all its own. *Koetsu sode-gaki* is a long, low, sloped fence used to divide various parts of a garden, while *Shiorido* uses shaved bamboo in long strips to make a diagonal latticework design.

But stones provide the backbone of the garden's design. Stones are not seen as lumps of granite but are instead thought of as being endowed with the spirit of nature, and they represent timelessness, quietness, and stability. There are correct ways to arrange them: A large stone at the garden's center with a smaller stone at the two o'clock position is good, but if the smaller stone is moved to the three o'clock spot the arrangement is bad. If there are more than two stones, they should be broken into odd-numbered groups of three, five, or seven.

Even steppingstones have a history. They were developed by sixteenth century tea-ceremony masters to pave the way to the teahouse without causing damage to a silken slipper, a grass stain to a kimono, or injury to the surrounding moss gardens.

At Brooklyn's Japanese Garden, the steppingstones lead to Turtle Island. Here stones have been placed to look like a formation of flying geese, while Turtle Island itself on warm days is always populated by turtles sunning themselves. Turtle Island gets its name not from the turtle inhabitants but from its shape. Standing on Lotus Bridge, visitors to the Garden will see a cave in the center that signifies the turtle's mouth, and the stones on the island's sides represent its feet.

Artificial light is very important in Japanese gardens since they are also meant to be enjoyed at night. Stone lanterns were introduced by the tea-masters to light the way to ceremonies and were never put where light would not be needed. The most popular lanterns were those designed to view both the falling and the gathering of snow.

And water is sublime. The sounds and reflections of water are as important as the plants in the garden. And if water was not available at a garden site, lakes were built to contain it. If space was limited, ponds were used instead. If the garden was small, then stone basins were used. And if water was unavailable, a streambed could be constructed using a serpentine pathway of dry stones.

Even the outline of the lake had meaning, and the shore was always kept to an irregular design so a visitor's view was constantly changing, the eye never seeing the same thing twice.

The pond in Brooklyn's Japanese Garden has been designed to represent the Chinese character for heart or mind, which in Zen means "meditating center," expressing tranquillity. The waterfall represents the feeling of perpetual life.

A cascading waterfall leaps over echo caves. The original designer of the garden, Takeo Shiota, is recorded as not liking the sound coming from the caves when first built, and so the stones were rearranged.

The focal point of the Japanese Garden is the red torii that rises from the pond waters. It is modeled after the famous camphorwood torii at Miyajima, which stands in the sea off the coast of Japan. A torii announces the presence of the nearby shrine, and this garden is dedicated to Inari, the Shinto god of harvest. The red color of this flattened arch is a dramatic counterpart to the shades of green so prevalent in this garden.

Construction of the Japanese Garden began on May 17, 1914. By the spring of 1915, a grove of honey locusts (Gleditsia triacanthos) was planted north and west of the Garden, and on June 6, 1915, the garden was opened to the public. An incredible amount of work had been accomplished in one year.

The *Brooklyn Botanic Garden Record* reported: "Without question, this garden will be the most striking feature, and one of the most beautiful, in the Botanic Garden, and will undoubtedly be the most unusual artificial landscape design within the limits of Greater New York."

By 1919, the Austrian pines *(Pinus nigra)* were planted to the east side of the lake. In 1923 more improvements were made, and in 1925, the hill to the west was graded and readied for planting.

September 21, 1938, saw the most severe hurricane ever recorded in Brooklyn, and fifty-five trees were felled by the winds. Shortly thereafter, sixty-three yews (*Taxus* spp.) of twenty-four varieties were planted east of the Japanese Garden, to create an evergreen screen to buffer the sights and sounds of Washington Avenue.

Nationalism also came with the force of a hurricane, and in 1938 the shrine was razed by fire. (In 1960 a new shrine was built and dedicated, constructed by Garden carpenters using blueprints of the original building, requested from Japan.)

In the spring of 1941, the Kwanzan cherries were planted in the Esplanade. The United States entered the war on December 7.


## THE JAPANESE GARDEN'S GARDENER

The man in charge of the Japanese Garden is Robert Gundacker. We met him one July afternoon. After walking through the entrance to the Japanese Garden, we looked past a Japanese aucuba *(Aucuba japonica)* that was as large as a small tree and saw him pruning trees on the hill. The pond shimmered in the hot summer air and the comments of many visitors were mingled with the gossiping quacks of the Garden's ducks.

His career at the Garden began twenty years ago, and because of his interest in bonsai and Japanese gardening in general, he was apprenticed to Frank Okamura. The bonsai master worked with him for a few months, then, suddenly, this garden was in Mr. Gundacker's hands.

"My knowledge," he said, "came from reading and observing and from the application of bonsai techniques to landscape gardening. When I first came here, there were many plants that did not belong; some had been planted and others just seeded themselves."

Many other important elements of the Garden were missing,

too. The idea of reintroducing the wooden lantern and mugho pine, an important part of today's garden, was obtained by examining old photographs.

"Many flowering plants had to be eliminated," he said, "because one of the chief dangers of a Japanese garden in the hands of American gardeners is the temptation to convert it into a flower garden. Basically such a garden is made up of forms and shades of green. It should be well landscaped, relying on winding paths that with each turn give visitors a different perspective. The scene is always changing. There is usually one main viewing area for the whole garden but even from it you can't see everything. The charm of a Japanese hill and pond garden is that you must go through and discover it; it should never be obvious."

Originally, the landscape consisted largely of plants indigenous to Japan, and it featured Japanese maples, flowering cherries, azaleas, barberry, and hollies; today Mr. Gundacker has restored this garden to its original intent.

He cares for the entire garden by himself, with only an occasional volunteer during the busy times of early spring and fall.

"But," he adds, "the new plantings are definitely being geared toward lower maintenance."

## PRUNING AND SHEARING

Today's visitors will observe the pleasing and dramatic shapes of many of the shrubs, accomplished by using a pruning style called cloud pruning—literally what the name suggests. All growth is removed from the bottom of each horizontal branch and the foliage on top is pruned to a rounded shape to simulate that of a cloud. The process is simple, but in order to maintain the shapes, the maples are pruned three to four times a year.

All the other plants are also kept neatly pruned and under control. Mr. Gundacker uses a narrow pruning shears for the delicate work—it resembles a needle-nosed pliers—and regular pruning shears for the heavier pruning.

In addition to the maples, the pines are also pruned regularly —"Once a year, in June," he said. "But it should be done earlier if that's possible."

Hollies (*Ilex* spp.) and the azaleas (*Rhododendron* spp.) are pruned after they bloom. Those azaleas involved in cloud pruning are cut back twice a year, with the second cut in mid-August, as

• One year an annual border at the Brooklyn Botanic Garden (above) was planted with a softly harmonious combination of violet-blue salvia, pink petunias, and silver-leaved artemisia.

• This lovely hybrid tea rose, *Rosa* 'Elizabeth Scholtz' (below left), is named in honor of the distinguished Director Emeritus of the Brooklyn Botanic Garden.

• In the annual border near the outdoor water lily pools (below right), two *Celosia* cultivars, 'New Look' and 'Century Series Mixed', are artfully paired with giant red zinnias and an ornamental foxtail grass, *Pennisetum setaceum* 'Burgundy Giant'.

• The Shakespeare Garden includes a bench in the shade where visitors can sit to take in the garden's colors and scents.

• In the Herb Garden (lower left), deep green hop vines are trained on a simple tripod of wooden stakes.

• The feathery plumes of this perennial ornamental grass, *Miscanthus sinensis* 'Gracillimus', can be seen in the Monocot Border in summer and fall.

- In the formal Knot Garden at BBG, crushed clay pots, charcoal, and marble chips provide the background color that sets off the plants.
- Dogtooth violets have naturalized around the base of a tree in the Local Flora Section of the Garden.

• In the Japanese Hill and Pond Garden, *Iris pseudacorus* lends its rich yellow flowers to the spring palette. This iris grows well in boggy conditions and is lovely planted at the edge of a pool or pond.
• Japanese anemones grace the Rock Garden (upper right) in late summer and fall. In home gardens they can offer a welcome change from autumn's ubiquitous chrysanthemums.
• The meticulous pruning evident on this azalea is representative of the idealization of form so important in a Japanese garden.

- *Euonymus alata* 'Compacta' can be grown as a low hedge, offering definition for garden areas and the bonus of brilliant red foliage in fall.
- Richly colored azaleas harmonize beautifully with the fragrant, pale violet blossoms of Japanese wisteria in spring.

- This venerable lilac, *Syringa × persica*, is a hybrid between two other species, *S. afghanica* and *S. laciniata,* and was introduced before 1760.
- *Berberis thunbergii,* barberry (lower left), is available in a number of attractive foliage colors. The two cultivars shown here are 'Atropurpurea Nana', left, and 'Aurea', right.
- The pink blossoms of this heather, *Calluna vulgaris,* are set off beautifully against the green foliage of a false cypress.

• Gardens take on a special, quiet beauty in winter. Here the Cherry Esplanade is seen from the Overlook. In spring the cherry trees are covered with clouds of soft pink blossoms; after a snowstorm the mood is one of serenity.

• Magnolias are an important part of the early spring display. The trees in the Magnolia Plaza are at the peak of their bloom.

• The broad, sweeping lawn in the Osborne Section of the Garden is bordered by, among other things, azaleas, viburnums, hollies, and crab apples. Japanese wisteria covers pergolas that arch over paved walkways to either side of the lawn area.

• This creeping juniper, *Juniperus chinensis* 'Prince of Wales', is found in the dwarf conifer collection. Its low, bright green branches spread across the ground instead of growing vertically.

- *Houttunia cordata* is a colorful, easy-to-grow ground cover, but it can become invasive and must be kept within bounds. The cultivar shown here is 'Chameleon'.
- These marvelous water cannas are the newly introduced Longwood hybrids.

that's the latest it can be done without harming next season's buds.

A weeping mulberry (*Morus alba* 'Pendula') that stands near the top of the hill next to a grove of crabapples is pruned twice a year.

There are four burgundy lace Japanese maples (*Acer palmatum* 'Burgundy Lace') that form a large hedge to the right of the viewing pavilion, a wooden structure that extends out over the pond and provides a shaded place to sit, out of the hot summer sun. Normally these trees would become quite tall, possibly up to twenty feet, but with a yearly pruning they are kept within bounds.

Weeping cherries (*Prunus subhirtella* 'Pendula') planted at the edge of the pond are allowed to grow until their branches hit the ground or the water. Unfortunately, once they reach into the water, they will die back a few inches. For the pruning of the water side, Mr. Gundacker waits for the pond to freeze over.

The pond is fifteen feet deep in the middle and fed by a spring so the water moves constantly; there are seldom any problems with algal growth. During the summer of 1989, some algae did appear, but Mr. Gundacker simply skimmed them off and the problem was solved. Because no chemicals are used in the water, the pond is a permanent home to both fish and turtles—they spend the winter underneath the ice—and to vast numbers of birds, including mallard ducks, and in late spring and summer, American egrets, blue, green, and black-crowned night herons, and all the other winged inhabitants of the Garden at large.

Every spring people who live within wind distance of any grove of trees—whether oak, pine, or even yew—are aware of pollen. Fast-moving clouds like a golden or yellow mist will drift across lawns, dusting leaves, lawn, or water and sail on through windows and open doors, covering floors and furniture alike.

Pollen settles on the pond, swirling on the slight currents from both the spring and the wind, looking for all the world like the marbleized endpapers found in old leatherbound books. It soon dissipates naturally.

At the far end of the pond is a large colony of water iris or yellow flags *(Iris pseudacorus),* beautiful in or out of bloom, their reflections waving back and forth in the wake of swimming ducks and geese. They are divided every twenty years and now need to be divided again. The constant clipping of the seedpods exercises some control on growth.

The bonsai techniques used to shape the trees in the garden include wiring branches to create special shapes and removing limbs to open up space between the living clouds.

A large Japanese black pine tree *(Pinus thunbergiana)* close to the pond's shore and near the torii is being trained to represent a sailing ship with a slanted form; it is shorn of foliage on the bottom of the branches. Wires are used (threaded through hose whenever they encircle living wood) to tie upper branches to lower branches, each being pulled in the opposite direction from the other. In Japan, the trees are trained by placing foundations of bamboo lattice under them and wiring their lowermost branches to that holdfast.

Even the ladder that is used to reach the upper branches of a bush or tree—whether for clipping, pruning, or cutting—is unique to this garden. It's in the shape of a tripod, one side having steps almost wide enough for two men to stand abreast. The other side consists of an inverted A, with the letter's point securely anchored in the ground.

As for fertilizing, Mr. Gundacker said: "I go through in the spring with 5–10–5. Then, if a plant is ailing, I use Job stakes. It's that simple."

And yet the Garden is not simple, and the care exercised in its keeping is not simple either.

Composed by Mr. Gundacker, an inscription on a plaque at the Garden's entrance reads:

> *This is a living breathing garden.*
> *Enter its beauty in awe—*
> *And let its meaning of life surround you.*
> *May your thoughts be as beautiful*
> *As what you behold.*

## • PLANTS FOR JAPANESE GARDENS

*Abelia chinensis.* To 5 feet; spreading deciduous shrub, often prostrate; small toothed oval leaves; terminal clusters of small white fragrant flowers from early August to frost. Full sun, in well-drained soil rich in organic matter. Originally from China. Not hardy in the northernmost U.S.

*Acer japonicum,* full moon maple. To 25 feet; deciduous tree or shrub with a rounded bushy broad form; many-lobed leaves, green in summer and red in autumn; clusters of small purple-red flowers in mid-spring. Full sun, in moist but well-drained soil of reasonable fertility.

*Acer palmatum,* Japanese maple. To 20 feet; deciduous tree or shrub with a rounded bushy form; deeply lobed green leaves turn brilliant red, orange, or yellow in autumn. Some cultivars have finely cut or deep wine-red leaves of very graceful appearance; clusters of small purple-red flowers in spring. Full sun, in moist but well-drained soil of reasonable fertility.

*Aucuba japonica,* Japanese laurel. To 10 feet; evergreen shrub with long glossy leaves; clusters of small purple flowers in early spring, followed by red berries; plants are dioecious, with male and female flowers on separate plants. Partial shade in well-drained soil rich in organic matter. 'Crotonifolia' has leaves splashed and mottled with various yellows. Needs wind-protected spot in USDA Zone 6. Not hardy in northern U.S.

*Berberis thunbergii,* Japanese barberry. To 7 feet; deciduous, arching, thorny, dense shrub with small leaves turning red in autumn; clusters of small pale yellow flowers followed by bright red berries. Various cultivars have gold, rosy, or red leaves all season. Full sun to partial shade; tolerates poor, dry soil. Can also be grown as a hedge.

*Cephalotaxus harringtonia,* Japanese plum yew. To 15 feet; evergreen spreading conifer, similar to yew, but with slightly larger needles, dark green above, gray beneath; oval red fruits; male and female flowers on separate plants. Adaptable to hot, dry climates. 'Prostrata' forms a wide spreading bush to 3 feet high. Not hardy in northern U.S.

*Chaenomeles* × *superba,* Japanese flowering quince hybrid *(C. japonica* and *C. speciosa).* To 4 feet; deciduous spreading shrub with thorns; red, pink, apricot, or white flowers, followed by yellow fruits, suitable for making jam. Full sun to partial shade, in moist but well-drained soil. Prune out dead wood. Flowers are produced on the previous year's growth, on new and old wood.

*Corylopsis sinensis,* Chinese winter hazel. To 15 feet; deciduous spreading shrub or small tree with fine-toothed leaves, bright green above, blue-green beneath; drooping clusters of bell-shaped yellow flowers in spring. Partial shade in moist, lime-free soil mixed with peat. Not hardy in northern U.S.

*Cryptomeria japonica,* Japanese cedar. To 60 feet in a garden (some cultivars are much smaller); evergreen coniferous tree of pyramidal shape with short needles, round brown cones, and interesting bark, foliage bronzing in winter. Full sun, but best with some late-afternoon shade, especially in winter, in moist but well-drained soil. 'Compacta', with blue-green needles, grows to 45 feet, and 'Elegans Compacta' has curly foliage turning mauve in winter and remaining the size of a large bush. Can be used as a hedge.

*Cupressus bakeri,* Modoc cypress. To 30 feet; evergreen, coniferous tree with small gray-green scalelike leaves and red-brown bark turning gray with age; small cones. Full sun, in moist but well-drained soil; also tolerates hot, dry soil. Not hardy in the northernmost U.S.

*Forsythia* spp. To 9 feet; deciduous shrubs grown for their bright yellow tubular flowers that are deeply 4-parted, blooming in early spring. Full sun, in any garden soil. Easy to grow. Pruning is best done by removing branches for forced flowering. Makes excellent open hedges.

*Hamamelis japonica,* Japanese witch hazel. To 25 feet tall; deciduous shrub or small tree; glossy green leaves turn yellow in autumn; fragrant 4-petaled yellow flowers with 4 ribbony petals in late winter or very early spring; full sun to partial shade, preferring moist soil but adaptable.

*Hamamelis mollis,* Chinese witch hazel. To 20 feet; deciduous shrub or small tree; toothed oval green leaves turn yellow in autumn; fragrant yellow flowers with 4 ribbony petals in late winter or very early spring. Full sun to partial shade, preferring moist soil, but adaptable.

*Ilex crenata,* Japanese holly. To 15 feet; evergreen shrub or small tree of densely branched habit with small glossy evergreen leaves; dull white flowers followed by small black berries. Full sun to partial shade, in any good garden soil. Hollies resent transplanting, so use containerized plants. Many cultivars available.

*Ilex serrata,* Japanese winterberry, finetooth holly. To 8 feet; deciduous shrub with glossy green toothed leaves; many bright red berries in autumn. Male and female flowers on separate plants. Full sun to partial shade, in any good garden soil. Hollies, as stated above, resent transplanting, so use containerized plants. 'Xanthocarpa' has yellow fruits and 'Leucocarpa' has white.

*Juniperus chinensis,* Chinese juniper. To 50 feet; evergreen conifer with many cultivars available in a wide range of sizes and in shapes ranging from pyramidal to columnar to mounded to low and spreading; young leaves are needlelike, mature leaves scalelike, with medium green, blue-green, gray-green, or golden foliage; peeling bark. Full sun; tolerates a range of soils and hot, dry, and city conditions. 'Ames' forms a broad-based pyramid reaching 6 feet and needing no trimming, while 'Kaizuka' (the Hollywood juniper), has a twisted form and makes an unusual hedge.

*Juniperus horizontalis,* creeping juniper. To 1½ feet; prostrate evergreen conifer with low spreading or creeping habit that varies from cultivar to cultivar; needle- or scalelike foliage of medium green, blue-green, or gray-green, often purple in winter. Full sun; tolerates a range of soils as well as hot, dry, or city conditions. Excellent ground cover; can be pruned back to promote bushy growth. 'Bar Harbor' is a popular form that follows the contours of the land and weaves between rocks, and 'Glauca' will completely cover the chosen site with a living carpet of blue-green foliage. Both are beautiful when hanging over the edge of a wall.

*Kalmia latifolia,* mountain laurel. To 10 feet; slow-growing ever-green shrub or small tree, abundantly branched, with oval deep green glossy leaves to 5 inches long; clusters of white or pink flowers (colors on individual plants are variable) blooming from late spring to early summer. Partial shade, in moist but well-drained acid soil, rich in or-ganic matter. Beautiful when planted at the edge of a woods.

*Larix kaempferi (Larix leptolepis),* Japanese larch. To 100 feet; decid-uous coniferous tree of spreading form; soft needlelike blue-green leaves turn yellow in autumn and then fall from tree; small cones. Trees are easily pruned and kept to garden size, a 10-year-old tree being 10 feet high and 5 feet wide. Full sun, in well-drained soil.

*Malus × atrosanguinea,* carmine crabapple. To 20 feet; deciduous shrub or tree; oval dark green shiny leaves; red flower buds open to rose-red blooms in spring; small deep red fruits. Full sun to partial shade, in moist but well-drained soil of average fertility.

*Metasequoia glyptostroboides,* dawn redwood. To 115 feet; deciduous conifer with upward-facing branches; soft needlelike bright green leaves, turning an orange-gold in fall. Full sun; best in well-drained soil, but tolerates some moisture. First described in 1941 from fossils—then in 1948 living plants were discovered in China. Will easily grow from cuttings and from seed; a tree will be 13 feet high and 6 feet wide in 10 years.

*Morus alba* 'Pendula,' weeping mulberry. To 45 feet; deciduous tree with weeping form; lobed glossy deep green leaves; inconspicuous flow-ers turn into edible berries in summer; attractive to birds but messy in the garden. Full sun; well-drained soil of reasonable fertility. Leaves used to feed silkworms.

*Orixa japonica.* To 9 feet; a deciduous shrub; shiny bright green leaves to 5 inches long; inconspicuous flowers and fruits; male and female flowers on separate plants. Full sun. The whole plant is very aromatic.

*Phyllostachys aureosulcata,* yellow grove bamboo. To 25 feet; ever-green clump-forming bamboo with hollow green stems ridged with yellow; green leaf blades are ¾-inch wide and about 6 inches long; Full sun to partial shade, in moist but well-drained soil. One of the hardier species in the genus, but not hardy north of USDA Zone 5; there it needs protection. Useful as canebrake and graceful landscape screens.

*Pieris japonica,* lily-of-the-valley bush, Japanese pieris. To 8 feet; evergreen shrub with oblong glossy deep green leaves; hanging clusters of small creamy white flowers in spring. Does best in full sun with mid-afternoon shade, or in partial shade; prefers somewhat acid soil rich in organic matter. Remove spent flowers to prevent seed formation.

*Pinus mugo* var. *mugo,* mugho pine. To 10 feet; shrublike evergreen conifer with many branches in a spreading form; long bright green needled leaves; small cones. Full sun; can tolerate dry, sandy soils. *P. mugo* var. *pumilio* forms a rounded bun of 15 inches in diameter in 4 years. Excellent landscape conifer with attractive silhouette.

*Pinus parviflora,* Japanese white pine. To 50 feet; evergreen conifer with widespread horizontal branches; twisted blue-green needles in groups of five in dense tufts; ovoid cones are pale brown. Full sun, in well-drained soil of reasonable fertility. Many unusual cultivars in compact forms including 'Glauca,' with decidedly blue foliage, and 'Gimborns Ideal,' which forms a large shrub. *P. parviflora* in all forms is a valuable plant for bonsai cultivation.

*Pinus strobus,* eastern white pine. To 120 feet or more; evergreen conifer forms a pyramid in its fast-growing youth, but eventually becomes a flat-topped and stately tree; long soft blue-green needles in groups of 5; 6-inch cones often white-tipped with rosin. Full sun, in well-drained soil of average fertility but adapts to very thin, moist, and poor soil. Transplant with care, making sure roots never dry out. Makes an excellent living hedge. There are many cultivars suitable for the formal Japanese garden and the rock garden. 'Horsford' is a dwarf form that grows in a bun shape with diminished needles; 'Prostrata' bears normal foliage but has a complete prostrate habit without a leader.

*Pinus thunbergiana,* Japanese black pine. To 130 feet; evergreen conifer with irregular form; rigid, deep green needles and conspicuous white buds; 2½-inch cones. Full sun to partial shade, in fertile, well-drained soil. Grows well in windy seaside gardens. Slow-growing with average 10 feet for 10 years without pruning. 'Oculus-draconis' has needles banded with yellow, most noticeable in autumn but effective all year.

*Prunus serrulata,* Japanese flowering cherry. To 35 feet, but usually 20 to 25 feet depending on cultivar; deciduous tree with glossy narrow leaves; single or double white, greenish yellow, or pink flowers in spring; some cultivars have colorful fall foliage. Full sun, in moist but well-drained soil. Not hardy in northernmost U.S.

*Prunus subhirtella* 'Pendula', weeping Higan cherry. To 30 feet; deciduous tree, a cultivar with pendulous and crooked branches making a graceful weeping form; pale pink flowers in spring. Full sun, in moist but well-drained soil. Not hardy in northernmost U.S.

*Pseudolarix amabilis (P. kaempferi),* golden larch. To 130 feet in nature; deciduous conifer with pyramidal, spreading form; feathery needlelike leaves turning gold in fall; reddish brown bark. Full sun, in well-drained, slightly acid soil. The BBG Bonsai Collection contains a beautiful dwarfed specimen of this tree.

*Pyracantha atlantioides,* firethorn. To 15 feet; evergreen shrubs with spiny branches; glossy oblong leaves; flat clusters of white hawthorn-like flowers in late spring followed by red berries in autumn, persisting into winter. Produces most berries in full sun, but also tolerates partial shade; moist but well-drained soil, can tolerate some dryness. Not hardy in northern U.S.

*Rhododendron catawbiense,* mountain rhododendron. To 20 feet; evergreen shrub or small tree; 6-inch-long oval green leaves, glossy above; clusters of lilac-purple bell-shaped flowers in late spring. Partial shade, in moist, acid soil rich in organic matter. Shallow-rooted, so be careful when cultivating; needs additional water during drought. A native American rhododendron, the parent of many Catawba hybrids, and valuable because of its hardiness, surviving in USDA Zone 5 or below.

*Rhododendron fortunei,* cloud brocade rhododendron. To 12 feet; evergreen shrub; broad leaves, glossy deep green above and smoky blue beneath; clusters of fragrant pink funnel-shaped flowers in spring. Partial shade, in moist, acid soil rich in organic matter. Not hardy north of USDA Zone 6.

*Rhododendron obtusum,* Hiryu azalea. To 4 feet; semi-evergreen, but often deciduous, dimorphic shrub having two sets of leaves: 1-inch elliptical dark green leaves in spring followed by more oval-shaped summer leaves. A few leaves persist to the following spring. Flowers in various shades of rose, magenta, red, or red-violet, depending on the cultivar, blooming in spring. Partial shade, in moist soil rich in organic matter, moderately acid. Not hardy in northernmost U.S.

*Sophora japonica* 'Pendula', weeping Japanese pagoda tree. Usually reaches 12 to 15 feet; deciduous and spreading tree with pendulous branches; ferny compound leaves; drooping clusters of pale yellow pea-like flowers in spring (trees may not bloom until quite a few years old). Full sun, in well-drained soil of average fertility; can withstand city conditions.

*Taxus cuspidata,* Japanese yew. To 40 feet; evergreen shrub or tree depending on cultivar; spreading and upright branches; soft flat narrow and lustrous leaves, dark green above, light green below; inconspicuous flowers in early spring release clouds of pollen followed by scarlet berries (really arils) in autumn. Male and female flowers on separate plants. Full sun to partial shade, in moist but well-drained soil on the alkaline side. The cultivar 'Nana', a low spreading bush 6 to 10 feet wide and 3 feet tall is often used for foundation planting. Responds well to trimming.

*Taxus × media.* To 8 feet; evergreen hybrid between the English yew *(T. baccata)* and *T. cuspidata;* cultivar 'Densiformis' has rounded form with dense lateral branches; hardier than the English yew; flat leaves; red berries. Full sun to partial shade, in moist but well-drained soil. Hardy in USDA Zone 5.

*Thuja standishii,* Japanese arborvitae. To 40 feet; evergreen tree with spreading form; flat sprays of lacy leaves. Full sun to partial shade, in moist but well-drained, fertile soil. Not hardy in northernmost U.S.

*Torreya nucifera,* Japanese torreya. To 75 feet; evergreen tree with pyramidal form; yewlike leaves, glossy dark green above; fruit is covered by a green fleshy aril that is eaten by the Japanese. Full sun to partial shade; moist but well-drained soil. Not hardy in the northern U.S.


## THE BONSAI COLLECTION

A new space houses the Bonsai Collection at the Garden. It occupies a wing all its own that runs off to the left of the entrance to the Steinhardt Conservatory. Here, in an atmosphere that is cooled in the summer—for Brooklyn summers can be very, very warm—bonsai stands of varying sizes each support a beautiful ceramic pot.

Bonsai is an art that seemingly is not constrained by time. It may take a few years, or it may take generations, for a bonsai to reach a state of perfection. The bonsai gardener may spend his whole life devoted to the care of a particular specimen. And yet there are an amazing number of plants that can be trained as bonsai without having to wait a lifetime.

The day we visited the Bonsai Collection, the Greater New York Bonsai Society—one of the oldest such societies in this country—was staging an exhibition at the Botanic Garden. In the Exhibition Gallery of the Steinhardt Conservatory, tables were covered with a range of the bonsai art form, and among the dwarfed oaks, pines, and Japanese maples were tiny dishes holding companion plants such as scouring rushes *(Equisetum hyemale* and *E. scirpoides),* sedums *(Sedum* spp.), dwarf maidenhair fern

*(Adiantum pedatum),* and Japanese blood grass *(Imperata cylindrica* var. *rubra).*

Kazuo Fujii has been in charge of the Collection since 1980, replacing Frank Okamura.

"I think," he said, in reference to the vast number of plants used for bonsai, "that once you are into bonsai, it doesn't matter how old the plant is or what it is. The important thing is your relationship with the bonsai: the style and the balance.

"Bonsai has become so popular that stores now sell a little tree that you are just supposed to prune or pot with no training and no style, not realizing that it sometimes takes years to make a good style and, of course, make it all look easy."

"Should people start with their own tree or plant to make bonsai?" we asked.

"Yes, of course, but first I want them to read a book on bonsai, to study the difference between indoor bonsai and outdoor bonsai. For example, outdoor bonsai need temperatures that change with the season, like outdoor weather."

He gestured to the neat rows of bonsai in the room behind him.

"Here we have no problem because we control the temperature. I bring the seasons indoors, for when it starts getting cold I just keep the room at the outside temperature. Then we have the Quonset greenhouse for storing many of the trees and keeping the temperatures just above freezing, so there are no problems. But people who do not have these facilities can place their bonsai in a cold frame in the backyard much like nurseries bury certain potted plants over the winter.

"Somehow the colors of autumn are much brighter when the trees are grown outside. Morning dew or mist or the other elements of nature intensify the colors when the time comes. I don't know the reason, but the leaves are distinctly brighter outside than when grown under glass.

"Once a week I water the bonsai from above with a sprinkler so it becomes rain as this helps to create nature for them. It also helps to dislodge dust and discourage insects.

"I think a good way to grow bonsai is to keep them outside whenever possible and then when you have a dinner party, bring one in for a centerpiece at the table."

For many years botanists have known that trees must be subjected to wind, the resulting movement enabling them to strengthen the tissues in their trunks. By keeping the bonsai outside, nature performs this task for Mr. Fujii. And poor air circulation can lead to disease—another problem that is more under control when plants are kept outdoors.

We asked him about the importance of a watering routine, and if he had heard of the American custom of adding ice cubes to potted plants, especially in hot summer months, to ensure that roots receive adequate moisture.

He laughed. "That is a very American thing.

"But," he continued, "I don't have that problem here because I can watch them every day and give them water when they need it. But for people who go away for a few days, one suggestion is to put their bonsai on a tray with pebbles and water. Some people put them on a pedestal over a bathtub full of water, but the best way is to have a friend water them as needed."

About drainage: "All bonsai need good drainage and one must be sure water never stands in the pot.

"A woman I met in Australia says she uses six-month-old cow manure and small pebbles for a soil mix, so that will be my next challenge, for I'm always looking for something new that might be an improvement on my usual methods."

"Should we talk a little bit about philosophy?" we asked.

"That," he answered, "is difficult to do."

After a few moments of thought, he said, "My philosophy of bonsai is patience, like we learn from nature and Zen philosophy: Just wait!"

For getting started in bonsai, Mr. Fujii suggested beginning with a plant either carefully taken from nature or, better yet, purchased from a nursery that understands the complexities involved.

"And," he continued, "anyone who tries to go into bonsai should join a local bonsai chapter or society if they can, and they will easily learn more than from any book."

# CHAPTER EIGHT

# ORNAMENTAL
# SHRUBS
# AND
# VINES

The botanical definition of a shrub (taken from *Hortus Third*) reads: "a woody plant that remains relatively low and produces shoots or trunks from the base, not treelike or with a single trunk; a descriptive term not subject to strict circumscription." The definition of a tree is: a woody plant that produces one main trunk and a more-or-less distinct and elevated crown. A bush is a low woody plant, usually thick with branches but without a distinct trunk. The word bush is often (erroneously) used interchangeably with shrub by home gardeners.

In reality a shrub can be fairly large, large enough to dwarf a small tree. A weeping birch, for example, which is definitely a tree, can often grow beneath the towering branches of an old common lilac, which is botanically a shrub. At the other end of the scale, the diminutive heaths and heathers, often thought to be herbaceous plants, are actually shrubs, even though a pair of typical gardener's feet could easily crush them to the ground.

The beauty of including shrubs in the home landscape revolves around their versatility, not only in terms of size or for their flowers and foliage but also for their speed of maturation. In the days of estate gardens, one generation of a family might plant a grove of trees and be content to know that another generation down the pike would reap the aesthetic reward of such plantings. Today, in a mobile world, when even the majority of the rich and famous do not have that sort of continuity among generations, it's obvious that the average gardener is also denied the same opportunity. But when we use shrubs in the garden, a look of age is relatively easy to obtain, and soon even very young lilacs, rhododendrons, azaleas, heaths, and heathers will bloom.

## USING SHRUBS IN THE HOME GARDEN

Years ago when a backdrop for a perennial border was needed, someone would build a wall. Winston Churchill spent most of his garden life at Chartwell building a wall of brick. A brick wall does make an effective setting for various flowers and plants, but it's labor-intensive and not at all cheap.

On the other hand, a wall of hybrid rhododendrons, or forsythia, or honeysuckle (*Lonicera* spp.), or clipped Canadian hemlock *(Tsuga canadensis)* can turn a mass of perennials from rather dull clods of color to an invigorating diorama by providing that dark background color that so many flowers need in order to be effective.

Shrubs in a rough row underplanted with ferns, hostas, or other perennials, or shrubs planted as hedges make great delineators that bring privacy to various garden areas, and create division lines around a property. For gardeners interested in pursuing the concept of garden rooms, shrubs and high hedges become "walls" defining the rooms. With the use of judicious pruning these "walls" can even have windows in them that allow glimpses into the room (garden) next door. If chosen properly, hedges can also be effective ways to stop most dogs from running rampant, at the same time concealing more effective but aesthetically ugly wire fencing.

Finally, a single shrub such as an attractive hybrid rhododendron can become a great focal point when used as a specimen plant, providing a mass of green that can unify other plants in the garden.

## BEFORE PLANTING A SHRUB

When you plant any shrub, consider that once installed it will be there for a good long time. Most shrubs are large enough after a few years of growth to make moving them an impractical pursuit, so the initial planning is very important.

Here the idea of a garden sketch or plan is very important. What is small usually becomes big. Nobody wants a beautiful shrub to be in a spot from which it eventually must be moved, or to be destroyed in order to allow the family to get to the garage in a rainstorm or to make a place for a swimming pool or other addition to the home.

And here's where a visit to a public garden like the Brooklyn Botanic Garden becomes important. There you can see what a particular shrub will look like after it reaches maturity and how it will look mixed with other plants. The Hedge Wheel at the Garden is also a very effective teaching tool for showing gardeners just how a hedge will look in the landscape. Here a number of plants, both common and uncommon, that are effective when used in hedges have been planted out, each species or cultivar becoming a spoke in a large wheel.

If your soil is on the acid side, most plants in this chapter (in fact, in this book) will grow successfully. If, however, the soil is alkaline, plants that need an acid soil like rhododendrons, azaleas, heaths, and heathers will either not live or at best do poorly.

Changing the pH of large amounts of soil is neither easy nor inexpensive. If your soil is alkaline but you wish to grow some acid-loving plants, the easiest and most inexpensive solution is to construct raised beds for them. Raised beds give you control over the nature of the soil.

Instead of digging down, mark out the area needed, then use a steel pole or pitchfork and make a number of holes in the surface of the ground that will be covered by new soil. Next build up low retaining walls of railroad ties (make sure they are pressure-treated and not soaked with creosote), fieldstone, or bricks. Usually a height of two feet is sufficient. Then fill in with soil of your own mixture.

If you live or garden on the side of a hill, this idea can be used to build terraces that will serve double duty: these beds will give you new soil in which to grow plants and prevent the rain from washing down the slopes.

When planting shrubs and trees, the old axiom of digging a twenty-dollar hole for a ten-dollar tree is very important. Unlike perennials, these plants should not continually be dug up because you are dissatisfied with their placement.

Since shrubs will be in one place for many years, the initial soil investment should be of high quality and the site carefully chosen.

While double-digging is always valuable, you should at least prepare the hole to the root depth of the plant and wider than the width of the roots of your new plant. Lay the soil to one side of the hole—plastic sheets underneath make sure that all the soil remains under your control—and with a pitchfork or other strong pointed tool, break up the soil at the hole's bottom. This is especially important if there is hardpan below your surface soil.


## SHRUBS AS HEDGES

A hedge is a living fence used to create a background or a barrier in the home landscape. The following plants are all found in the Hedge Wheel located at the Garden. They all make effective hedges, and are best kept at a height of one and a half to three feet. Note that the base of the hedge should be wider than the top in order to allow proper light penetration to the hedge's interior leaves, and to shed snow. The hedge should be at least as wide as it is high unless narrow columnar varieties are planted together. When establishing a low hedge, put the plants closer together.

The glossy abelia *(Abelia × grandiflora)* is a semi-evergreen shrub with glossy green oval leaves that reaches a height of five feet. Loose clusters of bell-shaped white flowers flushed with pink appear in summer. The origin of the plant is unknown but its first description came from a nursery in Italy. Full sun is best, and well-drained soil rich in organic matter. One of the hardier abelias, this plant will survive in USDA Zone 5.

The three-spined barberry *(Berberis wisleyensis)* is an evergreen shrub that grows about five feet high. Its yellow stems are armed with three-parted spines and lance-shaped, dull green leaves edged with spines. The yellow flowers are followed by black berries with a blue bloom. Full sun is preferred, but this shrub will adapt to light shade and will succeed in any well-drained garden soil of average fertility. Do any necessary pruning in spring.

The pygmy Hinoki cypress (*Chamaecyparis obtusa* 'Pygmaea') is a slow-growing cultivar of an evergreen coniferous tree that can top 120 feet in nature but here reaches a height of at best twenty-four inches in ten years' time. This lovely little shrub bears open fans of flattened and frondlike foliage on orange-brown stems. The leaves turn a beautiful green-bronze in the winter, when color is always at a premium. Give plants full sun in a well-drained soil of average fertility.

Dwarf Japanese cedar (*Cryptomeria japonica* 'Nana') has been in cultivation for over 140 years. Because it withstands pruning well, its cultivars have long been used for hedging. Being the dwarf cultivars of evergreen coniferous trees that can reach 150 feet in the wild, these cultivars grow to one and a half feet in ten years. The fine and feathery foliage of light green retains that color all year long. Provide full sun in a well-drained soil of average fertility.

The hollies have long been favorite plants of others besides gardeners, especially around Christmastime, when the berries are bright and shining. They are also valuable because they are tolerant of the many adverse conditions found in city gardens. A cultivar of the English holly (*Ilex aquifolium* 'Balearica') will grow to thirty feet if left unattended, but with pruning it is particularly valuable as a hedge. The evergreen leaves are thick with spiny or smooth edges of a glossy bright green. The flowers are white and fragrant, followed in fall by the bright red berries. These shrubs prefer full sun, and they produce more fruit when given plenty of light, but they will adapt to partial shade. Provide well-drained soil of average fertility. Hollies resent transplanting, so try to use containerized or balled and burlapped plants to minimize root disturbance. Do the necessary pruning in spring. English hollies are not hardy north of USDA Zone 6.

Many cultivars of the Japanese holly *(Ilex crenata)* are now available. *I. crenata* 'Microphylla' was introduced in 1864. Plants grow to fifteen feet without pruning and have evergreen, leathery deep green leaves, about three-quarters of an inch long. The flowers are white; the quarter-inch berries are black. Care is the same as for English hollies. In Japan these plants are used for bonsai. With protection, they will survive in USDA Zone 5.

The lily-of-the-valley bush *(Pieris japonica)* has been in cultivation since 1870 and originally came from Japan. The cultivar 'Dorothy Wyckoff' is an evergreen shrub with oblong, glossy, deep green leaves that turn bronze in winter, and it grows about eight feet high. Hanging clusters of small deep pink flowers appear in spring. They bloom best in full sun but will also adapt to partial shade, preferring somewhat acid soil rich in organic matter. Remove the spent flowers to prevent unnecessary seed formation.

Japanese black pines *(Pinus thunbergiana)* will reach 130 feet in the wild but are so slow-growing as to be without threat to the average garden. They are evergreen coniferous trees of irregular form, the branches bearing rigid deep green needles and conspicuous white buds. The cones are two and a half inches long. Give full sun to partial shade, and fertile, well-drained soil. These trees grow well in windy seaside gardens, although on eastern Long Island they are dying off in great numbers due to disease. Since they are slow to grow, they will average ten feet in ten years without pruning.

The hardy orange *(Poncirus trifoliata)* is a deciduous tree that will reach fifteen feet. Stout, spiny stems bear white flowers that appear before the leaves, which in turn are glossy and three-parted. The fruits resemble small two-inch-wide oranges, and the hardy oranges have long been used as a stock for citrus to make them more hardy. These trees need full sun in fertile, well-drained soil. They make a very effective hedge against small animals; when planted close together they are almost impenetrable. Remove any dead wood in early spring but prune for shape in early summer. Unfortunately they are not hardy north of USDA Zone 6.

Lace shrubs *(Stephanandra incisa)* grow to eight feet. They are deciduous, with finely cut, deeply lobed and toothed bright green leaves that turn a bright orange-yellow in autumn on branches that become a rich brown in winter. Clusters of small greenish-white flowers appear in early summer, but it is for the leaves that this shrub is used in gardens. Give full sun in any well-drained but moist garden soil of average fertility. Prune after flowering. Lace shrubs are hardy in USDA Zone 5 but need protection from bitter winds in snowless winters.

Japanese yews *(Taxus cuspidata)* can reach a height of fifty feet. These are either evergreen shrubs or trees, depending on the cultivar. Branches are spreading and upright with soft, flat, narrow and lustrous leaves, dark green above and light green below. The inconspicuous "flowers" in early spring are followed by scarlet-red berries (really arils) in autumn. Male and female "flowers" are on separate plants. Full sun to partial shade, in moist but well-drained soil on the alkaline side. The cultivar 'Nana' makes a low, spreading bush, six to ten feet wide and three feet tall; it is often used for foundation planting. Yews respond well to trimming.

*Taxus* × *media* is an evergreen hybrid between the English yew *(T. baccata)* and the Japanese yew *(T. cuspidata)*. The cultivar 'Densiformis' grows to 8 feet, in a rounded form with dense, lateral branches and is hardier than the English yew. The leaves are flat, the berries red. Full sun to partial shade, in moist but well-drained soil. Hardy in USDA Zone 5.

The eastern or Canadian hemlock *(Tsuga canadensis)* will often reach a height of one hundred feet in the wild. These are evergreen coniferous trees with soft green needles and small dainty cones, often growing with more than one leader. In the forest, plants will remain up to thirty-five years as small seedlings until a nearby tree dies and the forest canopy opens up for their further development. Give full sun to partial shade in moist, but well-drained, acid soil of average fertility. These trees are slow-growing and respond well to pruning in spring. Hardy to USDA Zone 3.

The dwarf European cranberry bush or Guelder rose (*Viburnum opulus* 'Nanum') is a deciduous bush about six feet high, with maplelike leaves that turn red in autumn. The flat-topped clusters of scented white flowers resemble a lace cap and are followed by red translucent berries. Give full sun to partial shade in moist garden soil of good fertility and plenty of organic matter. Prune these bushes after flowering. They are hardy to USDA Zone 4.

Four other shrubs found in the Hedge Wheel—*Buxus sempervirens, Cotoneaster divaricatus, Euonymus alata* 'Compacta', and *Forsythia suspensa* 'Variegata'—are described in the table Ornamental Shrubs to Grow, on page 160.

The Brooklyn Botanic Garden has a special interest in three particular groups of shrubs—lilacs, rhododendrons and azaleas, and heaths and heathers—and we spoke to the gardeners in charge of these collections. These shrubs are among the most popular and versatile for home gardens as well, so we are giving special consideration to them in this chapter. We were also so impressed by the tree peonies growing at the BBG that we had to give them special attention here. Tree peonies deserve to be better known among gardeners than they are—their flowers are absolutely breathtaking.

## LILACS AT THE GARDEN

"When lilacs last in the dooryard bloomed," wrote Walt Whitman in the mid-1800s. But there have been lilacs in the dooryards of America since the middle 1600s, when colonists brought the common lilac *(Syringa vulgaris)* over from Europe and England. In a letter of 1737, Peter Collinson, an English Quaker botanist, wrote to John Bartram, the famous plant explorer: "I wonder that thou should be sorry to see such a bundle of white and blue lilacs. That wonder might have soon ceased, by throwing them away if you had them already." So by then they were common enough to consider throwing them out. Lilac, by the by, is an old English word taken from the Arabic *laylak* and the Persian *nilak,* this last from *nil,* meaning blue.

Daniel Ryniec has worked at the Garden for thirteen years, and he took over the care of the lilac collection in 1981.

Since then he has been involved in the reorganization of the lilac collection, which at one time was planted according to color and whether the flowers were single or double. The reorganization was carried out with the cooperation of the Taxonomy and Horticultural Departments. After doing a survey of the entire collection to make sure of what was there, and after consulting old maps of the Garden, they eventually identified 95 percent of the plant material. The threefold goal of the collection was determined to be (1) to have a public display of lilacs that are correctly labeled; (2) to have the collection represent both species lilacs and the range of horticultural variation; and (3) to give individual specimens space for healthy and attractive growth.

Mr. Ryniec joined the International Lilac Society and began to collect a number of the newer hybridized plants.

"And this is the way you expand a collection?" we asked.

"Without a doubt," he answered. "On that hillside we have the Lemoine collection—the Garden actually received these plants from Victor Lemoine, the French nurseryman, and his wife and son, who carried on their business well into the 1930s from a beginning in the middle 1800s. These French hybrids were developed by a process that involved growing about ten thousand seedlings and maybe selecting one choice plant and plowing the rest under. Today, many hybridizers are just not that selective.

"To give you an example, in 1960 there were about six

hundred known cultivars of lilac in seven distinct colors—white, violet, lilac, blue, pink, purple, and red. There is another color, a yellow-white introduced in 1949 with *Syringa vulgaris* 'Primrose', but purists think it's only a shade of white. These numbers include single and double flowered forms, plus twenty-three distinct species. Today there are about two thousand named cultivars still in the same original seven colors, and the same number of species. So you can see there has to be a lot of duplication."

At the same time, Mr. Ryniec talks of the marvelous work being done by Father John Fiala, who is famous for using colchicine on lilacs. Colchicine is an alkaloid derived from the plant often called the autumn crocus (*Colchicum* spp.) that disturbs the process of cell division, resulting in cells with a double set of chromosomes. This may lead to larger flowers. The results of this line of work have been some more vigorous and substantial plants with flowers that are larger and have a deeper color, and others tending to be dwarf, with a greater tolerance to disease.

There are about 150 lilacs in the Garden's collection, along with twenty-one species. Only two species are lacking to complete their species collection. Included in the collection are all seven colors of lilacs, demonstrating a season of bloom that lasts for up to six weeks. *Syringa vulgaris* and its cultivars make up the majority of the collection, and the better flowering varieties of *S.* × *hyacinthiflora* (early) and *S. prestoniae* (later) are also present.

"I wanted *Syringa afghanica* but according to a recent article, it will now be called *Syringa protolaciniata* var. *khabul.*" He gets a wistful look in his eye. "But along the western border of Pakistan there just might be the true *Syringa afghanica.*"

We asked about the hardiness of lilac trees and bushes, and which was the most unusual.

"First, there are only two tree forms," he answered. "*Syringa pekinensis* grows to thirty feet, and *S. reticulata* reaches a height of sixty feet. With respect to hardiness, they do fine in USDA Zone 3, which means that most American gardeners can enjoy them. As to the most unusual, that would be *S. pinnatifolia* from China. It has pinnate leaves and white flowers without much fragrance. Through careful observation and hybridizing the future trends will be toward dwarf, disease-resistant varieties. Cultivars that will flower well in warmer climates such as California and the South are also becoming available."

Pests that affect lilacs can usually be controlled by good cultural practices such as proper fertilizing, pruning, careful plant selection and, if necessary, applications of horticultural oils and soaps.

Lilac borer, virus, mites, and girdling from European hornets are some of the common problems with lilacs which need to be attended to when the problem is present.

With regard to powdery mildew, "We generally get powdery mildew about the same time, year in, year out," said Mr. Ryniec, "usually in late August, and for the most part we've stayed away from treating it. The problem is if you get it in June, and it keeps coming back year in and year out, it will eventually weaken the plant. Farther south they have more humidity and are forced to spray their plants.

"Bordeaux mixture is a fungicide discovered in France many years ago. It's prepared from copper sulfate and lime and was a standard until 1940, when it was replaced by the chemicals produced by the oil companies. It's still a cheap and effective fungicide which leaves a conspicuous but relatively harmless residue. Also, summer horticultural oils are being used for some insect and mite control.

Mr. Ryniec has been doing drastic pruning on many of the older lilacs. There will be fewer flowers in the coming year, but after that a fuller and healthier plant will result.

"Is the old wood good for anything?" we asked.

"Sometimes carvers come in. Years ago the wood was often used to make pipe stems. I thought that some day I might make myself a set of canes."

Among the hundreds of lilacs on the nursery market today, Mr. Ryniec recommends the following: *Syringa vulgaris* cultivars 'President Lincoln' (single blue flowers), 'Firmament' (single blue), 'Mme. Lemoine' (double white), 'Sensation' (single purple with white edge), 'Sarah Sands' (single purple), 'Charles Joly' (double magenta), 'Lucie Baltet' (single pink), 'Romance' (single pink), 'Victor Lemoine' (double lilac), *S. hyacinthiflora* 'Annabel' (double pink), *S. reflexa* (single pink), *S. reticulata* (single white), and *S. patula* 'Miss Kim' (single purple).

The most important thing to remember when planting lilacs is that they need full sun. Those in partial shade will bloom, but not to their best advantage.

Lilacs need a reasonably fertile, well-drained garden soil, preferably with a good organic-matter content. Alternate yearly applications of 5–10–5 fertilizer and, in the Northeast where soils are acid, horticultural limestone usually satisfy nutrient and pH requirements. A 1½ to 2-inch layer of organic mulch will conserve soil moisture, reduce weeds, and protect the plants from mechanical injury.

As far as pruning is concerned, many lilacs left to their own devices in the overgrown gardens of abandoned farms bloom year after year. But to maintain the best flower quality, diseased shoots, plus the suckers that grow around the base, should be cut out, beginning the process after flowering is over.

Finally, lilacs should be deadheaded, not only to save on energy for the shrub but for cosmetic purposes as well. But be careful when deadheading not to remove next year's flower buds, which are located on the two branches below the dead flower heads.


## RHODODENDRONS AND AZALEAS

When entering the world of the rhododendrons, one must be prepared for a world complete unto itself. Many gardeners have started with one or two plants and wound up abandoning all else and making these "rhodies" the object of lifelong pursuits.

The genus *Rhododendron* represents some eight hundred species of usually evergreen, sometimes semi-evergreen, and often deciduous shrubs—rarely small trees—found in the Northern Hemisphere, chiefly in the Himalayas, southeast Asia, and the mountains of Malaysia, but in fact almost everywhere except the continents of Africa and South America.

Those horticulturists who deal with these magnificent plants have divided them into various sections and categories based on botanical differences. But for most purposes it is only necessary to know that there are two major divisions in the group: rhododendrons and azaleas. Both belong to the same genus, but azaleas are either evergreen or deciduous and have flowers shaped like funnels, whereas rhododendrons are usually evergreen and have bell-shaped flowers.

There are over eight hundred rhododendrons and azaleas planted at the Garden. The following species and cultivars are recommended by Joyce Van Etten, curator of ericaceous plants at the Garden. The rhododendrons described below are all lovely in bloom, with attractive leaves and growth habits. They are hardy to $-15°F$ unless otherwise noted.

'Vulcan' and 'Mars' both have flowers of a rich red color and are stars in the garden. 'Blue Peter' is an old cultivar whose pretty near-blue flowers have a contrasting dark eye. 'Wheatley' has fragrant flowers of a lovely soft pink, and along with the other Dexter hybrids is among the best-performing rhododendrons at BBG. 'Blue Diamond', hardy to − 5°F, is a small plant (three feet tall by two feet wide) which needs more sun—at least a half day of direct sun—than larger-leaved types to flower well. It is covered with small blossoms of glowing blue. 'Baden-Baden' grows just one and a half feet high with a three-foot spread; its flowers are luminous red bells. *Rhododendron yakusimanum* and hybrids of *R. yakusimanum* and *R. smirnowii* are noteworthy for their silvery new growth and indumentum (downy covering) on the leaves.

A number of azalea cultivars have also proven to be outstanding at BBG. A new introduction from the National Arboretum, 'Pyrored', may not yet be widely available but is one to watch for. Its glowing red flowers and small evergreen leaves are particularly wonderful when paired with white flowering dogwood. Two Robin Hill hybrids, 'Sir Robert' and 'Nancy of Robin Hill', both offer large, frilly, pastel pink flowers on low, spreading, semideciduous plants. They are reliably winter hardy. *R. kaempferi* 'Othello' flowers profusely, the blossoms a soft warm pink with a lot of orange. The plant has good autumn color. Many of the Exbury hybrids are spectacular two-tone blends such as 'Salmon Orange'. 'Gibraltar' is an especially good glowing orange. These hybrids look wonderful when planted near other flowers in related colors.

Many older azalea cultivars are also quite lovely, and are veteran performers in the Garden, but may be difficult to find in commercial nurseries. For interested gardeners they are worth the search. Two of the choice old Glenn Dale hybrids are 'Kobold', evergreen with rich burgundy blossoms in midseason, delightful against a white background, and 'Tomboy', with profuse flowers of pink or pink and white. 'Bouquet de Flore', a Ghent hybrid, has bright pink flowers, good fall foliage color, is deciduous, and needs a half day of direct sun.

Cultural requirements for rhododendrons and azaleas are the same: a well-drained acidic soil composed of leaf mold combined with sphagnum peat moss; heavy clay and alkaline soils are slow death to the whole group.

They prefer a location that protects them from the continuous heat of a summer sun and harsh winds in both summer and

winter. The high shade of deep-rooted trees such as oaks is beneficial. Their root systems are shallow and thinly branched so
plants need a soil that remains continually moist.

May is the best month for rhododendron displays, but a lot
of the dwarfs bloom in April.

Though some species are quite hardy (to $-25°F$) even when
exposed to bitter winter winds in the northern part of the country,
most prefer winter temperatures above $0°F$.

Generally rhododendrons should be planted out in the early
spring; the plants are then waking from winter slumber and ready
to shoot into growth and flowering. This schedule is especially
important in the north, since it gives plants adequate time for
settling in before the coming winter.

Planting preparations are much the same as for other balled
and burlapped or container-grown shrubs: the hole must be large
enough for the roots to spread out. Loosen the outer roots of
container-grown plants to encourage rooting into the new soil.
Position the rootball so that the crown is at the same depth it was
in the container. It is essential to keep plants at the same depth
they were growing before—their roots will suffocate if planted
too deep. Ms. Van Etten mixes the soil from the planting hole
with equal amounts of sphagnum peat moss and compost and
plants the shrubs in this soil mix. Firm the soil, mix carefully
around the roots to remove large air pockets, but don't pack so
hard that you compact the soil (never tread with your feet to firm
the soil). Water thoroughly after planting. Keep the soil moist and
follow a careful watering schedule for the remainder of the growing season.

When rhododendrons are planted next to a masonry wall of
brick or stone, especially if it is newly constructed, lime is leached
out by the action of rain over the years, and eventually the soil
becomes alkaline and the plants suffer. Adding ferrous sulfate or
sulfur should rectify the situation for a time, but consult your
local Extension Agent for a correct reading of the soil pH and the
right amount of chemical to add. Do not be tempted to use aluminum sulfate—it can have an adverse effect on rhododendrons.

Remove the spent blossoms to prevent seed formation and to
channel the plant's effort into next year's crop of blooms.

Unlike most evergreens, rhododendrons can be moved with
relative ease since their root systems are shallow and so close to
the stems. Just remember to take enough soil and use enough
water to settle the new plants in.

Ms. Van Etten gives the following advice on pruning: In general, rhododendrons and azaleas require very little pruning. In early spring branch tips of the most vigorous shoots might be pinched back to encourage compactness, if needed. Dormant vegetative buds are located all along azalea branches, but only above leaf rosettes on rhododendrons. Therefore, rhododendrons should be pinched back to a point just above a rosette of leaves. On azaleas the pruning cuts can occur anywhere. That is why azaleas, for example, can be sheared, as is often practiced in Japanese gardening. This practice is not recommended for most gardens, as it results in an unnatural appearance.

To rejuvenate old, lanky rhododendron specimens that have lost their lower leaves, cut branches back to one foot very early in spring, before flowering. Cuts should be distributed more or less over the entire plant so that even regrowth results. Retain some of the leaves—at least twenty-five percent. Weak, unhealthy trunks unlikely to resprout can be removed at the base. Azaleas are treated somewhat differently. If specimens are old and lanky, rejuvenation pruning is undertaken in early June, after blooming. Branches can be cut back to six inches or entire old branches can be removed at ground level to encourage new shoots. On either plant dead wood can be removed anytime.

## TREE PEONIES

When the talk at garden parties eventually leaves the subjects of insect attacks, the depredation of rodent damage, tent caterpillars, and bagworms, too much rain and too little rain, plus the weather in general, and finally turns to gardening with spectacular flowers, some experienced person in the group will mention tree peonies.

The genus *Paeonia* is known for its beautiful flowers, but tree peonies, chiefly *Paeonia suffruticosa, P. lutea,* and *P. delavayi,* first cultivated in China in the sixth century A.D., can cause even the most hardened of gardeners and garden visitors to gasp involuntarily. When we saw a bed of them at the Garden we were literally stunned by their shimmering blossoms. Even though the flowers come and go within a week or two at best—especially when spring is overly warm—they are worth the effort. Of all the plants worthy of contemplation, this is surely one.

The English were introduced to the tree peony in 1669 (the

year of Rembrandt's death), but the first flowering plant—a double pink—was not seen until 1787, when it bloomed in the gardens at Kew.

The tree peony is not really a tree but a shrub, usually reaching a height of about five feet and a spread of up to six feet. Individual flowers are usually between six and eight inches wide, but some of the more striking of the Japanese cultivars can be a foot across. Unlike other peonies, the branches develop a bark and they should never be cut off unless you are pruning an old plant.

Because of the spectacular nature of this plant, it should be the focal point in any garden, placed so that you can walk up to it and, ideally, see it from inside the house as well. Luckily the soft green foliage is also attractive. Even a small city yard should have a spot for a tree peony, complemented with small roses and hostas.

Tree peonies are expensive, especially when you buy grafts that are at least three years old, but these older plants are more established and usually succeed where younger grafts fail. They are also chancy in climates colder than USDA Zone 5 and will need extra protection and care if they are to survive temperatures below −20°F. If your winter provides these lows for any length of time, it's a good idea to cover the tree every year with a wooden box filled with dried leaves or straw.

Among the many cultivars available, the Garden recommends the following: 'Age of Gold', winner of the Gold Medal of the American Peony Society and one of the most popular and beautiful tree peonies, blooming with fully double, creamy golden blossoms with a light red tracery on some of the petals; 'Angelet', semidouble yellow flowers edged with rose; 'Black Pirate', with single, deep maroon flowers; 'Godaishu', a large semidouble, with globe-shaped pure white flowers with a yellow center; 'Hesperus', single rose-pink flowers with yellow overtones; 'Ori-hime', with double blossoms of Chinese red; 'Shinshium-ryo', a semidouble with deep purple flowers with fringed edges; and 'Yuki Doro', with double white flowers having red markings in the center.

New tree peony plants want a deep, sandy, rich soil, neutral or slightly acid, with plenty of added humus and compost plus a cup of bonemeal per plant. If your soil is too heavy, lighten it with the addition of builder's sand. Dig a hole about two feet deep and three feet in diameter and fill it with the prepared soil well before planting time, giving the mix a chance to settle. Since these plants have been known to live for over eighty years, it's worth the effort to properly plant them.

The best time to plant is late September or early October, depending on your climate zone. Set the plants at the same depth they were at the nursery, making sure that you use plenty of water and muddy-in the roots with a slurry of water and soil. Since most tree peonies are grafted onto regular peony roots, the graft junction should be about six inches below the ground level so the graft will develop its own root system. For a time, your peony may send up two kinds of leaves. The deeply cut leaves are the tree peony. Any other shoots growing from the rootstock should be cut off. If planting more than one, space them at least four feet apart.

Keep the plant well watered until frost. For the first winter, cover the new plant with an inverted bushel basket topped with a stone, or some such housing, to protect it from bitter winter winds.

Since the tree peony develops a strong system of feeder roots close to the soil's surface, you must use care in cultivating. Every spring, scratch in a cup or so of bonemeal.

Sometimes an old plant, or one that suffers from excessive winter damage, can get tall and straggly looking. In early fall the branch that offends can be cut back, forcing new growth in the spring.

Every so often the branch of a tree peony will wilt without any obvious cause. The problem is a fungus blight called botrytis. Quickly sever the wilted branch and burn it. Pick up any leaf litter around the plant and remember to remove all the old plant debris in the fall. Botrytis usually will not bother plants that have good drainage and plenty of air circulation.

Ants are attracted to the sweet sap on peony buds but are not known to cause any damage.


## HEATHS AND HEATHERS

We arrived at the Heath and Heather Collection of the Garden on a 90°F day in mid-August. There, in a border subjected to the burning rays of the afternoon sun, plants were blooming that are usually associated with either the Scottish moors or New England rock gardens in late fall and early winter.

One heather (*Calluna vulgaris* 'Tib') was covered with purple double flowers, while next to it the cross-leaved heath (*Erica tetralix* 'Alba Mollis') bore white blossoms. Behind them was another huge mound of a magnificent gray heather (*E.* 'Silver Knight').

Although both heaths and heathers are botanically considered to be evergreen shrubs, gardeners usually think of them as plants useful for the perennial garden and border because of their profuse flowering, their low stature, and their evergreen habit.

The heaths belong to the genus *Erica,* shrubs (occasionally low trees) that bear small, evergreen, needlelike leaves and pretty little flowers like grains of puffed rice, each with a scalloped edge. The heathers, also called lings, are represented mainly by one genus, *Calluna.* They too are evergreen, but the leaves are shorter and squatter, overlapping each other, and the tiny flowers are usually bell-shaped.

As far as gardening goes, these are important plants. In a recent article in *The Garden* magazine of the Royal Horticultural Society (April 1990), there is a plea to retain the present botanical name of *Erica carnea* rather than changing it to *E. herbacea,* perhaps a more correct appellation, but in the minds of many gardeners an unnecessary change. The authors, Christopher Brickell and David McClintock, point out that "Enquiry showed that it was not unreasonable to estimate world production of plants of cultivars of this species to be in the region of no fewer than 15 to 20 million a year, nearly all being sold as *E. carnea,* which clearly constitutes major economic importance."

Joyce Van Etten is in charge of the Heath and Heather Collection at the Brooklyn Botanic Garden.

"These plants are tricky," she told us. "It has taken four years and three plantings with a fourth planting coming in order to complete the Collection. This collection of the Ericaceae is part of the Garden's systematic collection. We presently have heathers, heaths, *Kalmia, Pieris,* and eleven other ericaceous genera, plus the Cornaceae, or dogwoods, because they look good with azaleas and rhododendrons."

She pointed to an area behind the systematic collection walkway that included a large magnolia tree in a horticultural planting.

"And here I hope to add more magnolias. This particular tree is a *Magnolia fraseri.* And over here I have a whole wilderness that was once a compost heap and general storage, to be developed. There are some fine conifers back there."

We asked about the culture and the blooming time of the heaths and heathers.

"They bloom during the spring and summer," she said. "But even when they don't bloom, they are great in the garden because of the color and texture of the foliage. If you don't have to cover them in the winter, they are very attractive. And we don't cover them here, except the young plants. Those are protected with evergreen branches. But we have mild winters here with temperatures rarely below 0°F.

"We use a gritty sort of soil, a lot of grit, a lot of peat moss, no fertilizer, and it's important to get them in the right exposure."

The exposure is important, especially where winters are cold. Most of these plants will do well in USDA Zone 4 if protected from bitter winds, either by natural or artificial windbreaks or by the inimitable spruce boughs. This is especially important in areas (or years) that receive little or no snow cover.

According to Ms. Van Etten, all of the heaths and heathers need an acid soil and good drainage. If your garden is heavy or uncut clay, add sharp sand or gravel and peat moss to the soil. These plants also need full sun. Cut them back in early spring (she does this the first week of April at BBG) so that any branches killed over the winter are removed. If you are gardening in USDA Zone 5 or colder, transplant only in the spring, allowing the plants plenty of time to settle in.

A well-planted display of these plants becomes a refined patchwork quilt of color, and if the gardener uses just a bit of restraint in mixing the colors, the resulting display has a quality unlike any other group of plants.

"Color is important to me," she said. "I like the subtle combinations, the subtle gradations of color. I don't like very strong 'Day-Glo' colors, harsh, bright colors that are found in some azalea pinks and rhododendron purples. Strong colors only work if they're handled right. For example, the *Impatiens* 'Tangeglow' mixed with that purple salvia in the Garden's 1989 annual displays is a weird color blend, but the intensity of the colors is the same so they work together."

Ms. Van Etten walked over to the edge of a small pond screened by shrubs from the main walkway.

"Someday this will be a Monet pond with water lilies but I haven't taken on this project yet. But this is a perfect setting for one. I'll also plant things that will reflect in the water.

"And I am in charge of a horticultural area consisting of ninety-seven rhododendrons and azaleas planted in 1965 near the other end of the Botanic Garden. In 1985 this area was enlarged by the addition of two acres. Here I envision a landscaped garden displaying a world class rhododendron collection, a daffodil collection, a lily collection, and a holly collection, since we already have the nucleus of a good collection of hollies in this area.

"We need an angel, a person of vision, who can look at that area up there, look at our plans for development, and help us to achieve what it could be."

Ms. Van Etten recommends the following heaths and heathers for interested home gardeners.

These are cultivars of *Erica carnea:* 'King George' (which Ms. Van Etten says is probably the best one) grows one foot high and blooms from January to May with rosy crimson flowers. 'Springwood White', a dependable cultivar, grows eight inches high and blooms from January to May with white flowers. 'Springwood Pink' grows eight inches high and produces pink flowers from February to April. 'Pink Spangles' grows one foot high and bears deep pink flowers in late winter, usually from February to April.

*Erica tetralix* is one of the hardiest heaths, with gray foliage and rosy flowers blooming from late June to October. 'Alba Mollis' has gray-green leaves, grows about fifteen inches tall, and blooms with white flowers from early June to October.

The following are all cultivars of *Calluna vulgaris:* 'Gold Haze' has lovely golden foliage but insignificant flowers. 'Mullion' has deep pink flowers starting in late July and remaining through September. 'County Wicklow' grows one foot tall, with pink flowers in summer. 'Tib' is easy to grow and blooms prolifically from July through October, with lavender flowers; and 'Blazeway' is recommended for its red foliage in fall and winter.

## SOME ADVICE ON GROWING SHRUBS

Here is some general advice on planting and caring for shrubs; these methods are either currently used or described in BBG publications.

Plant bare-rooted plants from the nursery in early spring, while the plants are still dormant. Container-grown plants can be planted anytime during the growing season when the weather is not too hot and stressful. Balled and burlapped shrubs are best planted early, but they can also be planted later, like container-grown plants.

To plant balled and burlapped plants, dig a hole one and one-half to two feet wider than the soil ball and at least as deep. Loosen the soil in the bottom of the hole. Put a shovelful of compost in the hole's bottom before planting, mixing it in. If your soil is sandy or heavy clay, you can improve the excavated soil by adding sphagnum peat moss up to a one-one mix. Place the plant in the hole. Stabilize it by filling the base of the hole with excavated soil or soil mix. Then loosen the burlap wrapping at the top of the ball and lay back the ropes (or nails, if they are used). The top of the rootball should be level with the surrounding soil. (Use the rootball, rather than the soil ball, as a guide because some nurseries plant too deeply.) Fill in around the ball with soil; water well; add more soil if necessary.

To plant bare-rooted plants, dig a hole large enough to comfortably accommodate the roots. Remove any broken or damaged roots. If the plant has spreading roots, make a mound of soil in the bottom of the hole. Set the plant on the mound and gently spread the roots over it and down the sides. Plants with a taproot or deep central roots can simply be set in the hole. Work soil around the roots carefully with your fingers. Fill the hole halfway with soil; water well; fill the rest of the hole, and water again.

To plant container-grown plants, remove plant from pot and examine the root system carefully. If any roots wrap around the soil ball, and especially if the shrub is severely potbound, tease some of the larger roots out of the ball, or make several vertical cuts up through the rootball. Set the plant in a hole large enough to hold the rootball, at the same depth the plant was growing in the container. Fill in around the roots with soil; water, and add more soil as needed.

It is important to mention again the business of watering newly ensconced shrubs and trees for a couple of years. Keep it up and do it well, especially in areas of low rainfall and above-average heat. Remember, too, that day after day of wind will quickly dry out the soil.

Feed shrubs once a year with an all-purpose fertilizer. Spring is the best time to fertilize most shrubs.

Water deeply during dry weather throughout the first growing season, while the plant is establishing itself in the garden.

and 'Black Knight', the latter with blue-black flowers. *B. alternifolia,* fountain buddleia, grows to 12 feet and has narrow gray-green leaves and pale lilac flowers; will adapt to dry soil. Blooms on previous year's growth, so prune after flowering. Excellent growing on banks and slopes. Hardy to USDA Zone 5.

*Buxus* spp., boxwood. From less than 3 feet up to 25 feet, depending on species; evergreen shrubs and trees with small, aromatic, glossy deep green leaves; flowers are insignificant. Full sun to partial shade, in any reasonably good garden soil. Slow-growing, takes clipping well, and is often grown as a hedge, but needs a burlap screen for winter protection in the northernmost U.S. *B. microphylla* is a compact shrub some 3 feet high, but the variety *japonica,* the Japanese boxwood and its cultivars, is usually offered. *B. sempervirens,* the common box, is a shrub or tree to 15 feet and is found in a number of cultivars of varying height including "Suffruticosa', the edging box, a dwarf form with smaller leaves.

*Callicarpa bodinieri,* beautyberry. To 8 feet; deciduous shrub with oval dark green leaves; clusters of star-shaped lilac flowers in midsummer, followed by clusters of pale blue-purple fruits that persist well into fall. Full sun, in fertile soil. Not hardy in northernmost U.S. but will generally survive in USDA Zone 5, with shoots dying back to the ground each winter.

*Caryopteris* × *clandonensis,* bluebeard. To 3 feet; deciduous shrub with attractive gray-green toothed leaves; spikes of tubular blue flowers in late summer to early fall. Full sun, in well-drained soil of moderate fertility, but partial shade in the South. Makes a beautiful hedge or edging in a large formal border. Stems may die back in cold winters, but crowns will survive with mulching. Prune back in spring. *C. incana,* or the blue spiraea, is a deciduous shrub to 4 feet with the same rules of cultivation.

*Chaenomeles speciosa,* flowering quince. To 6 feet; deciduous shrub with thorns; glossy green leaves; clusters of lovely flowers, red, pink, or white according to cultivar, similar to apple blossoms in spring; yellow-green fruits are hard but have excellent flavor for jelly. Full sun, in well-drained soil of moderate fertility. Plants work well as hedging. A number of cultivars are available. Hardy to USDA Zone 4. *C. japonica,* lesser flowering quince, grows to 4 feet; deciduous shrub with short spines; flowers are red to salmon to orange; the small fruits can be used like crab apples to make excellent jelly.

*Clethra alnifolia,* sweet pepperbush. To 9 feet; deciduous shrub with oval toothed green leaves turning yellow and orange in autumn; spikes of very fragrant white or pink flowers in mid- to late summer are followed by black fruits that resemble peppercorns. Full sun to partial shade, in moist soil of reasonable fertility. Good for seaside gardens. Hardy to USDA Zone 4.

*Corylopsis pauciflora,* buttercup winter hazel. To 6 feet; deciduous shrub with oval toothed leaves, smooth above but with hairs beneath; small, charming, fragrant bell-like yellow flowers in late winter or very early spring. Full sun, in well-drained, slightly acid soil rich in organic matter.

*Corylus avellana* 'Contorta', contorted hazel, Harry Lauder's walking stick. Old specimens to 15 feet; deciduous shrubs with curled and twisted stems of great character; almost round soft downy leaves; pendulous catkins appear in early spring. Full sun, in moist but well-drained soil of average fertility. Always a source of comment in the garden. Branches often used in floral arrangements.

*Cotoneaster* spp. Woody plants from less than 1 foot up to 12 feet, depending on the species and cultivar; small rounded leaves, evergreen in some species; 5-petaled white or pink flowers followed by small berrylike bright red fruits (orange or gold in some cultivars) that persist into winter. Full sun to partial shade in well-drained soil, with many forms excellent in dry conditions. *C. apiculatus,* cranberry cotoneaster, is under 3 feet and resembles *C. horizontalis* but with less irregular branching; hardy to USDA Zone 5. *C. dammeri,* bearberry cotoneaster, is a prostrate evergreen with roundish leathery leaves; white flowers in spring eventually become ¼-inch red berries; usually grown as a ground cover; needs moist soil; hardy to USDA Zone 6. *C. divaricatus* is deciduous with spreading branches; to 6 feet; shining dark green leaves; pink flowers followed by bright red fruits; hardy to USDA Zone 5. *C. horizontalis,* rockspray, or herringbone cotoneaster (so named because overlapping opposite branches resemble fishbones), is a semi-evergreen under 3 feet high, bearing roundish leaves, glossy green above, with a horizontal habit of growth; white to pinkish flowers become bright red berries; works as a ground cover, or espaliered against a wall, or tumbling down a bank; hardy to USDA Zone 5. *C. salicifolius* is usually evergreen with arched branches, and reaches a height of 12 feet; white flowers appear in clusters, forming bright red ¼-inch berries. Hardy to USDA Zone 6.

*Cytisus scoparius,* Scotch broom. To 6 feet; a deciduous shrub with slender arching evergreen branches; compound leaves; covered in spring with small pealike, brilliant yellow flowers. Full sun, in well-drained soil of average to low fertility. Not hardy in the northernmost U.S., but will often survive in USDA Zone 5 if given a protected spot on the side of a hill or slope. Established plants are difficult to move. Prune flowering shoots immediately after blooming stops.

*Daphne* spp. To 5 feet; deciduous or evergreen shrubs; oblong deep green leaves; clusters of fragrant white, pink, or light purple flowers in spring. Full sun to partial shade, in light, well-drained soil rich in organic matter. *D.* × *burkwoodii*, to 3 feet, can be evergreen, semi-evergreen, or deciduous, depending on climate; fragrant pink flowers in spring. *D. odora*, to 3 feet, is evergreen; fragrant red-purple flowers appear from late February into April depending on the severity of late winter weather. Neither is hardy north of USDA Zone 6. *D. cneorum*, garland flower, to 1 foot, is evergreen; fragrant rose pink flowers appear in mid-spring; this last is a perfect plant for the rock garden.

*Deutzia* × *rosea*. To 3 feet; deciduous shrub; narrow, oblong leaves; loose clusters of pale pink flowers in spring; full sun to partial shade, in any well-drained soil. Flowers appear on previous year's growth, so prune after flowering, but only when necessary. Easy to grow. Hardy to USDA Zone 5.

*Elaeagnus* spp. To 18 feet; evergreen or deciduous shrubs or small trees; oblong leaves, silvery underneath; creamy white or off-yellow flowers, usually very fragrant; silvery brown, yellow, or red fruits. Full sun, in well-drained soil; tolerates dry, windy sites. *E. angustifolia*, Russian olive, deciduous small tree; very fragrant small flowers; yellow fruits streaked with silver, beloved by birds; hardy to USDA Zone 4. *E. pungens*, thorny oleaster, to 15 feet; a thorny evergreen with very fragrant flowers in the fall; berries ripen in spring; hardy to USDA Zone 7. *E. umbellata*, to 18 feet; fragrant flowers in late spring; scarlet fruits are silvery when young; hardy in USDA Zone 5. Prune after flowering.

*Euonymus alata*, winged or cork-barked euonymus. To 8 feet; deciduous shrub with corky wings along the twigs; oval leaves turn bright red in autumn; inconspicuous flowers form small oval orange berries. Full sun to partial shade, in any good garden soil. Can be grown as a hedge, and kept smaller by pruning. Will seed about. 'Compacta' reaches 3 feet.

*Forsythia* spp. To 15 feet; deciduous shrubs; oval leaves slightly toothed; loved for their bright yellow 4-petaled flowers that appear before the leaves in early spring. Full sun, in any garden soil. Easy to grow. Excellent for use as an informal hedge. Thin out old shoots by cutting branches for forcing. Prune when necessary immediately after flowering, when weak shoots should be removed. *F.* × *intermedia* (a hybrid of *F. suspensa* and *F. viridissima*) can reach 15 feet, with sharply toothed leaves and many blossoms on previous season's growth. There are a number of cultivars. *F. ovata* reaches 5 feet, has smaller flowers, and is the earliest to bloom. *F. suspensa* reaches 10 feet and has a weeping form; many bright yellow fragrant flowers are produced on well-ripened wood of the previous season's growth; many cultivars are available including 'Variegata,' whose leaves are edged with yellow.

*Hamamelis* spp., witch hazel. To 25 feet; deciduous shrubs or small trees; toothed oval leaves turn a lovely yellow in autumn; fragrant yellow or orange flowers with 4 ribbony petals in late fall, late winter, or very early spring. Full sun to partial shade; prefers moist soil, but adaptable. Prune after flowering. *H.* × *intermedia,* a hybrid between *H. japonica* and *H. mollis,* has produced a number of attractive cultivars. *H. mollis,* Chinese witch hazel, to 30 feet; golden yellow flowers are very fragrant, blooming from January to March. *H. japonica,* Japanese witch hazel, to 30 feet; yellow flowers bloom in early spring. *H. virginiana,* American witch hazel, to 15 feet; blooms in late autumn; bark used for astringent skin lotion. Excellent in a wild garden.

*Hibiscus syriacus,* rose of Sharon. To 10 feet; deciduous shrub; oval leaves; large tropical-looking flowers, pink, blue, or white, in summer. Full sun, in fertile, moist but well-drained soil. Easy to grow, but self-sows, and seedlings can become something of a pest. The cultivar 'Diana', introduced by the U.S. National Arboretum, is a white-flowered triploid that seldom produces seeds, and is recommended by BBG. Can be pruned to shape in March and grown as a hedge. Hardy to USDA Zone 5.

*Hydrangea* spp. To 20 feet; mostly deciduous shrubs; broad, oval, green leaves; clusters of small flowers, pink, blue, or white, in summer. Full sun, in fertile, moist but well-drained soil. Many do well in seaside gardens. Prune back every spring to promote new growth. The flowers dry beautifully for winter bouquets. *H. arborescens* 'Grandiflora', hills of snow, to 4 feet; deciduous shrub; oval, toothed leaves to 6 inches long; snow-white balls of flowers; hardy to USDA Zone 4. *H. macrophylla,* to 6 feet; deciduous (evergreen in mild climates) shrubs; in acid soil, blooms are various shades of blue, in neutral soil both pink and blue can be present; to make flowers blue, add about 1 tablespoon of aluminum sulfate per plant; hardy to USDA Zone 6. *H. paniculata* 'Grandiflora', peegee hydrangea, to 18 feet; deciduous shrub; terminal panicles of large creamy white flowers aging to copper-pink; can be pruned in early spring to produce larger flower clusters; hardy to USDA Zone 4; these shrubs often found in old cemeteries. *H. quercifolia,* oak-leaved hydrangea; to 8 feet; deciduous shrub; leaves resemble those of an oak; upright panicles of beautiful white flowers; makes a striking backdrop for a flower bed; hardy to USDA Zone 5. Will tolerate partial shade and still produce good flowers and fall color.

*Ilex cornuta,* Chinese holly. To 9 feet; evergreen shrubs or small trees; glossy, rectangular, spined leaves; female plants bear red berries. Full sun or partial shade, in moist but well-drained soil of reasonable fertility. Not hardy north of USDA Zone 6. 'China Girl' and 'China Boy' are new cultivars said to be hardy to −20°F. One of each is needed for berries.

*Lagerstroemia indica,* crape myrtle. To 20 feet; deciduous shrub or small tree; small oval leaves of medium green turning reddish-brown in fall; clusters of flowers produced on new growth, in shades of pink, rose, red, purple, or white in summer. Full sun, in moist but well-drained, fertile soil. Many cultivars available. Prune in late winter or early spring; may be cut to the ground to keep shrub size and will still bloom. Difficult to transplant when large. Can be grown in pots and brought indoors over winter. Not hardy below USDA Zone 6.

*Leucothoe fontanesiana.* To 6 feet; evergreen shrub; arching stems with glossy, deep green leaves, evergreen in the South, semi-evergreen in the North (turning golden bronze in the autumn). Full sun to partial shade to shade in the South, full sun in the North in moist but well-drained soil with an acid pH. Prune after flowering, removing 2- and 3-year-old canes to promote new growth.

*Leycesteria formosa,* Himalayan honeysuckle. To 8 feet; deciduous shrub; heart-shaped leaves on green stems; white flowers backed with red-purple bracts hang in chains, followed by red-purple fruits loved by birds. Full sun to partial shade—but fewer fruits in the shade—in any good garden soil. Easily grown from seed. Prune established plants to the ground in early spring. Not hardy north of USDA 6. A splendid garden shrub.

*Ligustrum* spp., privet. To 15 feet; deciduous or evergreen shrubs; small oval leaves, green or variegated with yellow; clusters of strong-smelling flowers, liked by some, abhorred by others. Full sun to partial shade, in any decent garden soil. Easy to grow and widely planted as a hedge. *L. amurense,* to 15 feet tall; deciduous or semi-evergreen; is hardy to USDA Zone 4, doing well in northern gardens. *L. japonicum,* Japanese privet, to 10 feet; evergreen with leathery 4-inch leaves; flowers have strong odor; good for topiary and seaside gardens. *L. obtusifolium,* border privet, to 9 feet tall; spreading or arching form; hardy to USDA Zone 4. *L. ovalfolium,* California privet, to 15 feet; deciduous in areas of severe winters. Good choice for city conditions; a number of cultivars are available. Prune in spring.

*Lonicera* spp., shrub honeysuckles. To 15 feet; usually deciduous; oval to oblong leaves; tubular flowers, creamy white or pink, often fragrant, in early or late spring, depending on the species. Full sun to partial shade, in well-drained soil of good fertility. Prune after flowering.

*L. fragrantissima,* winter honeysuckle, to 10 feet; fragrant white flowers touched with pink, bloom in late winter to early spring before new crop of leaves, evergreen in mild climates but hardy to USDA Zone 6. *L. maackii* var *podocarpa,* to 15 feet tall; spreading form blooming in late spring with white flowers, turning yellow with age. *L. tatarica,* Tatarian honeysuckle, to 10 feet, white to pink flowers in late spring, hardy to USDA Zone 5 and good for northern gardens. Prune after flowering.

*Osmanthus heterophyllus,* holly olive. To 20 feet; evergreen shrub; hollylike leaves with a few large spiny teeth; small fragrant white flowers bloom in early autumn. Full sun, in any good garden soil. Can be grown as a hedge. Not hardy north of USDA Zone 6.

*Philadelphus* spp., mock orange. To 10 feet; deciduous shrubs; showy white flowers. Full sun (partial shade will produce fewer flowers), in reasonably fertile, well-drained soil. Prune after flowering, as blossoms appear on previous year's wood. Can be pruned annually for small gardens. An old-time garden favorite for generations. Hardy to USDA Zone 5. *P. coronarius,* to 10 feet; terminal clusters of very fragrant yellow-white flowers; often found in old farmhouse gardens; many cultivars available. *P.* × *lemoinei (P. coronarius* × *P. microphyllus),* to 6 feet —French hybrid with fragrant white flowers. *P.* × *virginalis,* to 5 feet; double white flowers appear in June and July.

*Potentilla fruticosa,* bush cinquefoil. To 4 feet; deciduous shrubs; compound leaves; single flowers in shades of yellow and orange in summer. Full sun to partial shade (with fewer flowers), in moist but well-drained soil of average fertility. Prune in early spring, removing older wood. Excellent ground cover. A number of cultivars available. Watch out for Japanese beetles. Hardy to USDA Zone 3.

*Pyracantha coccinea,* firethorn. To 15 feet; evergreen shrubs; oval leaves on thorny stems; white flowers in late spring; brilliant orange-red fruits in autumn, persisting into winter. Full sun to partial shade, in moist but well-drained soil of average fertility. Prune after flowering. Good hedges to protect gardens from animals. Especially attractive when grown against walls. 'Mohave' grows to 10 feet; profuse fruiting; hardy to USDA Zone 6; resistant to scab and fireblight.

*Rhodotypos scandens,* jetbead. To 5 feet; deciduous shrub; sharply toothed, ribbed leaves; 4-petaled white flowers in spring resemble dogwood flowers; shiny black fruits like small peas in fall that persist into winter. Full sun or any degree of shade short of dense shade, in any average garden soil.

*Spiraea* spp., bridal wreath. To 6 feet; deciduous shrubs. Full sun, but will tolerate some shade; adapts to a wide range of soils, but moist soil is best. Prune old canes after flowering. *S. prunifolia* has finely

toothed leaves, turning orange in autumn; sprays of white double flow-
ers resembling tiny buttons on old silk blouses, bloom in spring. *S. japonica,* Japanese spiraea, oval to oblong leaves, gray-green beneath; clusters of pink flowers with many stamens, blooming in midsummer. *S. nipponica,* clusters of white flowers in late spring or early summer; hardy in USDA Zone 5.

*Viburnum* spp. To 20 feet or more; deciduous and evergreen shrubs. Partial shade, especially during the heat of afternoon, in moist but well-drained soil of average fertility, with a slightly acid pH. *V. carlesii,* Korean spicebush, to 5 feet, deciduous shrub with fragrant pink-budded white flowers in early spring, perfect for small gardens, hardy to USDA Zone 4. *V. cassinoides,* withe-rod, to 6 feet. This deciduous bush, with leathery green leaves turning red in autumn, is native to moist woodland areas (introduced to cultivation in 1761), with white flowers changing to interesting fruits, first red, then blue, finally black. *V. opulus,* see Hedge Wheel. *V. plicatum,* Japanese snowball, to 9 feet, round white flower clusters in spring, leaves turn bronze in autumn. *V. plicatum* var. *tomentosum,* doublefile viburnum, has flat flower clusters (known as lacecaps) and a horizontal branching habit, well suited to small gardens. *V. rhytidophyllum,* leatherleaf viburnum, to 10 feet; evergreen bush with lustrous dark green leaves, rusty brown underneath; yellow-white flowers followed by black fruits; good foundation plants, but too many planted together are oppressive.

*Vitex agnus-castus,* chaste tree. To 10 feet; deciduous shrub or small tree; silvery lance-shaped leaves, aromatic when bruised; dense spikes of fragrant lavender-blue flowers on new growth in summer; ¼-inch in diameter blue-black aromatic berries in autumn. Full sun to partial shade, in moist but well-drained soil of average fertility and near neutral pH. In garden can be cut back almost to the ground annually or every few years to keep compact—or may be left to become a small tree.

*Weigela floribunda.* To 10 feet; deciduous shrub; oval toothed leaves; clusters of 5-lobed deep red flowers on furry stems in spring. Full sun, in moist but well-drained soil of average fertility. Prune after flowering. In Zone 5 gardens use *W. florida,* bearing rose-pink flowers in late spring.


## VINES AT THE GARDEN

A *lang* is a covered but open-sided walkway in a Chinese garden, usually with a tiled roof held aloft by columns. Between the columns the weary walker will find benches that offer a shady retreat and a chance to sit down for a moment to reset the pace of a visit. There are parallel arbors that make us think of *langs* in the Brooklyn Botanic Garden. They run along either side of the great lawn in the Osborne Section of the Garden, but instead of being roofed with ceramics, here they act as supports for gigantic and venerable Japanese wisteria vines, and in summer the roof becomes an open but shaded tracery of leaves. In spring, hundreds of heavy clusters of fragrant violet-blue blossoms, many of them over two feet long, hang down from winding branches, all alive with the buzz of bees as they scent the garden air.

The trunks of these woody lianas twine around the arbors and have become so gnarled and twisted with age that, for a moment in a flight of fancy, a visitor can forget the distant murmur of automobiles on Eastern Parkway and imagine that sound to be the hushed murmuring of a distant river in a far-off land— or dream of ancient temples lost in steamy jungles where secret doorways, surrounded with these vines, open into shadowed and strange interiors.

Of course, it's one thing to wax romantic about the Garden's wisterias, forgetting that most of today's gardeners do not have either the time or space to develop such formidable vines. But with careful planning there should be room in any garden for a vine, and if it's not possible to have a wisteria there are plenty of other choices. And if the home gardener still yearns for a wisteria, it's possible to grow the plant as a standard and by dint of judicious pruning create a small tree that will bloom every spring in the backyard (see chapter nine, Ornamental Trees to Grow).

Vines are often overlooked in today's landscape. People forget that one of the easiest and most inexpensive ways to hide an undesirable view or object, especially in the garden, is to hide it behind a vine.

The Brooklyn Botanic Garden has a display in which a group of galvanized pipes arranged in tripods is set in a lawn, like an open wall. Along the base, Dutchman's pipes are planted, and as soon as the days begin to warm in spring, the vine begins its annual climb. In a few short weeks, this wall becomes an impenetrable hedge, effectively blocking out the view on the other side.

At most garden stores and nursery centers you can buy ready-made folding trellises of wood that expand to twelve feet in length, or supports made of plastic rods that screw together. A movable support can be made from a frame of one-by-threes by stringing plastic fishline on brass cup hooks, evenly spaced along the top and the bottom.

## VINES TO GROW

There are literally hundreds of vines grown throughout the world, and a surprising number are available from nursery sources (either seeds or plants) throughout the country.

The actinidias (*Actinidia* spp.) usually clamber to thirty feet. They are deciduous vines (really climbing shrubs), excellent plants for area screening, and easily grown on trellises and arbors. They prefer full sun but will adapt to partial shade, in any ordinary garden soil. Usually started from seed, the following species are hardy to USDA Zone 5.

The tara vine *(Actinidia arguta)* will reach thirty feet. The vines bear six-inch-long, glossy green leaves on red petioles or stems, and are often used for screening, since the small white flowers are not too decorative and the resulting fruits, although edible and tasty, are only one inch in diameter. The vines are dioecious, with male and female flowers on separate plants; to produce fruit you must plant both a male and a female plant.

The kolomikta vine *(Actinidia kolomikta),* is a native of China and Japan, usually reaching between fifteen and twenty feet. The charm of this vine is in the foliage; the upper halves of the five-inch-long leaves are blotched with creamy white and pink, especially on the male plants (like tara vine, this species is dioecious). Small clusters of fragrant white flowers appear in late spring and early summer, followed by three-quarter-inch fruits on the female plants. Cats are especially fond of rubbing against the bark. A beautiful plant when trained to run along a stone wall. A third *Actinidia, A. chinensis,* the kiwi berry, is also hardy at BBG and, like its relatives, dioecious.

From Japan comes the chocolate vine *(Akebia quinata),* quickly reaching twelve feet and bearing compound leaves of a heavy deep green, each with five deep green oblong leaflets, semi-evergreen in warmer areas. A twining shrub or vine. The brownish-purple flowers are small, not showy but interesting, as they are fragrant and they open at night; they appear in spring and are followed by edible (but insipid), purple-podded fruits. Full sun to partial shade, in moist but well-drained soil of average fertility. This vine can be easily trained up a wall but can also become invasive, with plant-strangling properties like those of oriental bittersweet *(Celastrus orbiculatus).*

Dutchman's pipe *(Aristolochia durior)* is a deciduous climbing shrub or vine that, once established, will surge up almost any support, soon reaching thirty feet. The medium green leaves are large and rounded, often one foot long, and overlap each other to provide efficient screening. Small yellowish flowers resemble toy meerschaum pipes but are usually hidden by the leaves. Full sun, in fertile, moist but well-drained soil. Lush growth makes this an excellent screen when trained on fences, trellises, or wires.

Trumpet creepers were once mistakenly put in the genus *Bignonia* but are now correctly known as various species of *Campsis*. There are two generally available and both produce handsome foliage and beautiful trumpetlike blossoms that are especially attractive to hummingbirds. These vines are perfect for climbing trees and walls, clinging like ivy, but, be warned—they can occasionally be blown loose by high winds; reattach loose vines with staples. A particularly fine use for these vines is in the wild garden; and in the Local Flora Section of the BBG a red trumpet creeper climbs in and out of the branches of a white birch to great effect. Both genera prefer full sun and should be planted in a good soil with additional organic matter in order to get off to a fast start.

*Campsis radicans* is a native vine that often becomes a troublesome weed in cultivated fields, but the prodigious quantities of scarlet, funnel-shaped three-inch flowers with five spreading lobes of bright orange are worth coping with most of their problems. *C. radicans* 'Flava' is yellow. *C.* × *tagliabuana* 'Mme. Galen' is a cultivar of a hybrid of *C. radicans* and *C. grandiflora* (imported from China) and produces apricot flowers tinged with orange that begin to bloom in June and continue throughout the summer. One of its most valuable characteristics is that it doesn't sprout indiscriminately like its parents.

Entire gardens can be built around the various species of *Clematis* and the many hybrids and cultivars available. Often reaching a height of twenty-five feet, these are deciduous woody vines, usually with compound leaves and curling leafstalks that act like tendrils; in the wild they will clamber rather than climb, running about tree branches. The clusters of small flowers are surrounded by large, showy sepals in shades of purple, pink, violet, red, yellow, or white, blooming in spring, summer, or fall, often with attractive seed heads.

There are also a few species, *Clematis heracleifolia* for one, that grow as small shrubs; or they may be allowed to grow against a mortared wall. Full sun to partial shade, in fertile, moist but well-drained soil, partial to an alkaline pH or with added lime. They also appreciate having a mulch or shade at the base of the vine to keep roots cool.

Clematis hybrids and cultivars that belong to the Florida hybrids bloom in summer on previous year's growth, so should be pruned after they flower; the Patens hybrids bloom on old wood in the spring; and the Jackmanii hybrids are summer and autumn flowers, blooming on this season's growth, and can be pruned in early spring.

The alpine clematis *(Clematis alpina)*, to six feet tall (Florida hybrid), has nodding violet-blue (sometimes white) flowers and is perfect against a wall in a small garden or rock garden; there are many cultivars. *C.* × *jackmanii*, to twelve feet, is the first large-flowered hybrid ever developed (1863) and now one of the many members of its namesake's group; violet-purple flowers are five to seven inches in diameter; there are a number of hybrids and cultivars. *C.* 'Nellie Moser', to nine feet (Patens hybrid), has pale mauve-pink flowers, usually with eight sepals, each with a pink bar down the middle; it was introduced in 1897.

The golden clematis *(Clematis tangutica)*, grows to nine feet; feathery leaves; four-inch-long, bell-shaped, bright yellow, pendant flowers, followed by plumy seed heads. *C. paniculata*, to thirty feet tall, is semi-evergreen, with lustrous foliage; many small, fragrant white blossoms, like stars, are followed by attractive seed heads. The virgin's bower *(C. virginiana)* grows to fifteen feet. It has compound leaves; small white blossoms, followed by plumelike seed heads. This plant is not for the formal bed or border but perfect in a wild garden. These last three bloom on current year's wood.

The climbing hydrangea *(Hydrangea anomala* subsp. *petiolaris)* will grow to sixty feet. The leaves are glossy green, oval to heart-shaped, and loose clusters of white flowers appear in the summer and look like typical hydrangea flowers. Full sun to partial shade, in fertile, moist but well-drained soil. Using small rootlike holdfasts, the stems will firmly attach to wood, brick, or stone. This vine will also clamber up a slope, so it can be used there as an excellent ground cover. This plant is slow to recover from transplanting, so try to use a containerized one.

Moonflowers *(Ipomoea alba)* will reach ten feet in one summer season. They are tender perennial climbers with broad oval leaves. Fragrant white flowers like large morning glories open at night. Full sun, in any reasonable garden soil, or in pots. They will bloom from seed the first year.

Jasmines (*Jasminum* spp.), will reach forty feet. They are mostly tender climbers or shrubs with small compound leaves and clusters of sweetly fragrant white, yellow, or pink flowers. Full sun, in loose, loamy, fertile soil. Often grown in the greenhouse in the north. *J. beesianum* may exhibit a shrubby form or will climb to six feet; rosy pink flowers in spring; not hardy north of USDA Zone 7. The winter jasmine (*J. nudiflorum*) has yellow flowers in winter or very early spring. Loosely branching, this jasmine is not a vine but an arching shrub and hardy in most of the U.S., but flower buds may freeze in northern gardens. Poet's jessamine (*J. officinale*) has slender branches that may reach forty feet and need support. The leaves are a glossy green, and plants bear intensely fragrant white flowers in summer; not hardy north of USDA Zone 6.

Honeysuckles (*Lonicera* spp.) grow to thirty feet. They are deciduous or evergreen perennial vines with oval-to-oblong leaves and tubular flowers, usually fragrant. Full sun, in well-drained soil of average fertility. Trumpet honeysuckle (*L. sempervirens*) has yellow-orange flowers from early spring until frost. Everblooming honeysuckle (*L. heckrottii*) has trumpet-shaped flowers that are reddish purple on the outside and yellow inside. Woodbine (*L. periclymenum*) is a woody climber to twenty feet; clusters of fragrant ivory-colored flowers all summer. BBG Director of Horticulture Edmond Moulin advises against planting Japanese or Hall's honeysuckle (*L. japonica* 'Halliana') because the plant is terribly invasive, especially in the South.

The silverfleece vine (*Polygonum aubertii*) will reach thirty feet in a single season. This deciduous vine is harmless to foundations, walls, and brick mortar because it clings by twining about, and not with suckers. Lance-shaped leaves flutter in the breeze and masses of small fragrant white flowers appear in late summer. Full sun to partial shade, in any average garden soil. Excellent for covering a fence or for a quick-growing screen; very easy to grow.

The Japanese wisteria (*Wisteria floribunda*) is a deciduous woody vine with possibly more cachet than any other vine in the garden. The delicate compound leaves are very attractive and the large drooping clusters of fragrant lilac, white, or pink flowers appearing in spring are show-stoppers. Full sun is best, coupled with moist but well-drained soil with an acid pH. These vines need frequent pruning to keep neat and under control; their strength can actually warp metal poles. Plants produced from seed will often not flower for years—and then flowers are second-rate. Hardy in USDA Zone 5, but needs protection from bitterly cold winds. Wisterias do not transplant well so buy plants propagated by cuttings and grown in containers.

The Chinese wisteria *(Wisteria sinensis)* is also a deciduous woody vine with delicate compound leaves and drooping clusters of lilac or white flowers in spring. Full sun, in moist but well-drained soil, not too rich in nitrogen, with acid pH. Needs frequent pruning to keep neat and under control. Not quite as hardy as *W. floribunda*. Cultivate as above and buy plants in containers.

# CHAPTER NINE

# ORNAMENTAL
# TREES

In 1943 Betty Smith wrote a novel about a young girl living in a Brooklyn tenement at the turn of the last century. It was called *A Tree Grows in Brooklyn,* and the tree was *Ailanthus altissima,* or the tree of heaven (originally from China and now naturalized over much of America). From the heroine's fire escape, the only green she could see was this particular tree; it became a symbol of her dreams and hopes. She eventually saw the tree destroyed—but her dreams and hopes did not die. The tree was tenacious and would soon appear in another Brooklyn backyard.

The ailanthus is not on our list of ornamental trees to grow, although it will do well in city conditions. It's best classed as a weed tree—its seeds will sprout anywhere they fall, even in cracks between city sidewalks—and should only be used when all else fails. In addition the male flowers have a distinct odor that is definitely unappealing.* But it leads to an interesting question: What trees are best for the home garden, and why?

Although one often gets a warm feeling from being altruistic, especially when it concerns helping the natural world, in the case of the ailanthus, there are many other trees that will do the same job but are more attractive, either in leaf or in flower or both, and better suited for the home garden.

Another example of unsuitability: Why should you not put an English oak *(Quercus robur)* on a one-acre lot with poor soil and sparse rainfall? Because it takes far too long to mature and will be out of scale for the size of the lot, reaching a height of eighty feet with a ninety-foot spread.

The point is that choosing to plant big trees in small backyard gardens that are really unsuited to them, or to choose a tree that will take fifty years or more to mature—especially when there is no guarantee in today's world that anyone will live in one place for his or her entire life—is impractical, to say the least. And planting such a tree just to save some time or money doubles the insult, both to the gardener and the tree. Hopefully the location for such trees will continue to be in public parks, botanical gardens like this Garden, and arboretums—places with a commitment to the future that allows for their stewardship and protection.

In the home garden there are a number of other questions to consider, the first being cost. From the viewpoint of time, money, and the gardener's energies, trees are not cheap. They represent a long-term investment on the part of the nursery that sells them; hence they cost a sizable amount of money to buy; even when small, they are ponderous to move; if something goes wrong they cannot be replaced with the ease of a hosta or a marigold; they require looking after when branches die or lightning strikes; they produce yearly litter; and whether from mistake in cultivation or age or disease they fail to flourish, they are expensive to treat, and expensive to remove when they die.

And there is an investment of time. If you cannot hire out the work involved with owning trees, you will be required to do the work yourself.

---

* The largest *Ailanthus* in America is out on Long Island, New York. It is 64 feet high, with a spread of 76 feet, and measures 238 inches in circumference at 4½ feet above the ground.

So why have a tree at all?

Easy. They are beautiful to look at. At all times of year the properly chosen tree is a glorious sight. With leaves or without, with blossoms or without, ablaze in autumn or green in spring, and endowed with ripening fruit or not, a well-grown tree can be the focal point of your garden. And if a family ceremony is held when it's planted, it will always evoke a memory of happy times.

Trees provide shade in summer, and in the winter, they—evergreens especially—are excellent windbreaks, dramatically reducing energy costs—a bonus in these energy-conscious times.

They can turn an ordinary yard into something unique; here's where you can outdo the Joneses, not with money but with imagination.

Trees provide the material for the majority of homes both for humans and wildlife, and for the paper this book is printed on.

There are environmental benefits, too. As the pundits argue over who is responsible for the greenhouse effect, acid rain, and pollution in general, there is one thing they all agree on: trees remove carbon dioxide from the atmosphere, replacing it with the oxygen that all living things require—and so are an essential link in the earth's cycle of life. Without them we would perish. So every time you plant a tree you make a commitment to the human future on this planet.


## CHOOSING A TREE

When walking around the landscaped grounds of one of the better botanic gardens, such as BBG, it's easy to forget the concerns of living next door to another family in a neighborhood. When the BBG was planned, the basic concerns were not those faced by most homeowners when planning a garden, but instead revolved around creating broad vistas, ambling walkways, and majestic views. At the same time the planners had to be both imaginative and knowledgeable enough to look decades in the future and know that what were once small saplings would eventually be mature trees of formidable height and girth.

So, when choosing a tree for the home garden, there are many points to consider that the home gardener would share with the staff at the Garden: Where would a tree do the best job? Is there a section of lawn that you are tired of cutting? Or do you have a yen to try growing plants that prefer shade? And just how much room do you have?

But there are other concerns, applicable only to the home owner: Is there a part of your property that needs a lift, or a part of the house itself that would benefit from some shade? Do you live in an area of the country with a more difficult climate than the northeast? Perhaps there are trees native to your area that are not only attractive but that you know are equipped to survive in your environment.

Color of the tree is important. If you own, for example, a pink stucco house, stay away from big trees with bright yellow leaves. Consider, too, your neighbors' planting. For example, if the people next door to your right have a grove of trees on their right, the best place for your trees would be on your left, so they blend in and add to the other trees. And never plant trees too close to, or right on, property lines; today's friend can be tomorrow's enemy.

It's a good idea before choosing or planting a tree to draw a map of your property. It is important to determine where north and south are in relation to your yard, so you can site the tree where it will not cast shade on flower and vegetable gardens, or on areas you want to turn into gardens (unless you plan to grow shade-tolerant plants). Set down the house, any outbuildings, pools and the like, the children's playground, your existing garden, and any other permanent landmarks. And if you have a septic tank, or know where water pipes are buried, add them to the map. Other trees beside willows will seek water and invade septic lines in a search for water, quickly clogging these up.

When planting, remember to leave enough room not only for the tree aboveground, but the roots below. Those roots will look for nourishment as the tree grows and will take what food they need to the detriment of whatever else is planted there.

Send for catalogs of nurseries that sell trees and check with your local Extension Service to see if they have any leads. Finally, visit the botanic garden in your area to see just what a mature tree of your choice looks like.

For more detailed instructions on planting trees, in addition to those in this chapter, check the instructions in the chapter Ornamental Shrubs and Vines; the same techniques apply.

## THE CARE OF TREES AT THE GARDEN

There are two "high pruners" at the Garden. Their title refers to their work at the top of many very old and lofty trees.

On a beautiful day in early October, we met with James Cordray. "In answer to your question," he said, "I had a list from the computer, but offhand I'd say there are about seven thousand trees here in the Garden including some that were growing here long before the Garden began. With that many trees our work is basically all year long. We start in the winter by caring for equipment that includes chippers, hydraulic sprayers, chain saws, ropes, and climbing equipment, so as soon as the weather breaks or it isn't snowing, we start pruning.

"About the end of March, when the night temperatures are above 40° F., we start spraying with dormant oil sprays, doing a good part of the Garden, especially the cherries, plums, crabapples, and a lot of the big oaks that are sprayed to control scale insects."

Horticultural oil sprays are made of emulsified oils that are applied to trees before the buds are open, or when the buds are dormant. Such sprays are very effective in controlling mealybugs, many scale insects, and killing the eggs of many other insects and mites. They are safer for the gardener than many insecticides.

The spray operation takes about two weeks. The next step is the application of a fungicide, usually Bordeaux mix—an old-time spray originating in France and prepared from copper sulfate and hydrated lime. At BBG it is used on the Austrian pines *(Pinus nigra)* for control of Diplodia tip blight.

## ON CUTTING TREES

The high pruners also have techniques for saving damaged trees that might otherwise be lost. Removing a tree is a last resort. Mr. Cordray explained that they try to save trees whenever possible.

"Usually we try our best. This is a champion tree before us and you can see a crack in the trunk between the two leaders. I'll have to get up there and cable it. With a tree having a weakened crotch, you usually go two-thirds up between the crotch and the treetop."

In such a case Mr. Cordray can actually attach lengths of heavy wire cable running from the strong main trunk to the outer branch, thus relieving stress on the crack.

"You can also solve the problem another way," he said, "by using a rigid rod with washers and nuts at the outside ends that goes through the crotch to help support the branches."

Heavy wire cables can actually be attached to various branches in a tree.

Mr. Cordray will often look at new trees planted in the garden to see if they too need his attention. Frequently after planting, young trees are left to fend for themselves (except for watering and mulching), so the pruners come around and start to shape them at an early age so they will not need drastic pruning when they are older.

Trees are trimmed for a single leader so the fledgling trunk will reach a decent height before beginning to branch out. On small trees the pruners will clip the terminal buds on the side branches so they do not become too long.

"You don't want to remove the side branches," he said, "like they do in nurseries, since the tree will not put on as much caliper growth without them, but the idea is to keep them under control. When you eventually decide to remove them, it won't leave such a large, gaping space.

"And when you tie guylines to stake a young tree, remember to leave enough of the upper part of the trunk flexible because the movement from the wind is important in building up the strength of the trunk."

"Any hints on that old problem of getting rid of the stump?" we asked.

"We use a backhoe or a stump grinder that grinds down below the surface. Then we plant grass on top. Most of the major tree services that a gardener would call have stump grinders."

"You're big on chipping?"

"It's the best way in the world to make mulch or cut branches and twigs down to the size that's best for composting."

## TIPS ON PRUNING TREES
## FROM THE HIGH PRUNER

"The most important thing to remember," continued Mr. Cordray, "is no more flush cutting of branches. This was a very popular and much prescribed method over many years that has now proved detrimental to the trees concerned. A collar (a thin segment of the branch) must be left when a branch is removed in order for callus to quickly form and to prevent opening up the trunk wood to disease."

On any large or heavy branch, make your first cut from below about one foot out from the trunk; stop one-third of the way through the branch. Make the second cut from above, about two inches out from the first cut and remove the branch. Your final cut removes the short piece that's left, leaving a collar.

Always use a sharp, clean knife, saw, or pruning shears. Never just break off a branch on your way through the garden.

Don't cover wounds with pitch or wound dressings; when the wound is covered and cut off from open air, the area around the seal becomes a haven for fungi and bacteria.

Mr. Cordray was most concerned about the safety of anyone involved with pruning trees and using power equipment. Always have another person on the ground when climbing a tree. Never, never undertake off-the-ground pruning when alone.

Be careful when using a chain saw, and never climb a ladder with a chain saw in one hand and the other hand holding the rail. Once aloft, use a rope to pull the chain saw or other equipment up to your level. That's the way the professionals do it.

Be careful to place the ladder securely against the tree trunk and tie it to the tree.

And finally, be careful when you work trees in the neighborhood of power lines. One slip can mean disaster!

## ON FERTILIZING TREES

"We have hydraulic feeders," said Mr. Cordray, "for feeding trees, just because of the sheer size and number of trees that we support. But there are other ways to fertilize.

"The home gardener can use tree stakes that are pounded into the ground with a mallet or hammer, or can broadcast granular fertilizers around the base of the tree or apply a liquid—but if there is grass, that will add to the amount needed. There is also a soil auger that can be used by hand and one that is motorized; either of these can prepare a hole to receive the fertilizer. There are also root feeders that attach to the garden hose, and after an attached chamber is loaded with fertilizer cartridges, you force the liquid down to the roots. In fact, even using plain water in an injection device is beneficial to the tree because so much of the soil is usually compacted, and the water breaks it up and aerates the soil around the roots.

"Although," he cautions, "the problem with injection feeders is the water pressure that's needed. Most call for one hundred fifty to two hundred pounds of pressure, and garden hoses do not supply that much."

Another method is to punch holes in the soil, using an old crowbar or an iron staff. Mark off two imaginary circles with the tree trunk at the center. The first should be located one-third of the distance between the trunk and the drip line. The second should extend about two feet beyond the drip line. Then punch a number of holes, between eight and ten inches deep and two feet apart. Then a couple of ounces of fertilizer is put into the hole, the sod pushed back, and the ground watered well.

Just remember that there are different fertilizer formulas for different plants. These mixtures are identified with three numbers: the first number indicates the percentage of nitrogen; the second, the percentage of phosphorus; and the third, the percentage of potash.

Nitrogen is the most important part of any fertilizer. It's essential for healthy growth and a good green leaf color. Phosphorous promotes flowering and helps to form fruits. Potassium, or potash, is important in strengthening tissues and building up resistance to disease. According to Mr. Cordray and Edmond Moulin, Director of Horticulture, a good mix for tree application would be 3:1:1 ratio, such as 30–10–10 for shade trees and a 3:1:1 ratio used at half the rate for evergreens, including azaleas and rhododendrons. BBG recommends supplying three pounds of actual nitrogen per one thousand square feet for deciduous trees and one and a half pounds of actual nitrogen per thousand square feet for evergreens. You can calculate the amount of actual nitrogen in a fertilizer by dividing the percentage of nitrogen into the total weight of the fertilizer. For example, if the fertilizer is 30–10–10, 30 percent of the fertilizer is nitrogen. A fifty-pound bag of 30–10–10 thus contains fifteen pounds of actual nitrogen.

"One more thing about fertilizing," said Mr. Cordray, "with very old trees or trees damaged by construction or trees that are newly planted, we cut the fertilizer strength by half, or use none at all during the first year the plant is in stress."

They also fertilize beeches at half the rate (or less) of other deciduous trees.

## SMALL CONIFERS FOR SMALL GARDENS

Small evergreens are plants that are dwarf (three feet high or under upon reaching maturity) or small (under twelve feet high upon maturity, although a few specimens might reach sixteen feet). There are a number of reasons why a particular plant might be so qualified: It could be genetically predisposed to be dwarf or small. Or the plant may just grow slowly; a western red cedar (*Thuja plicata*), might be comfortable in a small backyard for fifty or sixty years before it became too large. A particular plant might grow horizontally rather than vertically, thus seeming small. It could be pruned by man or continually browsed by animals. It could be an example of a chance mutation, keeping all the parent's qualities except a penchant for growth. And finally, it could be a "sport" or bud mutation, where only one branch of a particular species gives evidence of change.

The well-known witches' broom, a condition in which a congested branch of shortened shoots arises at a joint of a branch, or often at the tip of a normal branch, sometimes occurs on a variety of trees, especially larch, spruce, and pine. These growth variations are easily mistaken for birds' nests from a distance or, as folklore would see it, a witch's traveling aid.

Plants that are propagated by cuttings from the actual brooms grow into dwarf or small specimens, and many conifers now common in gardens were first reproduced in this manner. Whatever the initial cause of a broom—mutation, insect attacks, or virus infections—normal-size branches may also develop and unless removed will ultimately kill the smaller ones by choking off all light and air.

## EVERGREENS AT THE GARDEN

The needled evergreen collection that begins near the Fragrance Garden and winds along the path in front of the Shakespeare Garden, continuing across from the pond in the Japanese Garden, spiraling up and over in the direction of the Rose Garden and turning back to stop next to a big beech at the back of the Japanese pond is all under the control of Ira Walker.

Mr. Walker became curator of conifers back in 1983. In addition he is in his second term on the board of the American Conifer Society and has been its treasurer since 1989. He has been at the Garden for twenty years.

We visited the collection on a warm, sunny day in September. The three of us sat on a bench and watched a squirrel burying peanuts in a large patch of mulch surrounding a bed of unusual variation of the white pine *(Pinus strobus)*.

Mr. Walker discussed his methods and explained that he uses mulches extensively with the conifers. "I only use organic mulches," he said, "because they break down and benefit the soil. I use at least an inch with two inches as the maximum. I like mulches not only because they look good esthetically but they also keep the soil temperature constant in the summer and the winter. And they keep the weeds down."

We asked about a beautiful weeping white pine, seemingly being held up with a wire cable.

"That's *Pinus strobus* 'Pendula'. Do you see the cable? We moved the specimen from the old dwarf garden (an enclosed area where all the dwarf conifers were once grown) when they began the work on the new conservatory and I wanted to make sure it didn't fall over. It was a precautionary measure, but the wire's loose and it will be removed after one more winter."

A neat pile of conifer clippings led us to ask about pruning.

"The only pruning I do on these conifers is to take out the dead wood. Otherwise I let them grow naturally. In some areas, particularly the junipers—the low-growing and spreading junipers—they are starting to grow together so I will have to take time to clip them. It's okay if they butt together, but I don't like their growing into each other. A lot of people don't realize that you can prune them back.

"I had a spruce in the conifer family bed that died back. So I did what I could to make it symmetrical again. I just went in and cut material off all the way around—it was good material, but I just wanted to even the plant out. Today, you would never know I ever touched it."

He keeps abreast of all the catalogs and the various mom-and-pop nurseries, knowing that it's one way to keep up on the newest cultivars. Very few growers stock everything and a number of them specialize.

"I go to symposiums," he said, "to the American Conifer Society meetings, and I visit different gardens and arboretums. I've been looking for a certain form of juniper for the juniper bed. I had planted a *Juniperus virginiana* 'Sparkling Skyrocket', a variegated, upright pyramidal cultivar, but it disappointed me and I felt it should be replaced."

"Did it die down at the bottom?" we asked.

"It was browning a lot but I really wanted something with a variegation in that spot. I'm looking for an upright pyramidal juniper, either variegated or with a grayish hue to it. There's a western juniper called 'Gray Gleam', but I need something that doesn't grow as fast. The 'Skyrocket' was rather nice but the color was disappointing.

There's a bit of the artist in every gardener and as Mr. Walker talked about various nuances of gray against the myriad shades of green, it was as though a brush and a palette were in his hand.

"This plant, *Microbiota decussata,* is from eastern Siberia and makes a low ground cover. It's medium green in the summer and turns a beautiful bronze overlaid with purple in the winter. A lot of the junipers do. People should visit here in the winter and look at the junipers in the collection. They would be amazed at the different shades of purple."

As to fertilizing these plants, he said: "I used to do some light fertilizing. I never really did anything major. I find—and it's a consensus with people in the conifer trade—that you really don't, especially with the dwarf material. If you fertilize too much, you're going to get rapid growth and force the plant to put on growth it ordinarily wouldn't do. This is a good soil, a loam, so I don't really bother fertilizing it."

A short walk beyond the Fragrance Garden is one of Mr. Walker's special charges, a Sargent's weeping hemlock (*Tsuga canadensis* 'Pendula').

"That's one hundred years old," he said. "We got that plant when it was seventy-five years old, back in 1964. We have other old conifers, and some of the Austrian pines *(Pinus nigra)* are at least ninety years old.

"We have five of the weeping hemlocks in the Garden but this is the biggest and the oldest—" He stopped to yell at a squirrel. "But really, slow-growing and dwarf conifers are becoming more popular because people don't have the space; they have small gardens, especially in the city. And these plants are adaptable to city conditions."

"How about extra watering?" we asked.

"Up to a point," he answered. "This year was wet and we didn't have to water as much. I'm watering now because it's getting into fall, and I want these trees to go into fall and winter with ample water. You have to make sure that conifers go into the winter with ample water because if you don't, and you have a cold winter, without that extra moisture in the soil, they will suffer and it won't show up until the following spring.

"The best thing in the winter is snow; it is a natural mulch. We have to knock it off the weeping trees because of the weight, but the snow keeps the temperature of the soil constant."

"We're in the city," he said. "Look at the light. The angle of the sun as it gets into the fall is gorgeous. I love it. Just walking through the garden in this month, the middle of this month through October, I think the angle of the sun is just so beautiful."

## CONTINUING CARE OF DWARF CONIFERS

Even though they are tough plants and will survive under many adverse conditons, the dwarf conifers are always at their best when given proper attention and care. The following practices have helped to make the conifer beds at the BBG so attractive.

Winter cold combined with winter sun will cause troublesome heaving of unprotected or unmulched ground. The alternate freezing and thawing forces up shallow-rooted or newly planted trees and plants, exposing their roots to wind, cold, and sun. Exposed roots must be promptly pushed down into the soil once again. Winter mulching is the best prevention.

Promptly remove all weeds growing close to the evergreens, and keep all grass at least one foot away from the outside edge of any tree or shrub planted in your lawn. Grass and weeds take nourishment, water, and sunlight away from small trees.

Cover all exposed earth with a mulch—wood chips, pine needles, pine branches, and the like—to inhibit future weed growth and conserve moisture. Do not use sawdust, grass clippings, or sphagnum peat moss. They will pack down too tightly and, in the case of peat moss, will actually repel water.

Fertilize older trees with one of the methods described on page 180.

Remove dead branches with a sharp, clean pruning shears or

saw. Lawn mowers, weed trimmers, pets, and people can easily break branches and even scrape bark off the trunk.

Keep an eagle eye out for insects and disease. Dwarf conifers are very tough but even they can succumb to an army of insects ganging up on them, especially when they have been recently planted. For example, when the needles turn a dull green or are streaked with gray, look for spider mites, then use insecticidal soap or frequent blasts of just water to dislodge them. Aphids and caterpillars can be handled, either with spray insecticides or with some of the newer biological controls.

Evergreens, unlike herbaceous plants and trees, can suffer from drought during the first couple of years of being planted out. The needlelike leaves can lose moisture in winter through the combined actions of cold and winds. They are unable to replace it when the ground is frozen.

To lessen the possibility of drought you can make sure the new plantings are adequately watered before the winter begins. Then you can improvise screens for protection against the weather. Some possibilities are: small wooden pyramids to cover conifers, a low tent of evergreen branches (a good ending for the annual Christmas tree), snow fencing held up with metal posts, and screens made of poles and burlap.

Finally, anticipate the ravages of deer, dogs, rabbits, and mice. Deer in many parts of the country are enjoying a revival and when winters are bad (or even when they are not), these marauding Bambis will move right in and rape, pillage, and destroy. And remember, wildlife fans, that deer, mice, rabbits, woodchucks, and so forth, will continue to chew everything in sight even if they have plenty of food.

Nothing discourages wildlife more than the gardener taking early morning or late evening walks in the garden, such unscheduled meanderings generally upsetting the precise scheduling of most animals. Peter often goes out just before sunrise and enjoys the sound of deer snorting in rage because there are humans in the vicinity.

One of the charms of the smaller evergreen conifers is the comparative ease with which they can be grown in containers. And especially for those gardeners in the city who have nothing but a terrace or small lot in the suburbs, container gardening is a most satisfying pastime.

A container by definition could vary from a small pot to a sunken soapstone sink to a large raised bed in the backyard, constructed of fieldstone or brick. They all have one thing in common: the soil they contain will be mixed to your specifications and can be adjusted far more readily than an entire garden of poor soil.

There is one requirement: Evergreen plants in small containers will do best if sunk in the ground for the winter and allowed to endure the cold with the rest of the outdoors. If they are brought under shelter, they must have at least three months of temperatures of no more than 50°F in the daytime and 33°F to 40°F at night. If these conditions are not met, the plants will eventually die.

If you live in an area like USDA Zone 6 and have no backyard to store plants, you can put them behind a parapet or the like, a place where they are out of the direct wind and also away from the winter sun. Or you could put the pots in small boxes surrounded with Styrofoam pellets or foam insulation (the foam must remain dry).

When a potted plant is left outside without being buried or given some other protection, the bitter winds striking the pots will soon kill the plant's roots. If the winds don't do the job, the repeated freezing and thawing of the soil will.

When living in the colder parts of the country, there is the additional problem of clay pots that break when the water in their pores freezes and expands, so the best thing to do is use plastic pots and put them inside more decorative containers.

## • TREES TO GROW

All the following trees are best in full sun. (If adaptable to shade, this will be noted.) See the table in chapter 7, Plants for Japanese Gardens, for more outstanding trees to grow.

*Acer saccharum* and varieties, sugar maple. To 100 feet. Deciduous tree; upright form; leaves 4 to 6 inches long, with 3 to 5 lobes and coarsely toothed edges; dark green with gray undersides; green-yellow flowers followed by winged seeds; brilliant autumn foliage of yellow, orange, and red. Grows best in fertile, well-drained loam, but tolerates many soils. Source of sap used in maple syrup. A number of cultivars are available. Excellent shade tree. Hardy to USDA Zone 3.

*Albizia julibrissin* var. *rosea,* silk tree, mimosa tree. To 30 feet. Deciduous tree; spreading form; lacy leaves composed of lots of small leaflets; fluffy clusters of pink flowers with long stamens in midsummer. Grows in moist soils, and also does well on dry, rocky soil where few plants thrive. Good specimen tree for a lawn. Easily grown from seed. Young plants in the northern parts of the U.S. must have winter protection while getting started. USDA Zone 7. This tree is very subject to fusarium wilt, a soilborne disease. Once this fungus gets into soil, albizia should not be planted or replanted.

*Amelanchier canadensis,* serviceberry, juneberry, shadblow. To 30 feet. Deciduous tree; rounded form; young leaves are silvery; clusters of white flowers in early spring; blooms in the Northeast when shad come upriver to spawn; purple fruit is attractive to birds and rarely left to make a serviceable jelly. Best in well-drained loam, but tolerates a range of soils; a beautiful tree. "To see the real beauty of the juneberry is to see its frail blossoms intermixed with snowflakes on a stormy day in early spring—youth daring the tempest," wrote Jens Jensen, one of America's pioneer landscape architects, in his book *Siftings* (Ralph Fletcher Seymour, Chicago, IL, 1939). USDA Zone 4.

*Betula nigra* 'Heritage', river birch. Small tree to 30 feet. White outer bark peels to expose reddish-brown inner bark. Moist, slightly acid soil of reasonable fertility. This cultivar is resistant to bronze birch borer, which has become a tremendous problem in recent years for susceptible species like the weeping birch *(B. pendula)* and the paper birch *(B. papyrifera)*. Major borer infestations seem to occur cyclically, and until the current cycle ends it is unwise to plant this species. USDA Zone 4. *Betula populifolia,* gray birch, is a short-lived tree to 30 feet tall that grows in clumps, usually in very poor soil, and is especially suited to small gardens. It is so resilient that heavy snows bend it to the ground without breaking it. USDA Zone 4.

*Cedrus atlantica,* Atlas cedar. To 100 feet. Coniferous evergreen tree; pyramidal form; open branches have clumps of short needles (var. *glauca* has blue-green needles) that leave the trunk exposed—unusual and interesting appearance. Well-drained soil is essential; can withstand drought and windy conditions. Grow as a specimen tree. Variety *pendula* has weeping branches. *C. libani,* cedar of Lebanon, is very similar. USDA Zone 6 in protected spot.

*Cercis canadensis,* eastern redbud. To 30 feet. Deciduous tree; irregular form; red-budded pealike flowers appear directly on branches before the leaves; the flowers quickly turn rose-mauve, pink,or white. Heart-shaped leaves turn yellow in the autumn. Well-drained soil with slightly acid to near neutral pH. Best if it receives some shade in the heat of afternoon. Good tree for small properties. Difficult to transplant larger trees. USDA Zone 5.

*Chionanthus virginicus,* fringe tree. To 30 feet. Deciduous tree; irregular form; 8-inch oval leaves turn a bright yellow in autumn; 6-inch clusters of fragrant white flowers with 1-inch petals closely resembling fringe; fruits are blue berries. Moist but well drained soil with good fertility. Spectacular tree in flower and worth having just to see it in bloom. USDA Zone 5.

*Cladrastis lutea,* American yellow-wood. To 50 feet. Deciduous tree; rounded form; dense oblong compound leaves, turn yellow in autumn; smooth gray bark; drooping clusters of fragrant white pealike flowers in summer resemble wisterias. Grows best in full sun, in deep, fertile, well-drained soil, but tolerates a wide range of soils. Can withstand drought, heat, and cold. May not bloom every year. USDA Zone 4.

*Cornus kousa,* Japanese dogwood. To 25 feet. Deciduous tree; upright, spreading form; oval leaves; flower clusters surrounded by large showy white pointed bracts followed by berrylike fruits attractive to birds. Full sun in cooler climates, but likes open shade, too; light, well-drained soil rich in organic matter, preferably with an acid pH. USDA Zone 5.

*Cornus florida,* flowering dogwood. To 40 feet. Deciduous tree; branches are horizontal, so trees have a distinctive flat top; 4-inch oval leaves have sharp points; leaves turn scarlet in autumn; flower clusters are small, each set inside 4 large showy white or pink bracts, followed by red berries in autumn.

This is the native American dogwood, a tree of great beauty that unfortunately is dying in many parts of the country as a result of a plant disease called dogwood anthracnose; it is caused by several types of fungi and has been recognized since the late 1970s. The disease attacks trees both out in the woods and in home gardens, although the disease is worse in woodland plants; the environment is cooler and more humid there, while trees in home gardens usually receive better air movement and more sunlight, and thus are better at surviving. The first symptoms are spots on the leaves, followed by leaf scorching; soon the leaves die, yet remain hanging on the tree, carrying the infection. Sometimes an infected tree will grow a number of water sprouts and these sprouts will carry the disease back into the bark. The bark then gets cankers, like localized dead spots, so trees can be under a two-way attack. The disease is also worse when there is a wet spring, when humidity is high and leaves are often wet. The BBG's Research Center in Ossining, New York, is a leading center for the study of this disease. Dr. Craig Hibben, at the Research Center, suggests three aids to prevention:

1. Good sanitation and maintenance, which include pruning off dead twigs that carry the spores; watering trees during extended dry

spells (since they are shallow-rooted); and fertilizing every year in spring or late fall.

2. Spraying with a fungicide when the young leaves appear in spring and twice more at two-week intervals. (Check with your local County Agricultural Extension Agent for the latest fungicide recommendations.)

3. Replacing lost trees with the Chinese dogwood *(Cornus kousa),* a tree that is not immune but is resistant.

*Cornus mas,* cornelian cherry. To 20 feet or more. Deciduous tree; rounded, dense form; one of first plants to bloom in spring; fuzzy clusters of tiny yellow flowers; cherrylike fruit in late summer. Light, well-drained soil rich in organic matter. Use as a specimen plant or in the shrub border. USDA Zone 5.

*Crataegus* spp., hawthorn. To 30 feet. Deciduous trees; glossy, lobed leaves turn orange or red in autumn; clusters of white, pink, or red flowers in late spring or early summer; small fruits are red in autumn. Fertile, well-drained soil; tolerates dry soil and cold winters. *C. phaenopyrum,* Washington thorn, is best grown as a specimen tree; *C. laevigata (C. oxycantha),* English hawthorn and *C. crus-galli,* cockspur thorn, can also be used as hedges. *C. viridis* 'Winter King' has few thorns and a good growth habit, and is recommended as a good small tree for the home landscape or a suburban street. Most are hardy to USDA Zone 5.

*Fagus* spp., beech. To 90 feet. Deciduous tree; dense, pyramidal form; deep green foliage, toothed leaves, bluish-green above, light green beneath, turning yellow or bronze in autumn; attractive gray bark. Fertile, light, moist but well-drained loam. These trees are majestic planted as specimens on large lawns. *F. grandifolia,* American beech, is native to eastern U.S. USDA Zone 4. *F. sylvatica,* European beech, has numerous varieties with such qualities as weeping branches, purple foliage, or finely cut leaves. USDA Zone 5.

*Franklinia alatamaha.* To 20 feet. Deciduous tree; upright form; oblong, glossy green leaves turn beautiful orange-red in autumn; 3-inch white flowers with prominent yellow stamens in late summer or early fall. Moist but well-drained soil; can be planted along banks of a stream. The BBG recommends that this tree be given an eastern exposure with morning sun in preference to a western exposure with evening sun; it also likes open shade. Not hardy north of USDA Zone 6, but will send up new shoots every spring if crown is mulched against severe cold.

*Ginkgo biloba,* maidenhair tree. To 100 feet or more. Deciduous tree; irregular form; attractive fan-shaped light green leaves similar in shape to leaflets of maidenhair fern, turning yellow in fall; female trees produce small fruits that smell of rancid butter, so plant only male trees. Sun or shade, in practically any well-drained soil. Tough tree that does well in many parts of the country and withstands urban conditions. Kernels of "fruit" considered a delicacy in Asia. A living fossil, now found only in cultivation. Grow as a specimen tree. USDA Zone 5.

*Halesia carolina,* Carolina silverbell. To 20 feet. Deciduous tree; roundheaded, spreading form; 4-inch oval leaves turn yellow in autumn; small, dangling, bell-shaped white flowers in spring. Partial shade, in fertile, moist but well-drained loam. Avoid planting on windy sites, and in the North do not plant in low, cold spots where late frost may damage flowers. Use as a specimen plant or in woodland garden. USDA Zone 5.

*Kolreuteria paniculata,* goldenrain tree. To 30 feet. Deciduous tree; upright form; feathery, compound leaves that may turn yellow in autumn; long clusters of small fragrant yellow flowers in early summer, followed by attractive seedpods. Practically any garden soil; tolerates drought and wind. Grow as a specimen tree. Chinese make necklaces from pods. USDA Zone 5.

*Liquidambar styraciflua,* sweet gum. To 100 or more feet. Deciduous tree; pyramidal form; palmate star-shaped leaves turn a beautiful deep red in autumn; small inconspicuous greenish flowers; interesting seedpods persist after leaves drop. Full sun to partial shade, in moist, fertile, loamy soil. Trees produce aromatic balsam called styrax, important in medicine and perfumery. Grow as a specimen tree on large lawn. USDA Zone 6.

*Liriodendron tulipifera,* tulip tree. To 100 or more feet. Deciduous tree; pyramidal form with stately trunk; lobed leaves somewhat similar to maple leaves turn yellow in autumn; tulip-shaped flowers have greenish-yellow petals striped with orange. Deep, fertile, moist soil, but will tolerate a variety of soils. Good specimen tree for a large lawn. Known to live 500 years and reach 150 feet in height. USDA Zone 5.

*Magnolia* spp. To 20 or more feet. Deciduous, evergreen trees; rounded form; oval leaves; gray bark; large showy flowers in early spring; interesting bright red fruits for late summer and early fall; handsome in winter. Full sun is best, but tolerate partial shade; moist, fertile soil, rich in organic matter and with an acid pH. Withstand city conditions, but not hardy in northernmost U.S. Grow as a specimen tree in modest-sized yard, in shrub borders, or in front of evergreens, or mixed with rhododendrons. *M. grandiflora,* bull bay, southern magnolia. To 100 feet. Thick shining deep green evergreen leaves to 8 inches long; fragrant white flowers to 8 inches across; USDA Zone 7. *M × soulangiana,* Chinese or saucer magnolia, has cup-shaped flowers in white, pink, or purple, with a sweet, lemony scent; warmer part of USDA

Zone 5. *M. tomentosa (M. stellata)*, star magnolia, has double star-shaped fragrant white blossoms with floppy petals that resemble pussy willows in bud; usually hardy in USDA Zone 5 with protection from worst winds of winter.

The magnolia is an important tree to the Garden since a great deal of research into hybrids of this genus was carried on by Dr. Lola Koerting of the BBG research center in Westchester, New York. A number of very important cultivars have been bred and selected by BBG. They include 'Marillyn', 'Yellow Bird', and 'Elizabeth', the latter with clear yellow blooms that appear later than those of most other magnolias and escapes damage from unexpected cold snaps in spring.

*Malus* spp., flowering crab apples. To 30 feet, depending on the species. Deciduous trees; oval leaves, folded or rolled in bud; in spring covered with white or pink flowers, usually fragrant; small red or yellow fruits, liked by birds. Adapt to almost any soil, as long as it's well drained. Next to the Japanese cherries, these trees are stars of just slightly less magnitude. Many different forms and leaf, flower, and fruit colors available, with more to choose from every year. Excellent for the small garden. *M. floribunda* has red to deep pink buds opening to fragrant white flowers. *M. arnoldiana* has white blossoms that are pink inside. *M.* 'Red Jade' is a weeping form, covered with flowers that are white with touches of pale pink, followed by bright red fruits that persist after the leaves have fallen; developed by the Garden and patented in 1956. USDA Zone 5.

*Oxydendrum arboreum*, sorrel tree, sourwood. To 25 feet. Deciduous tree; pyramidal form; small glossy green leaves resemble mountain laurel, turning bright red in fall; drooping clusters of fragrant bell-shaped white flowers bloom in summer, followed by attractive seedpods in autumn. Must have full morning sun (best if given some shade in the heat of the day), in moist but well-drained, somewhat acid soil. Grow as a specimen tree or as the background for a formal border. USDA Zone 6.

*Picea breweriana*. To 100 feet. Coniferous evergreen tree with elegant drooping branches bearing flattened needles 1 inch long with white bands above; cones are orange. Full sun; well-drained but moist, slightly acid soil. A broad pyramid of drooping branches becomes the quintessence of all aspects of the brooding and romantic landscape; it can turn a suburban yard into a bit of Transylvania and the *Sorrows of Young Werther*. Will grow 10 feet in 10 years. Not hardy below USDA Zone 5 and needs cool summers.

*Pinus strobus*, eastern white pine. To 120 feet or more. Coniferous evergreen tree with soft blue-green 5-inch-long needles in bunches of 5;

long, drooping cones (4 to 6 inches). Fast-growing when young, easily a foot a year. Full sun, but young trees will take some shade; any well-drained or evenly moist soil on the acid side; very adaptable. This is the majestic pine tree of America. Straight trunks of virgin trees were used to make masts of sailing ships, as many grew to a height of 200 feet. Sadly they were raped for all their potential uses. A major pest is the white pine weevil, which kills the leader of a healthy tree when between 6 and 12 feet, thus causing the tree to send up (usually) two new leaders, rendering the tree less attractive. Can be trimmed in spring and kept as a very serviceable hedge of almost any height over 6 to 8 feet. Smaller cultivars are listed later in the table Dwarf Conifers for the Garden, page 195. Hardy to USDA Zone 3.

*Pinus sylvestris,* Scotch pine. To 75 feet. Coniferous evergreen tree with blue-green 3-inch-long stiff and twisted needles in bunches of 2; reddish trunk; 2½-inch-long cones. Full sun; any well-drained average garden soil. When young, their pyramidal shape is a welcome addition to any garden; when older they have a tall trunk with rounded growth on top. They make excellent Christmas trees. Smaller cultivars are in Dwarf Conifers for the Garden, page 195. Hardy to USDA Zone 2.

*Prunus serotina,* native black cherry, rum cherry. To 90 feet. Deciduous trees; many drooping branches; lustrous peachlike leaves; hanging clusters of small fragrant white 5-petaled flowers, followed by small cherries, first red but ripening to black. Tolerant of shade when young; any good garden soil. Excellent in the woodland garden. A beautiful tree overlooked by most gardeners. A very old tree is in the Local Flora section of the Garden. USDA Zone 4.

*Prunus padus,* European cherry. To 35 feet. Deciduous tree; pyramidal in form; leaves are dark green on top, dull underneath, turn yellow in autumn; long clusters of fragrant white flowers, often drooping, blossom in late spring, followed by small, black, bitter cherries. Will adapt to light shade; any reasonably fertile garden soil. Beautiful specimen tree, or planted in groups; good in woodland garden. USDA Zone 6. *P. serrulata,* Japanese cherry. To 25 feet. Deciduous tree; light green oval leaves with toothed edges turn yellow or orange in autumn; white, cream, or pink single or double flowers, depending on cultivar, bloom in spring. There are many, many beautiful cultivars offered by various nurseries. USDA Zone 5.

*Pseudolarix amabilis,* golden larch. To 100 feet or more. Deciduous conifer; open, pyramidal form; airy, soft, light green needles turn a beautiful yellow in autumn, then fall from the tree; small oval 3-inch cones. Moist but well-drained, somewhat acid soil. Lovely specimen tree for a lawn.

*Rhus typhina,* staghorn sumac. To 20 feet. Deciduous tree; round-topped form; tropical-looking, with large, pinnate leaves to 18 inches long, turning yellow, orange, and rich red in autumn; tiny greenish flowers in tight bunches become cone-shaped clusters of hairy fruits that persist on trees after leaves have fallen. Will adapt to light shade in any average garden soil; can be invasive, with searching suckers. A short-lived tree, rarely beyond 25 years or so, appreciated in Europe and largely ignored in America, its first home. Name "staghorn" comes from velvet found on young stems. 'Laciniata' has fernlike foliage with deeply cut leaves. USDA Zone 4.

*Tsuga canadensis,* hemlock. To 100 feet or more. Coniferous evergreen tree with dark shiny green needles having two white bands underneath; graceful arching branches; cones are small and brown. Full sun or partial shade; well-drained or moist average garden soil, slightly acidic; in times of drought, needles may fall, so give necessary soakings. Once mighty native stands were destroyed to provide the tannin used to make supple shoes for troops in the Civil War. Excellent lawn specimens, and also make effective hedges, responding to spring shearings; not too happy in city conditions. Smaller cultivars listed in table Dwarf Conifers for the Garden, page 195. Hardy to USDA Zone 4.

*Wisteria* spp. To 16 feet, but usually shorter. Deciduous vine, but when properly trained by pruning will become a small tree with a weeping habit; delicate compound leaves; large, drooping clusters of fragrant lilac, white, or pink flowers in spring. Full sun, in moist but well-drained soil with acid pH. Start a plant by picking one stem, staking it, and removing all side shoots; it will eventually reach the height you wish. Cut back shoots in early autumn to 2 to 3 buds. If there are any flower buds they will be at the base of the shoot; the pruning will encourage these buds to develop next spring. Difficult to achieve, but worth the trouble when finally in bloom. Specialty nurseries often have such standards in stock. Hardy to USDA Zone 5 but needs protection from bitterly cold winds.

*Zelkova serrata,* Japanese zelkova. To 90 feet. Deciduous tree; rounded, spreading form, similar to American elm; leaves turn rust-color in autumn. Does well in a wide range of soils, tolerates alkalinity, hot sun, and wind. Also tolerant of city pollution. Good substitute for elm in a large lawn; resistant to Dutch elm disease. USDA Zone 5.

# • DWARF CONIFERS FOR THE GARDEN

Note: AGR is Average Growth Rate per year; UH is Ultimate Height; US is Ultimate Spread. Unless otherwise noted, all trees need full sun for maximum color and healthy growth. Check the table Plants for Japanese Gardens, page 130, for more small conifers.

*Abies balsamea,* balsam fir. Evergreen conifer to 75 feet in its native habitat. Leaves are flat on the upper side with a deep blue-green color; cones mature during the summer, changing color from violet, blue, green, or yellow to brown, standing upright on the branch. Firs prefer good moist soil and resent shallow or alkaline ground; smaller trees benefit from a mulch, especially during hot, dry summers. These trees resent pollution and are not at their best in city gardens. The cultivar 'Nana', dwarf balsam fir, eventually makes a round bush with a diameter of 3 feet and an AGR of 2 to 3 inches. Hardy to USDA Zone 3.

*Abies concolor* 'Candicans', white fir. Evergreen conifer; to 200 feet in the wild. This cultivar has one of the most beautiful blues in the conifer clan; upper leaves are silvery blue, and tree is cone-shaped; cones are purplish before maturity. Culture as above but can tolerate some heat and dryness. Tree reaches 20 feet in 40 years with AGR of 6 inches. USDA Zone 3.

*Cedrus atlantica* 'Glauca Pendula', weeping blue cedar. Evergreen conifer; to 100 feet in the wild. Stiff, needle-shaped bluish leaves; upright brown cones take 2 to 3 years to ripen. Trees require fairly well-drained soil with a slightly acid pH. This beautiful tree is not a dwarf and must be raised as a standard or grafted onto a standard in order to prevent the foliage from growing flat upon the ground; most nurseries stock it as a 4-to-5 foot tree. After 50 years the diameter at the base will be 25 to 30 feet. Hardy to USDA Zone 6, with some protection from bitter winter winds.

*Chamaecyparis lawsoniana* 'Filiformis Compacta', false cypress. Evergreen conifer; to 100 feet in the wild. Threadlike sprays of aromatic foliage with a blue-green hue; cones are small, round, and brown. Trees do best in moist but well-drained, slightly acid soil. After 10 years will form a 3-foot-high bun with about the same width as its height. AGR is 3 inches. Perched on a bank, this plant is a fine accent in a small rock garden or evergreen planting. Hardy to USDA Zone 6, but needs protection from bitter winter winds.

*Chamaecyparis obtusa* 'Nana', Hinoki cypress. Evergreen conifer; to 100 feet in the wild. Dark green threadlike foliage identified by white lines that resemble stick figures on the leaf undersides. One of the oldest evergreens in continual cultivation, it has been used by the Japanese in rock and stone gardens for centuries. Culture as above. After 30 years tree willl be 30 inches high and 30 inches wide in a rough oval. Since it can be easily damaged by snow, it's a good idea to grow this in a pot. Hardy to USDA Zone 5, but needs protection from heavy snows that can break branches.

*Chamaecyparis pisifera,* Sawara cypress. Evergreen conifer; to 100 feet in the wild. These trees often exhibit 3 different types of foliage: juvenile, which is soft and feathery to the touch and termed "squarrosa"; intermediate, which is a compromise between soft and prickly, called "plumosa"; and the adult form, which is sharp to the touch, "pisifera." There is a fourth, or threadlike, leaf termed "filifera." Culture as above. 'Boulevard' was originally termed *Retinispora pisifera squarrosa cyanoviri-dis* when it was introduced in 1934. The color is blue-gray; growth is pyramidal in form, reaching a height of 6 feet in 10 years. AGR is 6 inches. It may grow 20 feet in 30 years. 'Filifera Aurea' has bright yellow foliage in summer that turns golden brown in winter and is so dense it's hard to probe the interior; UH is 12 to 16 feet, with an US of 5 to 8 feet, and AGR of 8 inches. A beautiful plant at home in most gardens. 'Filifera Nana' has medium green trailing threadlike foliage that weeps; will spread to 3 feet wide and 1 foot high in 10 years. All are hardy in USDA Zone 5.

*Juniperus chinensis,* Chinese junipers. Evergreen conifer. To 60 feet in its native habits. Juvenile leaves are awllike or needle-shaped, while adult forms are scalelike, clasping the shoot and overlapping; berrylike fruit that is really a modified cone coated with resin, and dusted with a bloom; used to flavor gin. Minimal soil demands; lightly acid to neutral pH; most do well in calcareous soils; need watering during extended dry spells and should be pruned in spring to remove winter-damaged branches. 'Iowa' has a blue-green color and grows in an upright manner; in 10 years, tree will be 6 feet high with a base of 3 feet. 'Kaizuka', Hollywood juniper, has normal growth that is upright, but the branches may be pruned with ease, allowing the tree to spread; it will grow 10 feet in 10 years with a bottom of 4 feet in width; UH is 25 feet; will withstand the rigors of climate from southern California to Iowa, and resists pollution. There is also a 'Kaizuka Variegated' that grows in a column, with various patches of creamy yellow, but looks more like a "sick and twisted thing" than a conifer, so best overlook this one. 'Mountbatten' is hardy to the frigid grip of USDA Zone 3, since it originated as a mutant seedling in a Canadian nursery. If not pruned back, it will reach an UH of 16 feet, attaining 10 feet of growth in 10 years, with a pyramidal growth form. 'Pyramidalis' grows in the shape of a pyramid, as its cultivar name implies, with an UH of 16 feet and a 5- to 6-foot-wide base, with typical blue-green color, making a very attractive specimen tree.

*Juniperus communis,* common juniper. Evergreen conifer; to 25 feet in the wild. A low shrub to a tree, growing on rocky hillsides and pastures in the cooler states of the northwest to the northeast. The bark is thin and sheds with ease; needles are sharp with a topside of blue-green and a gray-white underside; berries turn from green to dark blue as they ripen. Very picturesque in windswept locations. Culture as above. 'Echiniformis' is named after a supposed resemblance to a sea urchin but looks, in profile, more like a European hedgehog. This light green bun-shaped plant grows slowly to a 1-foot diameter and a height of 6 inches. 'Depressa Aurea' is a yellow-bronze carpet juniper that darkens to green with the approach of winter. Spread will be 4 feet in 10 years, rarely exceeding 1 foot high, and may be pruned to keep within bounds.

*Juniperus horizontalis,* creeping juniper. To 1½ feet; prostrate evergreen conifer with low, spreading, or creeping habit that varies from cultivar to cultivar; needle- or scalelike foliage of medium green, blue-green, or gray-green, often purple in winter. Tolerates a range of soils, as well as hot, dry, or city conditions. Excellent ground cover; can be pruned back to promote bushy growth. 'Douglasii' originated 135 years ago in Waukegan, Illinois, and is known also as the Waukegan juniper. Main branches hug the ground and side shoots swerve upward; color is blue-green in summer and purple-blue in winter. AGR is 15 inches. Good for seaside gardens. For other cultivars see table, Plants for Japanese Gardens, page 130.

*Juniperus procumbens,* Japanese garden juniper. To 1 foot; prostrate evergreen conifer, low and creeping habit; blue-green needles all year. Culture as for *Juniperus horizontalis,* above. Discovered in the mountains of Japan many hundreds of years ago; AGR is 6 inches, and a plant will eventually cover a circle with a 20-foot diameter in 30 years. 'Nana' (*Juniperus procumbens* 'Nana'), dwarf Japanese juniper. As above, but smaller. Color in spring is light green, darkening to a blue-green. Great bonsai subject as a very small tree or a cascade.

*Juniperus virginiana* 'Skyrocket'. Evergreen conifer; to 50 feet in the wild. Color is silvery blue-green; the tree is completely vertical in habit. This cultivar was found in 1949. In 10 years it will be 12 to 15 feet tall with an UH of 25 feet, but only 1 foot wide at the base. A great accent plant for almost any garden. Culture as for other junipers. Hardy to USDA Zone 3. *Note:* If your garden is in close proximity to an apple orchard, this tree is not for you as it is an alternate host for the apple-rust fungus.

*Picea abies,* Norway spruce. Evergreen conifer; to 150 feet in native habitat. Sharp needles are attached to branches with a tiny stem (sterigma), so when needles fall, the branch remains rough to the touch; cones are blue or green when young, ripening to brown, hanging down from the branch. Tolerant of most urban pollutants, doing well in a variety of soils, but prefers a mildly acid condition. The popular phrase "spruced up" is derived from the neat appearance of these plants. Hardy to USDA Zone 3. 'Nidiformis', bird's-nest spruce. Spring buds are light green against darker green of older needles. Young plants exhibit a slight depression in the center of the top that closely resembles its namesake; dense flat-topped tree with AGR of 3 to 4 inches; final diameter of 6 feet with a height of 4 to 5 feet. 'Pygmaea', pygmy spruce. Form is round, with an AGR of 2 inches, eventually making a globe about 1 foot in diameter after 10 years, then slowing growth by ⅓.

*Picea glauca,* white spruce. Evergreen conifer; to 100 feet in the wild. Needles are dark green with a bloom; a beautiful light green in spring. Good, well-drained moist soil. Height in 10 years will be 6 feet. AGR is 6 inches a year. Will grow slowly and stay small in a garden setting. 'Conica', dwarf Alberta spruce. Grass-green needles are so tightly packed that the tree looks like a solid inverted cone. UH is 15 feet but can be pruned to keep it smaller; AGR is 4 to 6 inches per year. A great accent plant. 'Echiniformis' is a true dwarf among dwarfs—a small pincushion of glaucous gray-green needles. The original appeared in France during the mid-1800s and it has been popular ever since. The UH is only 30 inches, with a spread of some 3 feet; AGR is 1 to 2 inches a year.

*Pinus densiflora,* Japanese red pine. Evergreen conifer; to 115 feet in the wild. Long graceful green needles in bundles of 2, 3, and 5; cones are large and woody. Although preferring full sun, will tolerate some shade; will grow in all kinds of poor soil, but should be planted deep enough to develop a good root system; it resents wet feet. Will usually grow about 10 feet in 10 years in the garden and can be kept small by pruning. With its stems that have a tendency to bend, and the beautiful red shade of young bark, plus the graceful needles, it makes a beautiful small tree. Hardy to USDA Zone 4 with protection from bitter winter winds. 'Umbraculifera', Japanese umbrella pine. Slow-growing cultivar with branches that grow up and around from the trunk like ribs in a wind-turned umbrella. After 35 years it will be 15 feet tall.

*Pinus strobus,* eastern white pine. Evergreen conifer; to 120 feet in the wild. Soft blue-green needles; long, brown, hanging cones. Full sun but will take some shade; any well-drained or evenly moist soil; very adaptable. Hardy to USDA Zone 3. 'Contorta' develops twisted branches bearing densely packed, twisted needles; in 40 years about 18 feet high. 'Nana' has needles so tightly bunched that the trunk is rarely seen; AGR between 2 and 4 inches; UH about 8 feet. 'Pendula', weeping white pine, can assume a height of 12 to 15 feet with a slightly smaller spread, with the trunk bent over and bearing weeping branches; AGR of 1 foot.

*Pinus sylvestris,* Scotch pine. Evergreen conifer; to 100 feet or more in its native habitat. Blue-green 3-inch-long stiff and twisted needles in bunches of 2; reddish trunk; 2½-inch-long cones. Any well-drained average garden soil. Hardy to USDA Zone 2. 'Fastigiata' has blue-green needles on a columnar tree that will reach 8 feet in 10 years, but with very little growth at the base; some 30-foot trees have a 3-foot spread, making it an excellent choice for a small garden; hardy to USDA Zone 3. 'Viridis Compacta' bears lighter-than-type green needles that are twisted and contorted; a slow-growing tree that will reach a height of 6 feet in 15 years. Hardy to USDA Zone 4.

*Sequoia sempervirens* 'Adpressa', dwarf redwood. Evergreen conifer; species grows to 300 feet or more in the wild. Medium green scalelike leaves, ½ inch long, with a bluish bloom underneath; new growth tipped with white; arching stems. Any well-drained good garden soil. This tree can be kept to a dwarf by removing any leaders that develop; will reach a height of 16 feet in a gardener's lifetime—certainly no threat to crowding. Can be grown in a pot, needing plenty of winter light, occasional watering, and temperatures between 35 and 40°F. A beautiful tree. Hardy to USDA Zone 7; best in a protected spot.

*Thuja occidentalis* 'Hetz Midget', dwarf white cedar. Evergreen conifer; to 60 feet in the wild. Dark green scalelike leaves in flattened branches; ¼-inch brown cones. Well-drained, lightly acid garden soil of average fertility. This plant is perfect for the rock garden or dwarf conifer bed, as it will only grow to a height of 2 feet in some 30 years. After 10 years it will be 1 foot high. 'Lutea' grows to 16 feet when mature with an AGR of 6 to 8 inches and an US of 3 feet. During active growth the tips of the branches are a creamy yellow and turn to a golden bronze with winter's advance.

*Tsuga canadensis,* hemlock. To 100 feet or more; evergreen tree with dark shiny green needles having 2 white bands underneath; graceful arching branches; cones are small and brown. Full sun but will adapt to some shade; well-drained or moist average garden soil, slightly acidic; in times of drought, needles may fall, so give necessary soakings. Hardy to USDA Zone 5. Responsible for over 70 recognized cultivars. 'Cole' is an absolutely prostrate tree that actually hugs the ground. Prefers some shade and will not do well in hot sun or an exceptionally dry position. AGR is 3 inches, and a plant will cover an area of a 4-foot circle in 10 years; can be grafted on a standard to form a weeper. Forming an irregular pyramid of very compacted growth, 'Jervis' has yet to grow larger than 30 inches in any direction after being under 30-some years of observaton. 'Gentsch White' has branches with a lacy look, the tips toned a silvery white; UH and US are 2 feet. 'Pendula', Sargent's weeping hemlock, the Rolls-Royce of the hemlock world, was discovered near Fishkill, New York, in 1860 by the first director of the Arnold Arboretum; mature trees resemble shining green mammoths without tusks; best for specimen tree set off by a sweep of lawn; UH is 12 to 15 feet, US is 12 to 25 feet, and AGR is 2 to 3 inches. An excellent specimen at the Garden.

## ESPALIERED TREES AT THE GARDEN

Alexander Pope said of the Earl of Burlington in his *Moral Essays,* "Behold Villerio's ten years' toil complete, His quincunx darkens, his espaliers meet." It's a poetic way to mark the passage of time in the Garden.

Espalier is from the French word *epaule,* or shoulder, thence *epaulet,* the shoulder strap, and the Italian *spella,* or *espalliera,* a special wainscot construction to lean the shoulders against. Through the continual manipulations of language, it came to identify the process of growing shrubs and trees against flat supports or trellises either in front of, or upon, a wall. The quincunx in this case was not the title of a contemporary novel but referred to an old arrangement of planting trees where five trees make a square, four at each corner and one in the center.

The technique of espaliering began in Roman times and was perfected in Europe, where gardens were enclosed and space limited, conditions often cool and cloudy, and fruit trees such as apples and pears greatly benefited from being trained against a sunny and heat-retaining wall. Here in America the process has been used more for decoration than for fruit growing; such plantings have become living screens or have added interest to large blank walls and fences.

Honorio H. Ignacio is Superintendent of Horticulture at the Garden. There his primary responsibility is to work with the gardeners, especially if they have problems with projects they have envisioned, or what they plan to do during the Brooklyn winters; he deals with modifications of their gardens, if necessary, and with additional plantings they may be considering.

"If the gardeners need additional help," he said, "they have to advise me ahead of time because everything has to be timed to the season, including the gathering of all the leaves in the fall before winter sets in—we compost the leaves—and the care and ordering of supplies, especially fertilizers, lime, and mulches, since we order twenty tons a year."

But there is more to his job than that; Mr. Ignacio is the man in charge of all the espaliers in the Garden, including six weeping flowering crabapples.

"I prune those trees," he said, "right after they bloom, then again in early summer, and then again in late September. You have to get rid of the water sprouts (suckers that arise on the trunk) and any branches that sweep up instead of falling directly down."

We asked him how to begin to espalier.

"First," he replied, "if you don't want to damage a stone wall you must use a trellis in front of the wall. An advantage is that it's easier then to trim the tree. And in many walls you are limited to adding supports in the mortar between the stones, and this can be very limiting, so once again a trellis is better. And if the tree is too close to the wall, insects can hide behind the branches and actually find a place to escape insecticides in the crevices of the stone."

Another thing that is necessary for espaliering, according to Mr. Ignacio, "is a western or southern exposure. An eastern exposure is adaptable too, north of New York City. The plants chosen for the process must have small leaves—a leaf more than three inches wide will cast too much of a shadow. Then, the plant must have a long life span because of the work involved, and finally, it must be reasonably resistant to pests and disease."

Espaliered trees can be trained in the shape of fans, gridirons, pyramids, and in oblique, upright, or horizontal cordons; in fact, the only limits are those of imagination and the time that must be devoted to pruning and care.

"Let's say," he continued, "that you have all these things solved and you've picked a cherry, peach, apple, or crabapple. Right at the beginning you have to make a basic decision as to what form you wish to achieve. Next you must visit a nursery or a garden center and look for a suitable plant, free from insects, injury, dead branches, and since all the branches won't apply themselves to espaliering, you will have to know which ones to remove. And if there are any suckers, they also must be removed so that you have one single branch or trunk coming from the base.

"Sometimes you will find a single stem, but no side branches. It might be cheaper but it's no good for espaliering. Often the plant that is available will dictate the design you want."

## • A FEW SUGGESTED TREES FOR ESPALIERING

*Acer palmatum* cultivars
*Camellia japonica,* common camellia
*Cercis canadensis,* Eastern redbud
*Chaenomeles* spp. and cultivars, Japanese quince
*Cornus florida,* flowering dogwood
*Cornus kousa,* Japanese dogwood
*Cornus mas,* cornelian cherry
*Cotoneaster horizontalis,* rockspray cotoneaster
*Euonymus alatus,* winged euonymus
*Forsythia* spp.
Fruits, including apples, pears, plums, cherries, peaches, nectarines, and apricots.
*Hamamelis* spp., witch hazel
*Jasminium nudiflorum,* winter jasmine
*Magnolia grandiflora,* Southern magnolia
*Magnolia tomentosa (M. stellata),* star magnolia
*Malus* 'Red Jade', crab apple
*Philadelphus coronarius,* mock orange
*Pyracantha* spp. and cultivars, firethorns
*Taxus* spp. and cultivars, yews

### STEPS IN ESPALIERING

1. When choosing a design, remember that a more formal approach is usually better in the long run than an informal design. Fruit trees are especially good with the cordon design and U shapes, while yews are best as fans.

2. Since it is hoped that these plants will be in place for a

long, long time, the initial planting must be done with care, using good soil and a decent-sized hole prepared at least eighteen to twenty-four inches deep and up to thirty inches wide.

3. If you are not using a trellis, make sure the base of the plant is at least six inches away from the wall. Use plant stakes when the tree is young, until the branches are strong enough to support themselves.

4. Start with a three-foot shrub or tree as the branches of these are most easily bent to shape.

5. Use special soft ties, garden twine, rubber bands, etc.— but not wire—for holding branches.

6. When training, remember that twigs bend best when young, and should be held in place for a year or so until the branch growth has matured.

7. Only minimal pruning should be done in the first three years.

8. Prune lightly three or four weeks after blooming.

9. Prune if the new growth is over three inches long, to avoid breaking branches because of the weight.

10. The last pruning for the year should be minimal. It is done just as a precautionary measure because a severe winter could bring heavy snow and ice that could break branches. The last pruning is also called "winterizing" the tree.

11. It's a good idea to have a sketch of the desired result in front of you as you prune or you could inadvertently remove the wrong branches and shoots.

There was one final piece of advice from Mr. Ignacio.

"There is not always a guarantee," he said, "that what you buy is what you are going to get. The gardener should check the reputation of the nursery involved. After all, if you are going to invest time and money to have a special tree, it's important to investigate the source of your stock."

CHAPTER TEN

# LAWN GRASSES
# AND
# GROUND
## COVERS

There is a story, probably apocryphal, about two wealthy Americans touring an English estate.

"Goodness," said the wife as they trod the palatial lawn, "this grass is simply beautiful," and turning to the head gardener, she asked, "How in the world does one get a beautiful lawn like this?"

"Well, ma'am," he replied, "first you roll it for four hundred years."

John Kneisel hasn't been rolling the lawns for that long, but one way or another he has been involved in turfing twenty-two acres at the Garden since 1979. He bears the title of Grounds Gardener Turf Specialist (or GGTS for short).

When he began working on the lawns in earnest some five years ago, the problems were the same problems that face many homeowners: crabgrass, insects, grubs, and no individualized programs either for fertilizing or for the application of lime. This last was especially important; Mr. Kneisel counsels that when fertilizer and lime are applied together they can bind each other and be no help to the grass.

"We have split the fertilizer applications into programs," he said, "in March, in June, and September. Even though the grass is going into a dormant phase in winter, the addition of fertilizer in September helps it out next spring when it's ready to take off. And it's important to remember that if you live in a part of the U.S. where the soil is acidic, as it is in Brooklyn, you can add lime at a rate of fifty pounds per thousand square feet to maintain the pH. When more is required, make applications two or three times a year, if necessary; a good pH is between 6.2 and 6.8."

Mr. Kneisel explained that it's perfectly all right to apply lime at any time of the year.

"As for fertilizing, we used a 10–6–4 formula that we would apply in March and in June at half rate. We determined from testing that the nitrogen and potassium levels were low and the phosphorous was high in the soil here so we went to a 25–5–15 to build up the nitrogen and potassium and lower the phosphorous. Next year we'll test again and might try a new ratio. But we have tripled the nitrogen to three pounds per thousand square feet to keep the grass green and growing and to inhibit weed populations, since this garden is subject to high traffic."

Mr. Kneisel recommends using fertilizers that are time/temperature released instead of standard chemical fertilizers, because the latter release all their nutrients at once; that's usually more than the grass can use, and excess leaches into the ground, where it can find its way into the water table and eventually cause pollution.

And as we walked along various pathways that wound through what appeared to be verdant turf, Mr. Kneisel advised caution when applying fertilizers. If it doesn't go down evenly, the gardener will soon see yellow spots where he or she missed, and burned spots where the applications were too heavy.

We asked about the mix of grass seed that best suited the Garden.

"Last year," he said, "we bought five hundred pounds of seed—always buy certified grass seed—and developed various mixes using many grasses. For example, I'll get three varieties of bluegrass that do well in the sun, two bluegrasses meant for shade, two tall fescue grasses for drought areas, two fine fescues, and two narrow-leaf perennial ryes to use as starter grass. Then I'll mix the seed. For example, for the shadiest of areas, I will mix two fescues. For a location a little less shady I would use forty percent fescue (two different types), forty percent shady bluegrasses (two different kinds), and twenty percent rye grasses (again, two types). For a moderately sunny area, a good mix is twenty percent shady bluegrasses (two kinds), sixty percent sunny bluegrasses (three types), and twenty percent rye grasses (two kinds). A good mix for a very sunny location like that in the middle of the Cherry Esplanade is eighty percent sunny bluegrasses (a mix of three kinds) and twenty percent rye grass."

The grasses are also chosen on the basis of resistance to disease, drought, and insects. For a temporary cover he recommends the tall fescues, which are drought-tolerant, and cheaper than bluegrass. Later on you can reseed with a permanent grass mix, after first rototilling, then adding fertilizer, and leveling the area.

## RECOMMENDED LAWN GRASSES

The bent grasses (*Agrostis* spp.) are attractive in a lawn but require frequent mowing and thatch removal. The plants spread by stolons, growing well in humid locations, and do very well in the North but are prone to problems when weather is hot and muggy and they need regular watering and fertilizing. Velvet bent grass *(Agrostis canina)* is sometimes used for putting greens; redtop *(A. gigantea)* is used for both lawns and pastures; and colonial bent grass *(A. tenuis)* is also used for lawns. There are a number of cultivars on the market.

Buffalo grass *(Buchloe dactyloides [B. secundatum]),* on the other hand, is represented by only one species that is especially good in the dry midwestern plains. The low-growing narrow, gray-green blades are less than one-eighth inch wide and form a thick sod that requires little mowing. They can be mixed with other grasses or used to cover dry, exposed banks.

Bermuda grass *(Cynodon dactylon)* is fast-growing, spreading by runners. Although attractive, it needs lots of care, including thatch removal. Full sun is necessary, and as it is not hardy north of Tennessee, this grass is best for southern lawns.

Centipede grass *(Eremochloa ophiuroides)* is a medium-textured, spreading, handsome plant. It prefers soil of poor-to-average fertility, with an acid pH; does not do well in rich, alkaline soil. This grass can be difficult to grow and is best in the South.

Red fescue *(Festuca rubra)* is a fine-textured grass, spreading somewhat by rhizomes. Well suited to poor, dry soil and dry, shady conditions, it will also grow well in sun. Fescues do not thrive in hot, humid weather, but otherwise are very rugged.

Perennial ryegrass *(Lolium perenne)* makes a good starter grass, especially for covering bare soil. Fast-growing, it covers an area quickly, but since it grows in bunches, it is nonspreading. Unfortunately, ryegrasses are not quite as hardy as bluegrass, and do not make really attractive lawns when used by themselves.

The annual ryegrass *(Lolium multiflorum)* quickly sprouts and can be used as a temporary ground cover until there is time to seed a perennial lawn, but it also quickly goes to seed and then dies out.

Bahia grass *(Paspalum notatum)* is a medium-textured grass with flat or folded blades that spreads by runners. Not the best-looking lawn grass, but low in maintenance and adaptable to a range of conditions. Grows best in the South.

Kentucky bluegrass *(Poa pratensis)* is a beautiful, durable grass that recuperates well after winter, spreading by rhizomes. Both sun and shade varieties are available. It does well in northern lawns.

St. Augustine grass *(Stenotaphrum secundatum)* is a coarse-textured plant that spreads quickly by runners. Although growing well in the Deep South, it tolerates shade but is prone to thatch. (A variegated form, 'Variegatum', makes an excellent pot plant.)

The zoysia grasses *(Zoysia* spp.*)* are often the subject of full-page magazine advertisements and have been billed as "miracle grasses." They resemble Bermuda grass but are slow-growing and can be difficult to establish. Although slow to turn green in spring, they are attractive when the change occurs. Very tough and durable, but because of their density, they must be mowed with heavy-duty equipment. They are prone to thatch. Best for southern lawns.


## THE PROBLEM OF SHADE

As we walked the various pathways with Mr. Kneisel, we passed beneath a number of ancient trees with gnarled and protuberant roots and knowing that grass in such places is, at best, spotty, we said, "We have a friend who dotes upon his lawn and every year moans about the condition of the grass beneath a clump of stately old maple trees. Is there any advice for people who have old suburban lawns where the trees provide too much shade?"

"We have an area," Mr. Kneisel answered, "where the grass won't grow because of shade, and we've tried for three years to get something in the grass line to grow there, from shady blue-grass to fine fescues to rye grasses, but they just won't grow. The problem is that the area of lawn beneath a large tree with dense leaf cover suffers from a lack of sunlight, food, and water. Now you could cut off some of the lower branches—making it easier to get in with the lawn mower and adding a bit more light—but with the thickness of those leaves above, you will still have problems with grass. So the best idea there is to plant a shade-loving ground cover."

"How about leaving bare earth around a tree?"

"At one time we had a man who came around and sprayed glyphosphate around the base of many of the trees to remove the grass, but it turns out it's almost easier to cut it than to keep up with that. Eventually you will have weeds where the grass was."

He stopped to examine a patch of newly seeded lawn. At BBG, new lawns are cut three times before any sprays are applied.

"About chemical sprays," he said, "we are all extremely careful when handling them. And that reminds me about weedkillers. They are used in spring and fall—never during hot summer months, when they could damage the grasses. And you have to be careful, especially when the lawn borders a garden area."

## A WATERING SCHEDULE

When asked about watering a lawn, Mr. Kneisel said, "We recommend one or two inches of water a week, and the soil should be moistened to a depth of between four and six inches. Like everything else, a lot of people think that if a little water is good, more is better. But just as a lot of light waterings will encourage weeds and shallow grass roots that will burn on hot days, too much water will waterlog the soil, keeping oxygen away from the roots. Then the shallow roots are prime candidates for destruction, especially in drought conditions. Unless your lawn is on sandy and porous soil, it would be best to wait until the grass shows signs of wilting and then soak with as much water as the ground will hold."

Gardeners should remember that only three-quarter-inch-diameter hoses deliver enough water pressure to properly operate most garden sprinklers, and the sprinkler itself should release large drops of moisture—not a mist—because mist evaporates quickly and much of the water is lost before it reaches the ground.

The timing is important, too. The best times to water are early morning and early evening, to avoid the additional heat of the summer sun and the drying effects of daytime winds.

But how do you know that enough water has been used? Usually 0.6 inches of water will wet the soil to a depth of four inches, with sandy soils taking less, and heavy clay soils needing more. To obtain a four-inch depth of moisture, the gardener would apply 528 gallons of water per thousand square feet. At a standard water pressure of forty psi, using a three-quarter-inch, fifty-foot hose, the sprinkler would release 528 gallons an hour. In forty-five minutes, 375 gallons would be released, thus wetting a completely dry soil to a depth of four inches.

## CUTTING THE LAWN

As to cutting, Mr. Kneisel would mow twice a week in spring and fall if that were practical, but it's not. He does mow weekly, continuing to cut well into November. The cutting height is two and two-thirds inches at all times. By leaving the turf with a greater leaf surface, the plants hold more water and the leaves actually act as umbrellas, shading the roots from both the drying heat and the evaporation of high summer, and also shading out the weeds.

"You can cut shorter," he said, "in early spring and in the fall and keep it at three inches in the summer. You can, of course, mow shorter, but the depth of the rooting will correspond to the mowing height, so a lawn left with longer blades will have a longer and stronger root system that is especially good when water is short. And a longer lawn is less likely to get weedy.

"But," he cautioned, "never remove more than one-third of the leaf blade at any one time, since food is stored in the blades, and removing them also removes food from the plants."

And never forget the importance of a good mower that has sharp blades. Once the blade is dull on a modern rotary mower, it will just beat the grass back, leaving ripped and ragged tops that cause the plants to lose more water, become insect- and disease-prone, and look unsightly.

Finally, when cutting, remember that frequent mowings when the grass is one-third higher than the desired height means grass clippings can be left where they fall, to decompose and help the health of the turf, as well as decreasing trips to the compost heap or the local landfill.

In the authors' lawns, we bag only the clippings that would fall directly in the pathways through the garden and around the front and back doors, so they are not tracked into the house. Everywhere else they fall to the ground.

Mulching mowers are a new development on the lawn-mower market, but we've found that most regular mowers that enable the user to close the side shoot do a good job of returning the clippings to the mowed lawn, where they quickly decompose. If you are using a bagging mower and you remove the bag, remember that the opening must be closed to prevent objects from flying out at a high speed. To avoid pile-ups of clippings, never mow the grass when wet, and never remove more than one-third of the length of the grass blades in a single mowing. Finally, clippings on the lawn do not contribute to thatch buildup. Thatch is made up of tough grass stems and roots and doesn't decompose quickly, while grass blades are soft and quickly disappear.

Recent developments in disposing of clippings include a grass-clippings compost maker that will turn them into compost in less than thirty days. They can also be used to mulch garden beds.

Mr. Kneisel also believes in de-thatching the lawn, but only when this is required. Thatch is the buildup of a layer of plant debris that falls to the base of the sod before it can decay. Thatch makes it difficult (or impossible, if it gets bad enough) for water and fertilizers to penetrate to grass roots. There are machines and attachments for removing thatch. But earthworms are an excellent means of control—a good argument for avoiding the use of pesticides and herbicides at home.

"After you've picked up the thatch," he said, "you can seed needy areas and add a top dressing of a mix of topsoil and sand, and you'll have a beautiful lawn."

## THE CONCEPT OF LAWNS

Now that we've talked about caring for a lawn, just what is a lawn, and what importance does it have for the average home and garden?

Lawn is from the Middle English *launde* and originally meant a heath or moor. Eventually the word became "lawn" and signified an open space between the woods or, more properly, a glade. In 1260 Albert, Count of Bollstädt, wrote in his treatise *On Vegetables and Plants:* "The sight is in no way so pleasantly refreshed as by fine and close grass kept short"; so the idea that an area of open grass is an attractive thing to have is not new. Most likely, since lawns in those times were extremely labor intensive, ample lawns were a sign of wealth—unfortunately, they usually imply the same thing today.

Note also the word "English." England is an island washed by the warm waters of the Gulf Stream and graced with an overabundance of water both from streams and rivers, plus fogs and rain. Vegetation flourishes, and lawns are a thing of beauty—in England.

When the first settlers came to the Northeast and brought with them the idea of the lawn, it worked because both climates, while not exactly alike, had sufficient water to support the grass. But problems arise when the idea of a lawn is moved to the outskirts of Las Vegas or Los Angeles, where the climate is desertlike or Mediterranean, and a lawn is not only unnatural but in these days of shrinking water reserves, also immoral.

Unfortunately, as mentioned before, the establishment of a large lawn is still seen as a sign of wealth. Often today's concept of a mansion (or for that fact, just a small home) is still visualized as perched in the middle of a gigantic expanse of green that requires both above and underground sprinklers, chemical weed control, and large riding mowers to keep it clipped and neat. The result is too much damage to the environment and too much use of water—this last a commodity increasingly in short supply all around the country.

Some communities, in fact, have recently passed ordinances not only to curtail the use of water for lawns and gardens but also to control the roar of dozens of engines from dozens of rotary lawn mowers all going at the same time on Saturday mornings and piercing the suburban air with both noise and exhaust.

But the question remains: Is a small area of lawn a worthy enhancement to the home and garden? In our opinion, yes, but with the following stipulations: (1) where the climate is receptive and the water is available; and (2) where the lawn is small and treated as another perennial plant, something to add color and texture to the garden. But if that available water comes from a water table or a community system already in short supply, the answer is a resounding *No!*

There are many ways to landscape and garden in a home employing drought-tolerant grasses and ground covers and plants native to the area, and with a skillful use of the landscape, a house, whether old or new, will become a home.

And if you do have a lawn, remember that, like anything else in this world, a good lawn is an investment in time. Perhaps four hundred years is not necessary, but allow at least two or three years for the grass to settle in. Then sit back and enjoy your effort.

## CARING FOR A LAWN

Start with soil in the best possible condition: cultivate before planting, mix in fertilizer, lime if needed, and organic matter. Prepare the soil this way whether you are seeding or sodding. This last process is the result of buying rolled-up squares of earth already planted with mature lawn grasses and laying them on bare earth.

Test the pH before planting; many people over-lime their lawn.

Choose the right combination of grasses for your climatic conditions; there are grasses for warm climates, cool climates, sun, shade, and humid or dry conditions.

If you sow seed, mulch with straw, loose burlap, or pine branches to keep seeds from washing away or clumping up in the rain, and to hold needed moisture.

Early spring and early fall are good times to seed a lawn. Seedlings should appear two to three weeks after planting. Sod will take about six weeks to establish new roots; keep it moist throughout the rooting period.

John Kneisel recommends fertilizing in March, June, and September with a high-nitrogen fertilizer that supplies one pound of actual nitrogen per thousand square feet.

When applying fertilizers, be sure to spread them evenly.

Otherwise you will find yellow spots where the fertilizer missed, and burned spots where it was applied too heavily.

As a general rule, lawns need one to two inches of water each week. When you water, do it thoroughly. Lots of light waterings are necessary when grass seed is germinating and beginning to take root; this may take three weeks. But thereafter, shallow watering will encourage weed growth and will promote weak root systems on grass plants. Less frequent—but using enough water—waterings are better.

Mow the lawn once or even twice a week throughout the growing season, continuing into mid-fall. Mow to about two and a half inches; cutting too short keeps root systems smaller.

If you use weedkillers, be extremely careful! Follow the label instructions explicitly. Apply herbicides in late spring, when the weeds are young, or in fall. BBG gardeners wear protective gear when applying herbicides and pesticides in the Garden.

De-thatch the lawn once a year, if necessary. Seed any empty spots, then top dress the lawn with a mixture of topsoil and sand.


## GROUND COVERS

There are many reasons to turn to ground covers in the garden: too much lawn to cut, and consequently a need to cut back on maintenance; covering an area of ground unreceptive to grass; a desire to construct living areas of color to set off the rest of the garden; cutting back on the job of weeding; and covering the ground after spring bulbs have finished blooming.

We must confess to preferring islands of green in shady spots, areas covered with ivy or pachysandra or luxuriant hostas rather than endless expanses of mown grass. And while steppingstones are attractive, they are even more so when surrounded by creeping thyme or tiny mountains of Scotch moss. And as an alternative to risking dismemberment by Rube Goldberg methods of guiding power mowers up and down steep grass-covered slopes, planting ground covers does an infinitely better job without the effort.

Almost any plant will work as a ground cover given sufficient time and money, but just as in other parts of the horticultural world, certain plants will do a faster and better job of covering the earth than others.

Prepare the soil for planting just as you would when setting out perennials or putting in grass. Add sufficient humus to poor soil, as even tough ground covers like the common daylily will do infinitely better in better soil.

## • GROUND COVERS

Low-growing cotoneasters and evergreens, ferns, hostas, and spreading herbs like sweet woodruff and thyme can make excellent ground covers, and many are mentioned below.

*Aegopodium podograria* 'Variegatum', goutweed, bishop's-weed. To 14 inches. Deciduous, with divided leaves, edged with white; clusters of tiny white flowers on tall stems in early summer. Any below-average garden soil in full sun or partial to full shade; leaves often burn at tips in full sun. Good underplanting in open woods or on banks or slopes. *Warning:* This plant can be very invasive, spreading by the tiniest piece of root or seeds that sprout with ease. Use it only in an area where such behavior is welcomed.

*Ajuga reptans,* carpet bugle. To 4 inches. Evergreen in warmer climates, with oblong leaves, green, purple, variegated, or crisped, depending on the cultivar; small spikes of violet, pink, or white flowers in late spring. Partial shade to full sun, in any average garden soil, dry or moist. Water during long spells of dry weather, especially if growing in full sun. Good underplanting for shrubs; easily spreads and must be kept under control with a barrier.

*Arctostaphylos uva-ursi,* bearberry. To 5 inches. Evergreen, with small oval leaves turning red-violet in autumn; small white or pink flowers like overturned urns followed by red berries that are attractive to wildlife. Full sun to partial shade; tolerates a wide range of soil, including sandy soil of low fertility; needs very acid pH (5.0 or lower) to do well. Tough and durable, withstanding seaside conditions.

*Asarum europaeum,* European or wild ginger. To 8 inches. Evergreen, low-growing and spreading; heart-shaped leaves; purplish or brown flowers like little jugs at base of plant. Partial shade to shade, in moist soil rich in organic matter. Lovely in woodland gardens.

*Convallaria majalis,* lily-of-the-valley. To 8 inches. Deciduous, upright, pointed oval leaves appear at plant's base; spikes of little bell-shaped fragrant white flowers in spring. Partial shade to shade; tolerates a wide range of soils. Easy to grow and spreads quickly. One drawback is that leaves lose their good looks as summer progresses and may die back before frost, but worth it for the look and smell of the flowers in spring.

*Dennstaedtia punctilobula,* hay-scented fern. To 30 inches. Deciduous fern with narrowly triangular leaves; fronds are sweet-scented when crushed or drying; turns a beautiful light golden brown in autumn. Full sun to partial shade; adaptable to almost any soil, withstands drought, and will do well among rocks and boulders, making it a good choice to carpet a bank or slope. Too invasive for the formal garden.

*Dichondra micrantha (D. repens).* Prostrate and creeping. Evergreen rounded leaves under 1 inch in diamater, spread by underground stolons; flowers are inconspicuous. An effective ground cover in areas of low traffic in USDA Zones 9 and 10; plants are killed when ground freezes to 4-inch depth; especially popular in California. Full sun to partial shade. Soil on the acid side with plenty of organic matter; resents heavy clay soil; needs frequent watering. May be mowed if it starts to look uneven; especially good for areas between steppingstones.

*Epimedium* spp., barrenwort. To 1 foot. Evergreen/deciduous depending on the climate; oval heart-shaped leaves, light green when new, often bronzing as season progresses; clusters of odd-shaped tubular flowers in early spring, in pink, yellow, orange, red, or white, depending on the species. Partial shade, in moist but well-drained, fertile soil. Excellent in rock gardens. Transplants easily, especially in spring, and should be divided every few years.

*Euonymus fortunei,* wintercreeper. Trailing or climbing by rootlets. Evergreen leathery oval leaves; creeping stems, but will climb trees; tiny flowers. Full sun to partial shade; not fussy as to soil but performs best in good garden soil. One of the best ground covers for flat or sloped areas, but it will also climb walls and trees. There are a number of varieties, cultivars, and forms, many with interesting variegations and colors.

*Festuca ovina* var. *glauca.* To 14 inches. Deciduous grass with slender blades covered with a bluish bloom, growing in clumps; flowers are attractive but insignificant. Full sun or partial shade; good garden soil. Since it's a clump-growing grass, individual plants will never meld, but make an interesting and unusual display. Best used as a pattern ground cover allowing the earth (mulched or not) to show between plants.

*Hedera helix* and varieties, English ivy. To 10 inches. Evergreen lobed glossy deep green leaves, in various sizes, variegated with white or yellow in some cultivars. Sun or shade, in any average garden soil. Spreads and can become invasive or "too much of a good thing," but easy to grow, durable, and attractive in both warm and reasonably cold climates.

*Hemerocallis fulva,* common daylily. To 6 feet in bloom. Deciduous, 2-foot long, straplike leaves from central crown; brownish-orange lilies bloom in June and July, each blossom lasting but a day. Full sun to partial shade in any average garden soil. Excellent (and inexpensive) when used to carpet banks or slopes or flat areas at the edge of woods and shrubberies. The recommended plant is the common wild daylily, not one of the sophisticated hybrids. Remove scapes after bloom for a neater appearance.

*Hosta* spp., plaintain lily. To 3 feet in bloom. Deciduous, attractive rounded or pointed leaves from central crown; pleasing flowers in various shades of blue or white. Full sun to partial shade in any average garden soil, but attain larger size and better flowers in moist soil with organic matter. Easy to transplant. Marvelous ground covers, especially under tall trees; individual plants soon have overlapping leaves. Some cultivars better for sun than others, so consult nursery listings.

*Houttuynia cordata* 'Chameleon' or 'Variegata'. To 9 inches. Deciduous heart-shaped leaves, many variegated with yellow, pink, and red; small spikes of white flowers resembling fibrous begonia blossoms to some people and little white zinnias to others, bloom in early summer. Full sun to partial shade, in moist, or even wet, soil. Spreads by means of underground stolons and can be invasive and difficult to eradicate should you decide you don't like it. Easy to grow and quite hardy to −35°F.

*Iberis sempervirens*, edging candytuft. To 12 inches high. Evergreen subshrub with narrow leaves; small 4-petaled white (turning a bit pink with age) flowers with 2 petals longer than the other two bloom in racemes that lengthen with age in late spring. Trim back the plants after flowering. Excellent tumbling over walls and stones.

*Juniperus horizontalis*, creeping juniper. To 1½ feet high. Evergreen prostrate conifer with low, spreading or creeping habit that varies from cultivar to cultivar; needle- or scalelike foliage of medium green, blue-green, or gray-green, often purple in winter. Tolerates a range of soils, as well as hot, dry, or city conditions. Excellent ground cover; can be pruned back to promote bushy growth. 'Douglasii' originated 135 years ago in Waukegan, Illinois, and is known also as the Waukegan juniper. Main branches hug the ground and side shoots swerve upward; color is blue-green in summer and purple-blue in winter. Average growth rate is 15 inches per year. Good for seaside gardens. For other cultivars see table, Plants for Japanese Gardens, page 130.

*Lamium maculatum*, dead nettle. To 1½ feet. Deciduous oval green leaves are silvery or tinged with yellow or white in some cultivars; clusters of small red-violet, purple, or white flowers in late spring and summer. Full sun to shade, in any moist but well-drained soil. Plant has a spreading form and can cover sparse areas in woodland or perennial gardens. 'Beacon Silver' is especially popular. Attractive as an edging.

*Liriope* spp., lilyturf, mondo grass. To 1½ feet. Evergreen narrow grassy leaves, variegated with white or yellow in some cultivars; slender spikes of tiny purple, deep blue, or white flowers in mid- to late summer, followed by blue-black berries. Sun to shade in moist soil rich in organic matter; will also tolerate dry soil. Clump-forming plants will spread, and can be further increased by division. An especially good ground cover in mild climates. Can suffer winter damage if climate is too cold. Remove damaged leaves in early spring before new growth appears.

*Mesembryanthemum* spp., ice plant. To 4 inches. Succulent trailing and running plants with curved, cylindrical leaves, some with a marked crystalline appearance, hence the common name; dazzling, daisylike flowers of red, cerise, purple, yellow, pink, and white. Full sun in a good, well-drained soil. Excellent and striking ground covers in areas where winters do not fall below freezing. Many species and cultivars available.

*Pachysandra terminalis,* Japanese spurge. To 10 inches. Evergreen dark green 4-inch-long leaves whorled about stem tops; terminal spikes of off-white flowers. Partial shade to full shade in a wide range of soils from light and well-drained to heavy clay, as long as there is adequate moisture. Cannot tolerate full sun, especially in the South, as it will then turn an unpleasant yellow-green. 'Silveredge' is exactly what the name implies. Probably the most popular ground cover, and frankly a bit overused, but still more practical than most. *P. procumbens,* Allegheny spurge, is a native American species with dull green leaves, tinted with silver markings, deciduous in colder climates; fluffy white flowers in early spring. Beautiful ground cover, but usually overlooked.

*Parthenocissus quinquefolia,* Virginia creeper. To 8 inches when trailing. Deciduous vine with 6-inch wide deeply cut leaves, turn a beautiful red in autumn; insignificant flowers followed by attractive black berries. Full sun to partial shade in a wide range of soils including woodland to clay. Usually grown as a vine, but will ramble along the ground, its big leaves making a most attractive display, especially in a woodland garden. Extremely hardy.

*Pulmonaria officinalis,* lungwort. To 1 foot tall. Deciduous oval leaves (evergreen in mild climates), heavily spotted with white; white, blue, or pink nodding bell-shaped flowers. Partial to full shade, especially in the South, in moist soil with plenty of organic matter. Plants spread with an underground creeping rhizomes. Once thought to be a cure for lung diseases since the spotted leaves were thought to resemble lungs.

*Sagina subulata,* Scotch moss. To 4 inches tall. Evergreen plants with tiny leaves; little star-shaped white flowers in summer. Full sun in moist soil with organic content. Quickly spreading ground cover. Especially fine between steppingstones and flagstone pathways. *S. subulata* var. *aurea* has bright yellow-green leaves.

*Sedum spurium* 'Dragon's Blood', stonecrop. To 4 inches. Succulent leaves, 1 inch long; bright red starlike flowers. Full sun to light shade in almost any well-drained soil. Excellent running around rocks.

*Vinca minor,* myrtle, periwinkle. To 6 inches. Evergreen, glossy, deep green, oval leaves; single blue flowers in spring. Full sun to partial or open shade. Adapts to all soil types, spreading by means of runners. A pretty plant both in and out of bloom. A number of cultivars feature different flower colors.

# CHAPTER ELEVEN

# WATER GARDENS

The wonder of water gardens is that anyone who has room for a bunch of marigolds or a small clump of ivy can make room to install a plastic washtub to hold a tropical water lily, or half of a wine keg in which to grow a collection of small aquatics. One of the most imaginative water gardens we ever saw consisted of five such tubs installed on a slight slope, their even, circular edges hidden by pieces of flagstone and their waters connected by short lengths of plastic tubing that were hidden by other stones. The first tub in the line received a slight trickle of water from a garden hose, and that was enough for consecutive overflows, the last tub dripping its water around most of its circumference and wetting enough soil to host a lovely mixed planting of cardinal flowers *(Lobelia cardinalis)*, sensitive fern *(Onoclea sensibilis)*, and various species of primrose.

"Water in a landscape is as a mirror to a room," wrote Neltje Blanchan in *The American Flower Garden*, published in 1909, "the

219

feature that doubles and enhances all its charms. Whoever may possess a lake, a pond, or a pool to catch the sunbeams, duplicate the trees and flowers on its bank, reflect the moon, and multiply the stars, surely will."

## WATER IN THE GARDEN

At the Garden, the outdoor pools are under the charge of Bernard Currid, the same man who champions the Herb Garden and many of the other flower beds.

The conservatory pools are in the capable hands of Michael Ramirez, a gardener who also takes care of the orchid collection.

There, under a glassed-in sky, are large rectangular pools of water containing plants acclimated to, or belonging in, water. The day we met was very hot, but the plants were all doing well, including a spectacular example of the Egyptian papyrus plant, this particular specimen towering well above our heads.

"That's *Cyperus giganteus*," said Mr. Ramirez. "It was unidentified for a long time but our taxonomist was able to key it out."

We stopped to gaze at a bed of water cannas, their large red petals bunched atop long stems and surrounded by very slender leaves. These marvelous plants are the new Longwood hybrids of the water canna; they adapt to a moist environment—something that cannot be done with the typical canna (*Canna* × *generalis*).

On the window side of the walkway that surrounds the pools are small raised planters, rectangular wooden frames on legs that bring them waist-high. They contain trays of water and a number of smaller water plants.

"These are made of a laminated wood," he said, "and hold trays from the hardware store. Here I have a batch of water snowflake *(Nymphoides cristata)*. People could grow many tropical water plants in their homes just like houseplants, provided they have at least five hours of sunlight or other strong light each day." The trays holding the small plants are about four feet high, and would provide easy access for gardeners in wheelchairs.

We then asked the question that most water gardeners ask: "What do you do to prevent—or don't you prevent—algae?"

"Algae," he answered, "are something you have to expect in any new aquarium or pool. Initially, you're going to get algae.

Usually when you begin such a garden, you may not have many higher plants that are established and growing and acting as competitors, so algae become the dominant vegetation. But later, once everything is planted, and fish are added (I try to avoid snails because, being vegetarians, they can disfigure plants), the water reaches a condition of desired clarity.

"Have patience and over time it will be difficult, or almost impossible, to get that pea-soup type of algae to repeat itself. You can use filters that will strain all that minute algae out of the water, but it's going to come back again once the pump is turned off, until it's all in balance."

A number of fish moved through the waters at our feet.

"Those are blue gouramis and paradise fish from tropical Asia. I chose them since they are air breathers. They can live in warm, stagnant water with very low dissolved-oxygen levels—goldfish couldn't tolerate that. And they're good at routing out larvae, mosquitoes, and also aphids that wash into the water."

"What is involved in maintaining those trays once you get things stabilized?" we asked.

"If an algal scum develops on those trays, every morning without fail I get out the hose and nozzle, adjust the spray, and carefully direct a jet across the surface of the water, breaking up the surface tension, then skim off the floating algae.

"And," he added, "it's important to realize that chlorinated water is bad for plants and fish, but the chlorine will dissipate if the water is left to sit for forty-eight hours or so, depending on the size of the container and the temperature of the water."

Another convenient thing about the water gardens is that all the plants are in individual black plastic pots and never planted directly into a submerged soil; the medium is ordinary garden topsoil. The water lilies in the big outdoor pools are in wooden containers. There they are planted in large square and rectangular boxes made of cypress, and those boxes last for years.

To fertilize the plants, Mr. Ramirez takes a handful of a 5–10–5 or a 10–10–10 granular fertilizer and puts it in cheesecloth—some people use newspaper—making a little ball that is pushed into the soil of the pots. The amount of fertilizer depends on the size of the containers. Fertilizing is done on a monthly basis during late spring and summer, when the plants are actively growing. He notes, however, that these fertilizers should not be used where fish are kept—the phosphate they contain may kill the fish. In water gardens containing fish, Mr. Ramirez advises using a fertilizer without phosphate, and adding bone meal to supply phosphorus.

As we left the aquatic houses, Mr. Ramirez was busy pulling dead and dying leaves out of the water.

"The most important thing to have," he said, "is interest, because when you're faced with little problems you have to solve them. And there is a daily vigilance you have to maintain in any kind of garden. Here it's freshening the water, removing dead and spotted leaves. There's a vigilance about the insects.

"Toward autumn there may be a problem that in fish pathology is known as "autumn disease." With the shortening days of fall and winter, vegetative growth slows down, and there is less utilization of available nitrogen by the plants. If the levels rise too much, conditions become toxic—that's why it's important to be able to flush the water and keep your eyes open for trouble. I replace a third of the old water with dechlorinated water."

## THE WATER LILIES

Outside of the Aquatic House, the long pools that front the new wing connecting the old Administration Building with the new conservatory are so full of blooming water lilies that it's difficult to believe that autumn or winter will ever appear again.

Occasionally a green heron will dart across the surface of the water, and tiny drops fly into the air with a sparkling flourish, then roll down the leaves of the lotus plants the way beads of mercury roll down a piece of glass, while dragonflies flit from lily pad to lily pad.

"The water lilies," said Bernard Currid, "do very well. I treat them with 10–6–4 fertilizer by making satchels of burlap that contain several handfuls of fertilizer, and in the late winter I just take aim and throw a bag into each planter box. The tropicals get fertilizer when they are planted.

"The pool's chief problem is all the leaves that fall into the water, and also dead leaves left by the lilies. I also use the green or black dye used in food coloring that helps to keep down the algae by cutting back on the light."

We asked when was the proper time to plant tropical lilies.

"Tropicals," he answered, "should be planted when the

water is above 70°F, and hardy lilies when the water is above 60°F. The fish, by the way, stay out all winter. They are perfectly all right as long as the pool is sufficiently deep.

"And remember that water lilies will go into a rest period if confronted with a sudden drop in water temperature, so when changing water in an ornamental pool, make sure the coldness is cut by adding lukewarm water."

## THE HARDY WATER LILIES

Hardy water lilies are perennials and can be left outdoors the year round as long as the water in your pond does not freeze to the bottom. If they cannot have such protection, the best thing is to lift the pots from the pond and store them for the winter in your basement, where the roots should be kept cool and moist until the following spring.

All the plants grown in the pools need five or six hours of direct sun a day. The blossoms—many kinds are fragrant—float upon the water's surface, opening in the morning and closing in the afternoon; they last three or four days before dying. A healthy plant will continue to produce buds throughout the season. Many water lilies make good cut flowers.

Some good, hardy water lilies are listed below.

*Nymphaea* "Marliacea Albida' is a superb fragrant white, with a 6- to 8-foot spread, needing full sun and excellent for the small pond; *N.* × 'Virginia' produces non-fragrant white double flowers and will spread up to 12 feet.

*Nymphaea* 'Fabiola' has a classic pink flower and a 6-foot spread; it has a slight fragrance and needs full sun. *N.* 'Pink Sensation' will spread up to 12 feet, needs full sun, and bears large, light pink flowers that remain open until late in the afternoon.

*Nymphaea* 'Charlene Strawn' is a beautiful yellow-gold fragrant flower, spreading to 12 feet, holding the blooms above the water's surface, and needing a bit less sun than those about to flower. *N.* 'Sunrise' bears very large yellow flowers that stay open later in the afternoon and spread to 12 feet; it needs full sun.

*Nymphaea* 'Ellisiana' bears many-petaled, deep red flowers on plants especially suited for small ponds, spreading up to 6 feet and needing full sun; they are best for northern ponds as temperatures above 95°F cause the flowers to burn. *N.* 'James Brydon' has a glorious and fragrant cup-shaped red flower on plants that spread up to 12 feet but are also at home in the smaller pond. These need full sun.

*Nymphaea* 'Graziella' is called a "changeable" lily, as it's nearly yellow when it first opens, then changes to a copper bronze with age; spread is about 6 feet, and a bit less than full sun is needed for flowering.

## THE TROPICAL WATER LILIES

Tropicals are tender plants and in climate zones colder than USDA Zone 10 are usually treated as disposable annual flowers. They can be taken up and stored under water in a warm greenhouse, and with the increasing daylight of spring new leaves will appear. But not many home gardeners have the facilities or space for this sort of storage.

The flowers are either day-blooming or night-blooming, needing five to six hours of direct sunlight. The very fragrant blossoms stand above the water's surface and will bloom all summer. Tropicals all make excellent cut flowers.

Among the night-bloomers recommended by the Garden, *Nymphaea* 'Juno' is a beautiful large white, needing a bit less than five hours of sun to bloom and spreading to twelve feet; 'Red Flare' has red-tinged foliage and flowers with dark red petals and stamens of deep maroon. It needs full sun.

The following day-blooming tropicals are in the Garden's pools:

*Nymphaea* 'Mrs. George H. Pring' bears large white flowers that rise above lightly speckled leaves, taking slightly less than full sun and spreading to twelve feet. *N.* 'Evelyn Randig' has classic deep magenta flowers and variegated foliage, needing full sun and spreading to twelve feet. *N.* 'Daubeniana' is blue; it takes slightly less than full sun and spreads a little over six feet; it is also viviparous, forming small plantlets where the leaf blade meets the leaf stalk.

## THE MAGNIFICENT LOTUS

A noble and majestic flower, the lotus is the blossom in which Buddha sits, steeped in the fragrance of far-off lands. After

slabs or other stone. If you want a formal look, you could lay stone paving on a bed of mortar. If you intend to put fish in the pool, let the water settle for a week before they join in the swim. You can use a siphon to empty the pool, but it is perfectly all right to leave such an installation all season long.


## MAKING A BOG GARDEN

Even if you do not wish to have an open pool, the same liners can be used to make an area of land that will become boggy and wet, thus opening up the garden world to a large number of plants that are especially happy at the water's edge.

The concept is the same as with pools, but here you excavate to a depth of one foot and replace the soil after the liner is in position.


## TIPS ON PLANTING
## AQUATIC PLANTS AND POOLS

When planting any of the following water plants, do not use commercial potting soils or mixes, as they often contain various materials such as vermiculite, perlite, and numerous other fillers that will float. Instead, use good garden soil on the heavy side.

Start the lotus rhizome in shallow water. The rhizome is banana-shaped and should be planted at an angle with the bud pointed up. Do not damage the bud; if it breaks, another may not sprout. Rhizomes need rich soil and plenty of room. Use a thirty-quart plastic tub and fill it halfway with soil, adding fertilizer or prepared fertilizer tabs; then put in remaining soil. Make a slight impression in the soil and carefully place the rhizome in position. Cover the rhizome with two inches of soil at the heavy end and extend the growing end above the soil by a half-inch. Lower the contained plant into the water until the rhizome is covered with two inches of water. As it grows, gradually increase the depth to six to twelve inches. Lotus are perfectly hardy as long as the water does not freeze.

To plant water lilies, fill the container half full of topsoil, carefully set the rootstock on the soil, then add more soil, pushing it around the roots, keeping the crown free of soil. Cover the soil with a half-inch of pea gravel or very small stones, still keeping the crown uncovered. Then saturate with water. Gently lower the tub into the water.

To plant bog plants, use good garden soil with some humus added. Fill container with soil, then push in roots of the plant, tamping the soil, and covering the surface with one inch of pea gravel or small stones. Saturate the pot with water, then lower gently into the pool or pond, setting the plant at the correct water depth. Use bricks or fieldstones to adjust the plant to the appropriate level.

Individual fertilizer bags can be made of cheesecloth, or even newspaper, filled with a handful of 5–10–5 or 10–10–10, and stuck into the wet soil.

If using chlorinated water, let it sit up to forty-eight hours before adding fish or plants.

Always remove dead and rotting leaves from the pool to prevent any chance of disease.

## • PLANTS FOR OUTDOOR WATER GARDENS

*Acorus calamus* 'Variegatus', variegated sweet flag. To 2½ feet high; slender sword-shaped leaves, striped with yellow, fragrant when crushed (used in hair oil); flowers on a green spadix. Full sun to partial shade, in boggy soil or shallow water to 6 inches deep. Can also be grown indoors. Roots have a spicy-sweet scent. *A. gramineus* 'Variegatus', miniature variegated sweet flag. To 18 inches high; swordlike leaves arranged like a fan with lengthwise stripes of white and green arise from rhizome that is not aromatic. Small and beautiful.

*Caltha palustris,* marsh marigold. To 2 feet. Succulent heart-shaped leaves; loose clusters of bright yellow flowers an inch across bear 5 waxy petals, blooming in early spring. Full sun until leaves appear, then partial shade; moist soil, but will luxuriate in a few inches of water. Early settlers ate new greens like spinach. Plants go dormant in summer.

*Canna* hybrids and cultivars, water canna. Rhizomes similar to the well-known favorites, but suited to wet conditions. To 6 feet. Large upright leaves; spikes of showy large-petaled flowers in various warm colors in summer. Full sun, in boggy soil or up to 6 inches of water. A group of newly introduced hybrids developed at Longwood Gardens is especially lovely, with slender leaves and flowers of salmon, yellow, or red. 'Endeavour', a clear red; 'Erebus', pink; 'Ra', like the Sun God, and yellow; and 'Taney', a bright orange. Store roots indoors over winter everywhere except USDA Zone 10.

*Chelone glabra,* turtlehead. To 4 feet. Narrow oval leaves to 6 inches long; clusters of white (sometimes pink) flowers, which resemble snapdragons but are well named "turtlehead." Full sun to light shade, in moist, humusy soil; best along the water's edge.

*Eleocharis tuberosa (E. dulcis),* Chinese water chestnut. To 3 feet. Clumps of tubular stems; straw-colored catkins in summer. Its corms are the water chestnuts used in Chinese cooking. Full sun to partial shade, in boggy soil or up to 1 foot of water. Not hardy north of USDA Zone 9.

*Eleocharis montevidensis,* spike rush. Perennial, to 1 foot. Quill-like leaves grow in a clump; flowers are brown buttons. Full sun in boggy soil or up to 2 inches of water. Very attractive, unusual plant. Hardy to USDA Zone 6.

*Equisetum hyemale,* horsetail, scouring rush. Perennial to 4 feet. Grows along streams, lakes, ditches, and the edges of old railroad beds. Evergreen shoots grow from a perennial rhizome and have such a high silica content that in pioneer days they were used to clean and polish pots and pans. Conelike caps produce spores, not seeds. Full sun to partial shade in boggy soil but will grow in a few inches of water. *Warning:* make sure you section off the area, as these ancient rushes are very, very invasive. In addition to the larger types, there are some that remain very small. *E. scirpoides,* the dwarf scouring rush, has 3-inch-high threadlike stems, perfect for miniature water gardens and bonsai applications. Also invasive in the garden.

*Eupatorium purpureum,* joe-pye weed. Perennial to 10 feet; toothed leaves and large terminal clusters of tiny purplish flowers. Roots once had medicinal uses including treatment of kidney problems. Full sun to partial shade; moist, fertile soil; best planted at the water's edge. Grows wild throughout much of America. Large and striking in perennial border and magnificent at the edge of a small pool or pond.

*Iris pseudacorus,* yellow water iris, yellow flag. To 5 feet. Sword-shaped light green leaves; yellow iris flowers. Full sun; moist or boggy soil. Especially fine at the water's edge, and in up to 10 inches of water. The Garden has a large collection of these plants in the lake in the Japanese Hill-and-Pond Garden.

*Iris sibirica,* Siberian iris. Perennial to 3 feet. Clumps of sword-shaped leaves; flowers in many shades of blue and an excellent white. Full sun to partial shade, in any good garden soil, but adapts with ease to moist, boggy conditions or water depth of 4 inches.

*Marsilea mutica*, water clover. Foliage floats on water. Leaves are four-leaf clovers marked with yellow patterns; this is a water fern and bears no flowers. Full sun to partial shade in water depth up to 1 foot deep. Hardy to USDA Zone 6.

*Matteuccia struthiopteris*, ostrich fern. Perennial to 3 feet. Large fronds resemble ostrich feathers and grow from central crown. Partial to woodland shade; moist soil rich with organic matter. A group of these plants will brighten the edge of any pond or pool.

*Miscanthus sinensis* 'Gracillimus', maiden grass. Perennial to 7 feet. Thin arching blades with narrow white centers; flowers in plumes with metallic cast before opening. Full sun; moist, fertile soil; best planted at the water's edge. Many ornamental grasses do well in moist soil, some planted directly in the water, but maiden grass has just the right look and grace for the water's edge.

*Nelumbo lutea* and *N. nucifera* and cultivars, lotus. To 5 feet. Large round leaves that repel water; big showy fragrant flowers in many warm colors, standing above the water's surface, blooming for 6 to 8 weeks in summer. Flowers are followed by distinctive seedpods, good for drying.

*Nymphaea* cvs., hardy water lilies. Perennials with floating, round leaves, mottled in many varieties; floating blossoms all summer, some fragrant, in shades of red, pink, yellow, and white. Full sun, in water 6 inches to 1½ feet deep.

*Nymphaea* cvs., tropical water lilies. Large floating round leaves, mottled in many varieties; blossoms usually on stems above water, some opening at night; shades of red, pink, purple, blue, yellow, and white. Full sun, in water 6 inches to 1½ feet deep. Grow as tender annuals except in USDA Zone 10. Good for cut flowers.

*Nymphoides peltata*, floating heart. Perennial with floating 3-inch leaves variegated with maroon; 5-petaled yellow flowers sit above water surface. Full sun to partial shade in up to 1 foot of water.

*Osmunda regalis*, royal fern. Perennial to 5 feet. Long fern fronds from central crown. Light shade in moist soil rich with organic matter. Start with young plants, as mature specimens are difficult to move.

*Pontederia cordata*, pickerel weed. To 3 feet. Glossy green heart-shaped leaves; spikes of tiny blue flowers in midsummer. Full sun to partial shade, in boggy soil or water up to 1 foot deep. Good cover plant for fish.

*Scirpus tabernaemontani* 'Zebrinus', variegated bulrush. To 2 feet. Round stems with sharp points resemble porcupine needles and are banded with white; leaves are brown sheaths at base of stem. Full sun to partial shade, in boggy soil or shallow water. Striking plant for the water garden. Not hardy north of USDA Zone 6.

*Thalia dealbata.* To 6 feet. Graceful broad oblong leaves similar to cannas, to 3 feet on tall stems; spikes of light blue-violet flowers in summer. Full sun to partial shade, in boggy soil or up to 1 foot of water. Beautiful plant and does well in a pot set inside a larger pot full of water. Not hardy in northern U.S.

*Typha* spp., cattails. To 7 feet, depending on the species; upright slender grassy leaves; large brown catkins in summer. Full sun to partial shade, in boggy soil or up to 10 inches of water. *T. latifolia* is typical wild species. *Warning:* care should be taken as this species is very invasive; cultivar 'Variegata', with vertical green and white stripes on the leaf, is safer and more attractive; *T. angustifolia,* narrow-leaved cattail, has more graceful leaves than *T. latifolia; T. minima,* miniature cattail, grows 2 feet tall, with very narrow leaves and small catkins.

## • *PLANTS FOR INDOOR WATER GARDENS*

The following plants are recommended for a water garden set in a greenhouse or a conservatory. They can all be used in northern outdoor water gardens but must be brought in over the winter.

*Anubias lanceolata,* water aspidistra. To about 2 feet. Lance-shaped leaves to 6 inches long; flowers cupped by white spathe; blooms in spring and summer, when plant is grown emergent (above water). Diffuse sunlight or shade, in any good soil, constantly, evenly moist; needs high humidity. Good plant for self-watering pot.

*Colocasia esculenta,* elephant's ear, taro. Rises to 3½ feet from tuber; large leaves shaped something like an elephant's ear, on strong upright leaf stalks; tubers are a source of poi. Sun, bright light, or indirect light, in boggy soil, or up to 12 inches of water. 'Illustris' has large velvety green leaves with black markings; 'Euchlora' has dark green leaves with purple margins.

*Crinum americanum,* bog lily, southern swamp lily. To 2 feet. Clusters of fragrant white flowers with long narrow white petals and usually several flowers on one stalk, blooming in summer; long narrow leaves. Bright to indirect sun, in boggy soil to 6 inches of water.

*Cyperus* spp., umbrella plant, Egyptian papyrus. Perennial from 2½ to 8 feet tall, depending on the species; variable form, but many have slender stems topped with umbels of flowers. Sun or shade, in boggy soil to 6 inches of water. Can also be grown as a houseplant in moist soil.

*Echinodorus* spp., sword plant. Perennial to 14 inches, depending on species. Rooted, submerged plant with upright pointed oblong leaves, wavy or crinkled depending on species. Bright to moderate light, from a few inches of water to completely submerged. The Amazon sword plant *(E. amazonicus)* has long been a staple of aquariums.

*Hydrocleys nymphoides,* water poppy. Perennial with floating leaves. Oval shiny leaves on surface of the water; 3-petaled yellow 2-inch-wide flowers are held slightly above the water and resemble poppies. Full sun to partial shade in water depth from 4 to 12 inches.

*Nymphaea* cvs., tropical water lilies. See descriptions above.

*Salvinia auriculata,* water fern. Perennial floating plant to 10 inches long. Boat-shaped leaves with stems and roots beneath. Safe to use in small pools and aquariums, but very invasive in a large pond or lake in the South.

*Vallisneria gigantea,* eelgrass. Perennial to 3 feet. Tape- or ribbonlike submerged leaves with longitudinal black and brown stripes; insignificant flowers. Filtered indirect sunlight. Not to be confused with *V. americana* and *V. spiralis,* both often used in aquariums.

*Zantedeschia aethiopica,* calla lily. Perennial to 3 feet. Arrow-shaped leaves of glossy green; elegant flowers with milky-white spathe and golden-yellow spadix. Full sun to light shade in boggy, even wet, soil.

# CHAPTER TWELVE

# GARDENING TECHNIQUES AND PRACTICES

The text of this book has assumed a certain amount of knowledge of basic gardening that many readers might not have had the opportunity to become acquainted with; we have, therefore, included in this chapter a brief introduction to some of the "nuts and bolts" of working in the garden. And since this information applies to all the gardens in this book, rather than repeat it in different chapters, we have put it all here.

## BASIC GARDEN DESIGN

Although the picture is beginning to change, due to the success of gardening in America today, the sight usually presented when you drive through any average suburb is the contemporary approach to landscaping and to gardening in general: a wide expanse of manicured lawn is dotted here and there with straight lines of meticulously clipped shrubs and/or some evergreens—and any shade trees on the property are plunked directly in the center of the lot. Flowers, if there are flowers, are confined to the three most widely grown plants in the United States: petunias, marigolds, and impatiens. If imagination is allowed to be used, it's usually found back in the vegetable garden where, for some reason, caution is thrown to the wind, and tepees of weathered branches hold verdant tangles of beans and peas, and the many shades of green of lettuce are mixed with the deep purples of eggplants and the bright red of tomatoes.

One of the lessons we hope can be learned from this book concerns the vast number and variety of plants available to the average gardener. We also hope to provide the impetus for you to use more of them in your own garden, whatever the size of either the land or the budget.

Of course, the first step in the making of any garden, however large or small, is a thoughtful design. And the first rule of garden design is: Take paper and pencil and sketch a simple map of the area to be developed and planted. The map need not be complicated or artistically pleasing. It is only a tool to help the gardener to focus his or her energies, and eventually it will save time and effort. Include on the map all permanent items in the landscape like outbuildings, fences, trees, and rocks. Also indicate the direction of the worst winter winds, possible obstructions to sunlight, and the path of the sun both in summer and winter.

At the same time you must think about just how much responsibility you want. Gardening is not easy, and it does take time and often a sizable investment of money, especially if you are forced to hire out any of the jobs that need to be done.

The next step is to decide on what kind of garden you want. Will it be a rock garden that bursts upon the spring with riots of color? A naturalistic wild garden full of American wildflowers? A perennial border full of old-time favorite blossoms? A combination vegetable and flower garden? A water garden? Or even a garden devoted to a favorite theme like an all-white garden, a desert garden, a rose garden, or, as found in the Brooklyn Botanic Garden, a plot devoted to the plants of Shakespeare?

## COLOR IN THE GARDEN

"My theories about color," said Joyce Van Etten, when we interviewed her about heaths and heathers, "are pretty much classic theories. I like the subtle combinations, the subtle gradations of color. I don't like blatant concoctions." The annual border planted by gardener Douglas Dudgeon in 1989 contained a combination of an orange impatiens with purple salvia that seemed as if it should clash—but because the intensities of the colors were the same, Ms. Van Etten thought the combination worked. So did we.

With her comments, Ms. Van Etten summed up pages and pages of garden theory. We quickly grow tired of flagrant colors, but subtle combinations are always new. However, so much depends on your climate and where you live in this broad country. Woodland gardens filled with shade call for a mix of more delicate colors, while sun-filled areas of sand and stone need bold, bright flashes of color or they will be washed out by the sun and sky.

Most colors work together if their intensities are the same. Picture a bed of orange, purple, red, and yellow flowers where the brightness of each flower matches that of the others. It may be a so-called riot of color, but it will work. In fact, most colors that are near one another on the color wheel usually harmonize.

Now imagine the same mix of flowers, but add some blossoms of pale blue. The blue flowers will be lost. A better partner for the blue blossoms would be pink, salmon, or pale yellow. Pay attention when you match colors in the garden, and you'll achieve the best results.

## THE OTHER RULES

In addition to making a master plan of your garden and paying attention to the matching of bright and pale colors, the following rules are just as important:

1. Pay attention to the eventual size of a plant, shrub, or tree. Try to visualize what it will become five years from the day you plant it.

2. Match the plant to the available conditions. Avoid planting a bush that requires perfect drainage in an area where soil is heavy with clay. It's not what's planted next to what that makes

the difference—it's giving plants what they need. You can probably rectify any mismatch, but it is often more trouble than the
effort is worth.

3. When planning, avoid straight lines unless you have the
acreage of Versailles; they are never found in nature and soon
become boring to look at and impossible to maintain. A gentle
and sweeping curve looks much better and is both easier to install
and to keep up.

4. Trust your own aesthetic judgment. After all, it is your
garden, and should reflect your likes and dislikes, not those of
some expert you don't even know.

5. Never use garden ornaments that are not in scale with
your garden. A small Japanese stone lantern, which could accommodate a candle or low-voltage light for evening viewing, would
probably look better in the average-sized garden than a six-foot
marble statue of David. If you wish to acquire garden sculpture,
keep in mind the specific requirements of your site. You will find
that scaled-down ornaments add depth to a garden view rather
than overpowering it.

## SOIL

If you are new to gardening, it's very important to understand what type of soil you have. The ideal soil is loam, which
contains both sand and clay, plus organic matter and minerals.
The more organic matter that soil contains, the better. Soils rich
in organic matter are both porous and moisture-retentive; the
particles of organic matter soak up water like microscopic
sponges, but the air spaces between the particles insure that the
soil also holds abundant oxygen for roots and will not become
waterlogged.

Sandy soil is light in texture because sand particles are large.
It drains very quickly, sometimes so quickly that it has difficulty
holding both moisture and nutrients. To correct sandy soil, you
need to improve its moisture-holding ability. Compost and peat
moss help build up sandy soil.

Clay soil is dense because the particles are tiny. It drains
slowly and feels sticky to the touch. It can easily waterlog. To
correct clay soil, you need to lighten its texture, improve its aer-
ation and drainage capacity, by adding organic matter (compost,
peat moss, shredded leaves, and well-rotted manure). You can

also add sand, but if you do, use sharp or builder's sand—beach sand is too fine and contains too much salt. If you want to add both sand and organic matter to clay soil, as a general guide add one part sand to six parts organic matter.

It's important for soil to hold the right amount of moisture. Roots need both oxygen and water from which they take up nutrients to fuel growth. In a soil that is too dry or drains too quickly, there's not enough moisture around the root zone for nutrients to be absorbed. When soil is too wet, plant roots (except those that are specifically adapted to survive in water) suffocate for lack of oxygen.

Throughout the book we have used terms such as "poor," "average," and "good" to define the characteristics of garden soil. Poor soil is usually a thin layer of dry soil over a base of rock or shale or often compacted clay—a type of soil often found in housing developments and usually the result of days and weeks spent under heavy construction equipment. But as you can see from observing any such site, soon weeds will appear, followed by short-lived or trash trees, and many attractive wildflowers and plants. This does not mean that you should not try to improve such soil, but shows that it *is* capable of sustaining plant life.

Average soil is usually a mix that is weighted toward the clay end of the scale, but has some topsoil, and can be worked with a shovel without too many trips to a chiropractor.

Good soil is evidenced by a reasonable concentration of organic material, and one's shovel can plunge right in without hitting large stones or requiring much preparation for formal planting.

## COMPOSTING

The best way to build good soil, no matter what kind you start with, is to add organic matter. As mentioned before, this can be peat moss worked into the soil (when used as a mulch, peat moss repels water), shredded leaves, well-rotted manure (often available by the bag from nursery centers), and compost.

Basically compost is started by selecting an out-of-the-way spot in your garden where you can pile up discarded vegetable matter collected from weeding, cutting grass, and vegetable kitchen scraps.

Here vegetable matter is placed in layers with soil. Once a week or so, the pile should be turned to keep the ingredients mixed and decomposition proceeding at an even pace. The gardener's other job is occasionally to add moisture, as a dry compost heap will not work. Bacteria will live and work in the moistened compost heap at high efficiency, breaking down this organic matter into a beautiful dark brown humus that is free of odor.

The only items not suitable for a home composting heap are human feces and those of cats and dogs, bones, meat products or animal parts, plant material heavily soaked with herbicides or pesticides, diseased plants, and other toxic materials.

## WATERING

The traditional rule of thumb is that gardens need one inch of water per week. Not many of us keep rain gauges in our gardens, and moisture needs vary widely with weather conditions (for example, there is more evaporation with high winds than without), soil type, plant type, and the growing environment. Generally, if you get a good soaking rain once a week, you probably will not have to water. But gardens in fast-draining sandy soils may need additional water, as may gardens in hot climates. Plants summering outdoors in pots will need to be watered daily, or perhaps even twice a day, depending on the size of the pot. Shallow-rooted plants need water more often than deep-rooted ones and new plantings also need even, constant moisture to establish new roots. The best way to tell when the garden needs water is to stick your finger into the soil. If it feels dry a couple of inches below the surface, it's time to water.

## WATERING SYSTEMS

Overhead sprinklers are the least efficient, especially in areas of high sun, high heat, and porous soil. Better are soaker hoses and drip irrigation systems that deliver water directly to the root zone. Soaker hoses have tiny holes that let water out slowly to soak the ground. Rubber types can be installed underground, under mulch, or placed on top of the soil. Trickle or drip systems use slender plastic tubing with tiny pores that allow water to ooze out slowly. Kits are available that give you all the parts you need. Attach the system to a water source, install a timer if you like, and you're ready to go.

All these systems can be connected to timers. There is also equipment available to regulate the pressure in the lines: higher pressure will create a gentle spray, lower pressure soaks the ground.

There are various kinds of timers. A simple windup timer turns off your hose or faucet after five minutes or after up to two hours. A computerized control will turn sprinklers or irrigation systems on and off even when you are on vacation. Really sophisticated systems will turn on the water in different zones of your property, allowing you to water some areas more frequently than others.

## THE IMPORTANCE OF DEADHEADING

Deadheading doesn't refer to the fan club of a certain rock band from the sixties. We are talking about pinching off faded flowers from herbaceous and woody flowering plants. Picking off flowers before seeds mature keeps plants looking good and also encourages them to produce more flowers. Herbaceous plants with branching form can also be pinched back to make them bushier.

## RECORD KEEPING

In the rush of planting and maintaining a garden, the job of record keeping often takes second place. You always think it's easy to remember a name and a date, but it isn't.

There is an inherent desire in most human beings, especially plant people, to know the correct name of everything, and if you ever plan on selling or trading plants, records and labels are a must. Keep information on three-by-five cards or in a small notebook. Note the botanical and common name (if any), the date you received the plant, its age, the nursery or plant supplier, its location in the garden, and any propagation attempts.

## A NURSERY BED

If your garden keeps expanding and you wish to try new plants, especially those grown from seed, try to include a nursery bed in your plan. It need not be large, but it should be in a protected spot, have good soil, and be out of the way so you are under no pressure to consider aesthetics. Here you can raise seedling plants to maturity before planting them out in the garden proper.

## MULCHING

Many of the gardeners at the BBG use mulches in the gardens under their care. Mulches decrease the amount of weeding necessary, help slow the evaporation of moisture from the soil, and, depending on the material used, improve the appearance of the garden by imparting a neat and orderly look (but eschew black plastic—it is bad from every account, except to hasten the ripening of a crop like melons, as the plastic soaks up heat and warms the soil). Mulch, for example, keeps mud from splashing onto plant leaves during heavy rains. But it can also provide a dandy hiding place for a number of garden pests, including slugs.

If you do decide to mulch your garden, we recommend organic mulches for the perennial beds and borders. These essentially plant-based materials gradually decompose, adding organic matter to the soil. Stone mulches are excellent for rock gardens and for drought-resistant plants, as the stones hold the warmth of the sun, radiating it slowly at night and often producing slight concentrations of moisture. It is not a good mulch for plants that like their roots kept cool.

Plastic mulches can hold in too much heat, and can make it difficult for moisture to penetrate plant roots. Covering an entire garden with plastic sheets topped with mulch, especially when they are run right up to tree trunks, can eventually cause the death of everything in the garden in a severe drought.

Ira Walker, curator of conifers at the BBG, uses mulches of pine needles, shredded cedar bark, pine-bark chips, wood chips, and licorice roots. All lend a natural look to plants.

The Garden has a display of different mulches that allows visitors to compare the appearance of each. This exhibit contains: pine needles; shredded cedar bark; pine-bark chips; salt-marsh hay; wood shavings; wood chips; cocoa-bean hulls; licorice root; buckwheat hulls; builder's sand; marble chips; bluestone; calcined clay; backed montmorillonite clay (marketed under the brand name of Terragreen and Turface); construction gravel; turkey grit (a crushed granite used in the poultry industry in three grades: starter, grower, and finisher); landscaping stone; crushed clay pots; coal; and black plastic. Marble chips, crushed pots, and coal are often used for background color in knot gardens.

## PLANT PROPAGATION

Sooner or later, after you become involved with plants, the collecting bug rears its ugly head and you begin to wish for more. When this urge strikes and the pocketbook rebels, the best and easiest solution is to grow your own plants, either from seed, cuttings, or the division of established plants usually provided by other generous gardeners. At the same time, seed propagation enables you to try many new plants ordinarily unavailable from the majority of commercial nurseries—a group that in recent years has never really been known for its spirit of discovery.

The majority of botanical gardens in the world, including the Brooklyn Botanic Garden, freely exchange among each other seeds gathered from the plants in their respective collections. Many of these institutions publish yearly seed lists, usually called the *Index Seminum* (the French term is *Catalogue des Graines),* and flipping pages from one such catalog can be an invitation to traveling around the world without ever leaving home.

Although this process is not open to the average gardener, there are alternatives. These include the seed exchanges provided by the various plant societies in the United States and Europe, and by the more obscure "Mom and Pop" nurseries, which by being small and having a low overhead, can provide unusual seeds and often unusual plants.

## THE PLANT PROPAGATOR

Robert Hays is in charge of plant propagation at BBG. There are three propagating rooms in his charge. Each is neat with tiny pots of seedlings and larger pots containing cuttings lined up in rows, each with precise labels as to the particulars of germination or the original source. Above the working area on his desk are shelves of reference books and files marked by the year containing the various seed indexes from other botanical centers.

By the south window of the greenhouse are innumerable tiny pots, each containing a number of marble-sized succulent plants.

"These were all started from seeds from the Kirstenbosch National Botanical Garden in South Africa. They are all different species of lithops (*Lithops* spp.) called living stones—and we'll keep them in these pots until they are absolutely bursting the seams."

Pointing to another group of these miniatures, he continued, "And here are agaves (*Agave* spp.), or century plants, also grown from seed. The lithops and cactuses like all the moisture they can get when young, but when they burst out of these pots, they will want dry conditions. We keep them in groups of ten while they begin to grow. When collecting and germinating seeds, it's almost like taking a plant expedition anywhere in the world without leaving home, and the cost is usually small or in many cases, a perk of membership in plant societies and other groups.

"You could build a collection of just lithops entirely from seeds if you wished. After all, this is where the Garden gets most of its really unusual plants. If you go back in the records, you'll find that most of the interesting and rare plants are *Index Seminum* plants. So I have a lot of fun going through the seed lists. Then there are the cuttings—when properly packed—that go from institution to institution through the mail or by United Parcel."

## GERMINATION OF SEEDS

Although found in a mystifying variety of shapes, sizes, and colors, all seeds consist of the embryo or baby plant surrounded by a seed coat or protective shell.

Within each seed, the embryo has a rudimentary stem, one or two seed leaves or cotyledons, and a tiny root. In addition, the seed stores food in the form of starch, sugars, fats, and proteins. At this stage the seed is essentially a young plant in a state of arrested development.

In order for germination to occur, three items are necessary: water, a favorable temperature, and oxygen. If any of these are missing, the seed will not germinate. In addition, after the first three conditions are met, light will play a key role.

Water softens the hard seed coat, making it easier for moisture to reach the embryo and for it to break through.

There is an optimum temperature for seed germination. For

many crop plants like peas and beans, it's 50 to 60°F, while most tropicals and houseplants need 65 to 80°F. And surprisingly, many seeds, like those of columbines (*Aquilegia* spp.), African violets (*Saintpaulia* spp.), and foxgloves (*Digitalis* spp.), need the stimulation of light for germination to occur.

Finally, many seeds are very small—there are approximately 200,000 snapdragon seeds to the ounce—and if buried too deeply in the soil, the seedling may perish before reaching the surface, or the seeds may not germinate at all.

We passed a tray of little palm trees, each with one unfurling seed leaf. They were planted in November 1988 and germinated on September 15, 1989.

"You have to be patient," said Mr. Hays. "The wish for instant gratification and wanting everything now doesn't work in the world of plants."

"What is the one rule you should always follow when growing plants from seed?" we asked.

"Easy," he replied. "Be clean! The mix you use must be sterile, and the containers used for germination must be clean to prevent the spread of molds, mildews, and those fungus diseases called "damping-off" in the trade. This is especially important for desert plants and for seeds that take a long time to germinate."

Records are important, too. "People never realize," he said, "until it's too late, just how easy it is to forget a date or a name. They think they will remember because it seems vital at the time, but two weeks later, they have forgotten. So labeling is most crucial. I write down the date of planting, and the assigned number of the seed, and I keep a journal for each year with every name, number, and the original source."

Even the way a label is written can be important, especially when that label is used outdoors. Most gardeners start at the outer edge of the label, writing in the direction of the pointed or soil end. That way the important part of the name is usually the first to disappear due to wind and rain. By starting the name at the end set in the soil, most of it escapes weather wear and is visible months or years later.

## SEED STRATIFICATION

One of the most surprising things we heard from Mr. Hays concerned his practice of sowing seeds for Temperate Zone plants. What doesn't come up in a month he puts in a refrigerator at 40°F. This stratification sends many of them into active germination.

Many plants that are native to the Temperate Zone will not germinate until they have passed through a period of dormancy. This protects the plant from sprouting during a January thaw only to expire in a February blizzard.

The two most common types of dormancy are impermeability of the seed coat, which prevents water from entering, or an internal dormancy within the embryo. In some species only one such mechanism exists; others may have both.

If a thick seed coat is the problem, it's easily solved. Either nick the seed with a file or soak the seed in warm water for 24 hours; many seed packets give this advice.

If internal dormancy is the problem, it's solved by a process called stratification. The seeds have to be placed in a bed of moist sphagnum or peat moss and exposed to temperatures of between 36 and 43°F for at least 90 days, with an average of 40°F.

## *FIVE RULES FOR PROPER GERMINATION*

The first rule is never to overwater your seeds, for by doing so you deprive the seeds of needed oxygen since they are unable to take oxygen directly from water. Often the seeds then begin to rot.

Rule two, on the other hand, stresses that the germination mix should never be allowed to dry out. The lack of moisture either disrupts the necessary steps of pregermination or kills the emergent seedling outright.

Rule three, use a mister or a fine hose for watering, as heavy sprays of water can often damage small seedlings and disrupt the germination mix.

Never sow seeds too deeply (rule four). If you are in doubt as to correct depth, just cover them lightly.

And rule five, keep seeds away from sunlight until germination is completed.

## SEEDLINGS

The young plant, a seedling, is now emerging from the soil. Before it becomes entirely dependent on food manufactured through its true leaves, the root system develops, and the reserve food supplies in the cotyledons (seed leaves) will provide nourishment for a time. At this point a seedling can exist in a sterile growing medium like sphagnum moss or other mixes, but once the true leaves appear, the plant will require a fertile soil or the addition of nutrients through the use of fertilizers.

Mr. Hays is responsible for starting all the bedding plants used in the various displays around the Garden. This is a major undertaking.

"As soon as the seeds germinate," he said, "I take the flats of seedlings down to what we call the production house and leave them alone for a few days so they become acclimated to their new surroundings. Then I prick them out to two and a quarter inch peat pots, using forty-two pots to a flat."

"The growing mix? I use a mix of ten parts pasteurized, composted soil, four parts Pro-Mix (a half-and-half mixture of peat and perlite), three parts sand, one cup of lime, and one cup of slow-release fertilizer."

For rooting cuttings Mr. Hays uses a blend of perlite, milled sphagnum moss, Terragreen (calcite clay), shredded Styrofoam, sharp or builder's sand, and #2 grit, which is like fishtank gravel, but he says that even bird gravel from the pet store will work amazingly well.

He pushed his finger into a small pile of the rooting mix.

"Frankly you could use this mix for longer than a year by just skimming off the top—since it's constantly moist, you get a good crop of moss growing on the surface—but for the sake of cleanliness, I start fresh every season."

## SUCCEEDING WITH SEEDS

Try to buy your seeds in early spring to take full advantage of the long growing season ahead. Although some plants may be started at any time of the year, the majority profit from matching their growth with the lengthening days of spring.

Don't be too smitten with the lovely catalog pictures. Limit your buying to what you have room and equipment for.

When seeds arrive, you will notice that many are packed in foil packets, with instructions on the label. To ensure their continued vitality, store the seeds in a cool spot away from radiators or other sources of heat.

Check to see if any of the seeds need stratification. If it's indicated, now is the time to start that procedure. Open the package and place the seeds in a slightly moist mixture of sand and/or sphagnum moss inside a small plastic bag, labeled as to date and contents. Store the bag in the refrigerator for at least six weeks. When the right time comes, the seeds and the medium can be sown as one.

Seeds can be sown in flats, usually made of compressed peat, wood fibers, or plastic. Smaller individual pots are available for limited sowings, including some that are one inch square and perfect for larger individual seeds.

Just about any container that will hold the planting mix, that is fairly waterproof, that has drainage holes at the bottom, and is at least two and a half inches in height, will work for seeds. That includes half-pint cream and milk containers with the tops cut off and a few holes punched in the bottom.

Moisten all germination mixes before use. An easy way to do this is to fill the pot or flat with the mix, set the container in a pan of warm water, and let it sit until the top of the mix is moist. Mr. Hays advises against the common practice of putting the mix in a bowl of water and kneading it with your hands to moisten it, because you could compact the mix and possibly contaminate it, too.

We know that seeds need water for germination, but they also need oxygen. If the mix is too wet, the seeds will be completely surrounded by water, the oxygen will not be readily available to them, and they will die.

It is also true that the mix must never be allowed to dry out because either the seed will die or the germination countdown will be interrupted and will have to be started all over from the beginning.

If you are worried about how deep to plant seeds, use the following rule to determine the depth of planting: Seed one-sixteenth of an inch or larger should be covered by the thickness of one seed. Tiny seeds, like those of begonias, need not be covered at all—just settled in with a light spray of water from a hand mister. When sowing smaller seeds, put them in a folded piece of paper, and tap it gently as you move it across the surface of the medium.

There are usually three reasons why seeds do not germinate: (1) They are too old and no longer viable; (2) they have not had proper stratification or enough time to germinate; and (3) the seedbed is too cold. Far and away the best solution is to provide a heating cable. These cables warm the soil to a preset temperature and keep it that way. They are sold with or without thermostats; get one with a heat control.

Once seeds are set, cover your containers with plastic wrap or glass, being careful to keep the wrap away from the surface of the medium. Drops of moisture can condense and form small swamps to drown the seeds.

Put these miniature greenhouses in a warm spot away from the direct rays of the sun. Soon they will want all the sun available —but not until they sprout.

A number of sources will tell you that complete darkness is necessary for germination. That is true only for a small number of seeds—nasturtiums and tithonias, for example. Most seeds will germinate in the presence of some light.

When the first green shoots appear, remove the covering immediately and move the containers into direct sunlight or artificial light of the proper intensity.

If plants are on a windowsill, turn them daily to prevent their growing toward the light.

After the true leaves appear, it's time to use a liquid fertilizer. Follow mixing instructions on the package but dilute the solution by one-half with water.

The pointed end of a pencil or a plastic plant label makes an excellent tool for transplanting. Just be gentle! Pick up the seedling by the leaves—never by the stem—and lightly cover the roots with damp, but not mucky, soil.

The plants should not be moved into larger pots until they have developed at least one set of true leaves.

## OTHER MEANS OF PROPAGATION

If buyers had to wait for growers to supply all the plants we desire from seeds, there wouldn't be enough plants to go around. Some plants take years to reach maturity, and someone would have to be responsible for providing "bed and board" for all that time. In addition, many plants are hybrids, the results of cross-fertilization or cultivars found by chance, and usually plants grown from the seeds produced by these plants will not come true —the characteristics that we want will not be there.

Luckily nature has accomplished an alternate method called asexual or vegetative reproduction, a process that gives most plants the ability to grow mature offspring from special cells found in leaves, stems, and even roots: One plant can manufacture hundreds of clones over its life span, each identical to the parent.

The Garden knows the value of reproducing choice plants asexually. Most budgets would never allow for the purchase of potted perennials to line long walkways or evergreens to fill out borders of one hundred feet or more. But using the methods described below—stem cuttings, root cuttings, and division—the gardeners can reproduce hundreds of plants almost immediately, or at least in a year or so.

"People," said Mr. Hays, "should not be afraid to propagate plants. That way you get many plants for very little money— usually just for your time and a bit of extra care. And if you start to overlap the propagations, within two years you'll start having new items each season."

## SUCCEEDING WITH CUTTINGS AND DIVISION

Plant cells resemble animal cells in many ways, and both use hormones to control and stimulate growth and development. Often a cutting that refuses to respond to the rooting process simply needs the additional stimulation of a plant-growth hormone. The wound on the bottom of the cutting is dipped into hormone powder just prior to planting. As with all such chemicals, please exercise care and follow package warnings when using these hormones.

### SOFTWOOD STEM CUTTINGS

This is the most common method of propagation. The term "softwood" refers to the soft green stem tissues found in the first season of growth, before the stem matures into woody tissue.

Late spring or summer is the best time to start cuttings, since at this season the plant has a good supply of food stored in its cells. If only a few plants are needed, the best method is to use a combination of small peat pots (2¼-inch) and small plastic food-storage bags. First, with a sharp knife or razor blade cut a healthy stem, about three to five inches long, with a sharp knife or razor blade slightly below the point where a leaf petiole (or stalk) joins the stem. Remove any damaged leaves and flowers and neatly slice off any bottom leaves close to the stem. Take the pot filled with growing medium or moist sphagnum moss and make a hole with a pencil or similar object to three-quarters of the pot's depth. Insert the cutting (after applying root hormone, if needed), making sure the base of the stem touches the bottom of the hole. Firm the medium around the stem. Now put the whole affair in the bag and seal the top.

The medium should be moist *but not soggy!* In about two weeks, give the cutting a slight tug to check if rooting has commenced. If it has not, pull out the cutting and see if the end has started to rot. If all looks well, try again.

### SEMIHARDWOOD CUTTINGS

Many plants are multiplied by taking cuttings from shoots of the current growing season in the fall of the year. The stems selected should not yet have hardened into wood, but should bend easily without snapping or pulling apart. Cuttings should be four to six inches long, with the soft tip removed, and the bottom cut just below a node. Place each cutting in a pot with moist growing medium, with about ⅓ of the stem buried, making sure that the base is in contact with the medium. To be doubly sure of rooting, dust the tip with hormone powder. Cover the pot with a plastic bag and subject it to gentle bottom heat of 65 to 70°F. The cuttings should begin to root within a month, when they can be transplanted to small pots.

### HARDWOOD CUTTINGS

Hardwood stem cuttings are made after the soft stem tissue has actually hardened into wood. Growth from the previous season is used. This method is usually associated with outdoor flowering trees and shrubs. Sections should be at least five inches long and up to ten inches long. The bottom cut is made at a slant (so you know which end is up when the twig is bare) just below a node, and the top cut about a half-inch above a node. The tip of the stem is generally discarded since that part is usually low in stored food. The bottom is dusted with hormone powder and planted in a flat of growing medium at least two inches deep, and left for three to five weeks with a gentle bottom temperature of 65 to 70°F and the tops exposed to open air. As roots develop, the stems should be transplanted into pots.

### TUBERS AND RHIZOMES

Although there is little resemblance, tubers and rhizomes are really modified stems. The most familiar tuber is the potato, but gloriosa lilies, gloxinias (*Sinningia* spp.), four-o'clocks *(Mirabilis jalapa)* and tuberous begonias are all tubers. To multiply tuberous plants, the tuber may be divided into as many pieces as there are eyes (or axillary buds). Use a sharp, clean knife, and set the cut pieces in a warm, dry place (about 68°F) for a day or two, allowing the cuts to seal over. Plant the pieces in a moist mix, with just the eye uncovered. When new leaves and roots appear, move to individual pots.

If a rhizome is cleanly cut into two sections, each piece with a growing tip or node, the cuttings will form new plants. Lightly cover the pieces with moist medium and transplant when new roots and leaves develop. Bearded iris, blackberry lilies (*Belamcanda* spp.), and water lilies (*Nymphaea* spp.) are rhizomatous plants.

### SINGLE LEAF CUTTINGS

Streptocarpus, gloxinias, and a number of succulent plants can be reproduced by using one of the following types of leaf cuttings: a single leaf, a leaf with the petiole attached, or the leaf, the petiole, and a section of the stem, including a leaf bud.

Leaves that are thick and succulent can be pushed into a moist medium without a petiole. Kalanchoes and other succulents will root and form new plants by this method.

Leaf petioles (of leaves with petioles attached) are pushed into the medium. This method works for African violets, most begonias, hoyas, and many other plants.

If either of these procedures is not applicable, try including the leaf bud and a bit of stem. The jade plant *(Crassula argentea)* will form roots from a leaf alone, but the leaf will never grow a stem unless the leaf bud is included.

### CUTTINGS IN WATER

An old-time method of propagation is rooting cuttings in a glass of water. It works for impatiens, ivies, coleus, begonias, inch plants, pelargoniums, and dozens more.

After healthy root growth has formed, start adding small amounts of sand or soil to the water every few days. That way you won't have a tangled mass of roots to sort out when ready to transplant, and the soil or sand will stimulate the roots to grow new root hairs, which are the true movers of food and water to the plant.

## PLANTS BY DIVISION

One of the easiest ways to produce new plants from old is by the division of the rootstock. Early spring is the best time, before new growth for the coming season begins. This process works with plants that form multiple crowns, like many of the ferns, hostas, daylilies, aspidistras, asters, and a host of others.

## RUNNERS

Any plant that produces runners with tiny plants at their tips, such as spider plants (*Chlorophytum* spp.) or strawberry geraniums (*Saxifraga stolonifera*), will make new plants if the tips are allowed to root. The easiest way is to anchor the small plantlet in a three-inch pot of soil using a paper clip.

## AIR-LAYERING

When a prized rubber plant (*Ficus* spp.) has reached the ceiling, it's time to either watch it bend or air-layer it. This is an especially valuable way to produce a mature plant in a short time and relieve that leggy look of the old plant.

Start the procedure in spring by making a diagonal cut, about one and a half inches long in the stem at the height you wish the new plant to be. Keep the cut from healing by inserting a wooden toothpick into the wound. The cut area is then surrounded with thoroughly moistened peat or sphagnum moss and wrapped with polyethylene, which is then tied top and bottom. Inspect the package every week or so for signs of new white roots. When roots are well developed, remove the plastic but leave the moss and cut the parent stem cleanly just below the new roots. Plant the rooted top in its own pot. The remaining stem will usually start to produce new shoots with leaves.

Air-layering is mainly used on woody-stemmed houseplants such as *Croton* spp. and *Dracaena* spp.

## CANE SECTIONS

Dracaena, dieffenbachia, and cordylines may be propagated by cutting their stems into three-inch sections, making sure that each section includes a leaf scar, then placing the sections horizontally on a bed of moist sphagnum or peat moss. When rooting is well along, the dormant bud will sprout, and a new plant is on its way.

# THE
# *PLANTS & GARDENS*
# SERIES

The *Plants & Gardens* handbook series published by the Brooklyn Botanic Garden covers over fifty gardening topics. Each single-topic, soft-cover issue is fully illustrated. The handbooks range from sixty to one hundred pages; they feature covers and inserts in color, some fifteen titles in full color, and include valuable references for further pursuit of your gardening interests. The following titles are currently part of the series:

Soils
Planting and Transplanting
Propagation
Plants for Problem Places
Beds and Borders
Perennials and Their Uses
Perennials: A Nursery Source Manual
Gardening for Fragrance

Ornamental Grasses
Bulbs
Roses
Rock Gardening
Flowering Shrubs
Dwarf Conifers
Flowering Trees
Culinary Herbs
Herbs and Their Ornamental Uses
Gardening with Wildflowers
Gardening with Wildflowers and Native Plants
Gardening for Wildlife
Ground Covers and Vines
Trained and Sculptured Plants
The Home Lawn Handbook
Gardening Without Pests
Low Maintenance Gardening
The Home Vegetable Garden
Oriental Vegetables and Herbs
Water Gardening
Japanese Gardens
Nursery Source Manual
Bonsai for Indoors
Bonsai—Special Techniques
Bonsai—The Dwarfed Potted Trees of Japan
Greenhouses and Garden Rooms
Indoor Gardening
Orchids
Container Gardening
Garden Ornaments
Dried Flower Design
Dye Plants and Dyeing
American Gardens: A Traveler's Guide
American Cottage Gardening
Garden Photography

# INDEX

255

About the Authors

Peter Loewer is an award-winning garden writer whose books include *A Year of Flowers* and *Gardens by Design*. He lives in Asheville, North Carolina.

Anne Moyer Halpin, author of *The Year-Round Flower Gardener,* owns and runs a garden-design business on Long Island, New York.